The Larousse Guide to
Animal
Tracks
Trails and Signs

R. W. Brown
M. J. Lawrence
J. Pope

W9-CPF-179

Larousse & Co. Inc.
New York

Authors' Acknowledgements

Over the years that we have been working on the book we have been helped by many people to whom we gratefully give thanks. We would also like to express our gratitude to those who have helped with material which either appears in or has been used as background for this publication: Antwerp Zoo; British Museum (Natural History); Chessington Zoo; Chester Zoo; Michael Clark; John Ferguson; Dr. Roger Fons, France; Asko Kaliola, Finland; David Lees, London Zoo; Professor Pucek, Poland; Dr. V. Rahm, Switzerland; R. Raymont, Stagsden Bird Garden; Stockholm Zoo; Professor Valverde, Spain; Professor Vogel, Switzerland. Particular thanks are due to Roger Coupland for checking at all stages of the work. Finally we would also like to thank our families for their tolerance and support during the preparation of the book.   R. W. B., M. J. L., J. P.

Artists' Acknowledgements

Roger Gorringe 208, 209, 211, 212, 213, 218, 228, 229, 231, 268, 271

Michael J. Lawrence 62, 90, 99, 104, 105, 125, 133, 143, 145, 147, 149, 150, 197

Kenneth Oliver 202, 203, 204, 205, 207, 244, 245, 249, 250, 253, 254, 256, 258, 273, 274, 275

David Thompson – Linden Artists 10–14, 257, 265, 269, 277

All other artwork prepared by Robert Mathias from material provided by the authors.

First published in Great Britain by Newnes Books, a Division of The Hamlyn Publishing Group Limited 84-88 The Centre, Feltham, Middlesex, England.

Published in the United States by
Larousse & Co. Inc.
572 Fifth Avenue
New York
N.Y. 10036

ISBN 0-88332-366-4
Library Congress Catalog No. 84-47822
© Newnes Books, a Division of The Hamlyn Publishing Group Limited 1984
All rights reserved. No part of this publication may be reproduced, stored in a retrieval system, or transmitted, in any form or by any means, electronic, mechanical, photocopying, recording or otherwise, without the permission of the Publisher and the copyright holder.
Printed in Spain by Artes Gráficas Toledo, S.A.
D. L. TO: 187 -1984

Contents

Introduction

We are, by and large, unaware of the large numbers of creatures with which we share our world: the more intelligent ones keep out of our way, for as a rule the presence of human beings bodes ill for them. Even so, we can often detect their presence and come to understand something of their way of life, for no animal can live and move about without leaving certain traces. The aim of this book is to show how to interpret such signs.

Some animals, such as birds and amphibians, are fairly conspicuous but mammals are largely nocturnal and secretive and are silent for most of the year, so their presence must often be deduced by their tracks and trails, feeding and grooming signs, the marks with which they delimit their territories and by their lairs. They tend to be the most difficult of creatures to see, but fortunately they leave the most definite signs of their presence or passage; this book is therefore very largely concerned with mammals.

Most mammals have a definite daily routine. This is a characteristic shared by man, for in general people are creatures of habit, taking the same route to work or to the shops each day, doing tasks in a particular order, and so on. It is the habit of taking the same route as they go about their business that provides the first clue to the presence of many animals. Grass does not need to be trodden down very heavily or frequently for a well worn track to be made, so we can often see narrow paths winding across fields and into woods. It may be difficult to tell exactly which animal has made the tracks, but the sharp cleaves of hoofed animals cut into any soft patch, suggesting the presence of deer or sheep, for example, while a stretch of mud may be imprinted with the pads and claw marks of badgers, foxes or many smaller animals. Badger trails may be confused with human pathways, although if running through a wood, sooner or later the track is likely to pass under a fallen branch with about 45cm clearance – a sure sign of badgers. Foxes are light on their feet and very wary, so they do not push through vegetation in the way some other animals do. Their presence is more difficult to discern unless the animal has passed that way fairly recently, in which case the powerful, throat-catching smell from its anal glands (over which the fox has no control) hangs heavily enough to be detected by even the human nose. In woods, deer may be discovered in a similar way, although the smell – a warm, cow-like odour – is quite different.

Even small mammals make tracks to and from their nests, usually appearing like tiny tunnels about 2.5cm in diameter in grass and undergrowth. The voles, mice and shrews which make these runs

Hazelnuts wedged into oak tree bark and opened by Nuthatch. Nuts wedged into bark by woodpeckers are opened with larger, coarser holes.

rarely leave them, for they represent a safe, familiar way through a world full of danger. In hedgerows and woodlands where the ground is more open, the runs of small mammals often take a course round the base of a tree, where they appear as narrow furrows, usually free from moss or other vegetation.

Most kinds of animal occupy territories, the boundaries of which are marked visually or with scent, and defended against others of their own kind. Within the territory will be the animal's den or lair, which may be no more than a sheltered spot where it habitually lies up, but especially with smaller animals it may be a well built nest or burrow. Many creatures change their home according to season, seeking better shelter in winter time. Birds' nests are nurseries, nothing more, and are left to fall apart or be taken over by other animals once the family has been reared.

Animals need to leave the safety of their homes to find food and water, to gather bedding or material to refurbish the nest, to win a mate, or simply for exercise and play. Many animals live in cramped dens, so the first thing that most of them do when they emerge into the open is to stretch and groom themselves. This usually consists of scratching and rubbing against a selected tree or post, and, especially during the moult, large tufts of hair may be pulled out. Badgers and bears, among others, may scrape their claws on a tree – the purpose of this may be to spread scent as much as to clean the talons. Its toilet complete, the animal will probably shake and lick itself briefly before setting off to forage. It will not go far, however, before it feels the need to relieve itself. Apart from foxes, animals which live in lairs are generally clean, and deposit their droppings away from the living place. In the case of some animals faeces are used to mark territorial boundaries; in others, such as badgers, they are left in open latrines, and in cats they are buried. Small mammals usually have latrine areas within their system of runs, so that the nest does not become contaminated or attract predators.

Once it has made itself comfortable the animal goes about searching for food. This may be easy for herbivores, although most have favourite places to browse or graze and often different sorts of food will be taken at different times of the year, so that the territory is used as fully as possible. Feeding signs will include browse marks on trees and branches and the tooth marks left by rodents, rabbits, deer or horses when they bark trees. Fungi may be nibbled by deer, rabbits or even slugs and on a larger scale the grazing line made by rabbits or other herbivores in vegetation near to a wood is often easy to see.

Many herbivores are untidy when it comes to food remains: the debris of a squirrel's feeding table leaves no doubt as to what has been taking a meal there, and the remains of nuts nibbled by mice or squirrels or hammered open by birds give a good clue to the

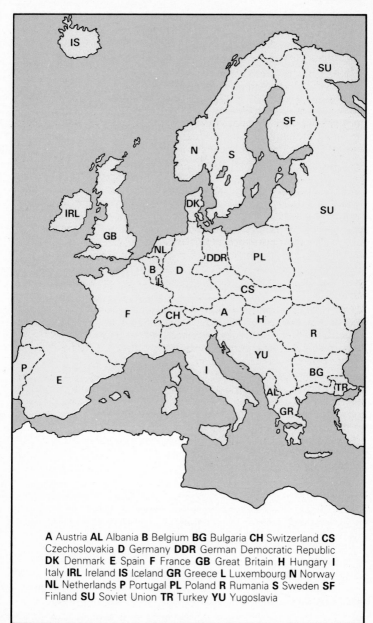

A Austria **AL** Albania **B** Belgium **BG** Bulgaria **CH** Switzerland **CS** Czechoslovakia **D** Germany **DDR** German Democratic Republic **DK** Denmark **E** Spain **F** France **GB** Great Britain **H** Hungary **I** Italy **IRL** Ireland **IS** Iceland **GR** Greece **L** Luxembourg **N** Norway **NL** Netherlands **P** Portugal **PL** Poland **R** Rumania **S** Sweden **SF** Finland **SU** Soviet Union **TR** Turkey **YU** Yugoslavia

identity of the feeder.

Hunters may have to travel further before they find a meal, and then have to eke out the flesh in their diet with invertebrates such as worms, snails and insects. They often leave shells, bones, fur or feathers: the identity of the prey and the way that it has been dealt with is often sufficient to identify the hunter. The presence of bats can sometimes be confirmed from the piles of insect legs and wings below their particular feeding perches. Even the feeding habits of small animals such as spiders and insects can sometimes be useful: the larvae of many insects will feed on only one kind of plant, and characteristic patterns of damage may indicate their presence.

Sometimes animals will make stores of food if it is not easily available throughout the year. Squirrels are perhaps best known for this habit, but many other rodents store nuts or other types of food – usually by burying it, although it may be hidden in an old bird's nest. Some birds also store food. Jays have been known to bury acorns as much as four miles from the nearest oak wood; but it is not easy to recognize such stores until groups of oaks or beeches are found growing well away from the nearest parent tree.

Carnivores too may store food. Foxes, wolves and bears will all return to eat any surplus which they have been able to accumulate, and they generally protect it against thieves by scraping earth over it, and sometimes spraying it with urine. Disturbed earth is the best clue to such hidden booty, but no such marker betrays the stores made by shrews, or the even bigger larders stocked by moles. The latter may collect very large numbers of earthworms, biting them at the head end to immobilize them.

After an animal has fed and made stores of any food surplus it will probably return home, perhaps guided by scent tracks laid down on the outward journey. The homeward journey may be broken by a period of play, although this does not produce any special sign (except for the mud or snow slides sometimes made by otters).

Some activities are seasonal in nature, particularly those associated with the rut in herbivores. Fallow deer make rutting runs in the autumn and at the same time most deer species advertise their readiness to mate by fraying young trees to spread the scent from the facial glands. In the early summer most male deer shed their antlers; these are rarely found intact, since the deer eat them to regain the minerals, but sometimes heavily gnawed antlers – or other highly mineralized materials – will be found.

Nests for bearing and rearing the young are also built in spring and early summer. Signs of this activity range from the jaw marks left by queen wasps on fence posts, from which they have scraped wood to make their paper comb, to the trail scrapes and torn fur of female rabbits which dig blind-ended burrows on the edge of the warren.

THE MAMMALS OF EUROPE

Many factors have affected the composition of the present day mammal fauna. There is a wide range of habitats, although many have been highly modified by man. A number of major climatic and geographical influences have also historically influenced the fauna. Finally deliberate attempts to eliminate some species and the introduction of others has further modified the picture.

Excluding whales, porpoises and dolphins there are about 170 species present in Europe. There are 60 Rodents, 3 Lagomorphs, 22 Insectivores, 31 Bats, 25 Carnivores, 18 Ungulates (Deer, Cattle and Sheep), 1 Primate and 8 Pinnipedes (Seals and Walrus). Within the voles and shrews some species are very similar and cannot be distinguished in the field, but there is generally great variety in body size, body form, habitat preference and way of life.

Some species have been greatly depleted. The larger carnivores, such as the Brown Bear, Wolf and Lynx have been greatly reduced in numbers by persecution. The Wild Boar was hunted out in many areas and the Beaver disappeared in all but a few river valleys and the lake complexes of Finland. Changes in agriculture have affected species such as the Harvest Mouse and in many places bat populations have been reduced due to accidental modification of hibernating and breeding roosts. Perhaps the saddest and least understood change of the last 20 years has been the complete disappearance of the Otter from large areas of Europe.

An estimated 22 species have been introduced in recent times, sometimes at the expense of indigenous mammals. The Grey Squirrel has replaced the Red in much of England and Wales, while the Raccoon Dog has found the wetter forests of Finland and eastern Europe an ideal habitat. The Sika, White-Tailed, Axis and Muntjac deer have been introduced with varying degrees of success.

MAMMALS PLATES

Insectivores and Bats
Hedgehog
  Erinaceus europaeus **c**
Mole *Talpa europaea* **b**
Common Shrew *Sorex araneus* **f**
Lesser White-toothed Shrew
  Suncus etruscus **l**
Water Shrew *Neomys fodiens* **e**
Greater White-toothed Shrew
  Crocidura russula **h**
Pyrenean Desman
  Galemys pyrenaicus **g**
Greater Horseshoe Bat
  Rhinolophys ferrum-equinum **k**
Pipistrelle
  Pipistrellus pipistrellus **a**
Common Long-eared Bat
  Plecotus auritus **d**
Daubenton's Bat
  Myotis daubentoni **j**

Carnivores – dogs, cats, bears, mongooses
Brown Bear *Ursus arctos* **a**
Wolf *Canis lupus* **d**
Fox *Vulpes vulpes* **e**
Raccoon Dog
  Nyctereutes procyonoides **c**
Egyptian Mongoose
  Herpestes ichneumon **f**
Lynx *Felis lynx* **b**
Carnivores – mustelids
Stoat *Mustela erminea* **f**
Weasel *M. nivalis* **b**
Polecat *M. putorius* **e**
Wolverine *Gulo gulo* **a**
Pine Marten *Martes martes* **d**
Otter *Lutra lutra* **g**
Badger *Meles meles* **c**
Rodents and lagomorphs
Brown Hare *Lepus capensis* **d**
Arctic Hare *L. timidus* **e**
Greater Mole-rat

Spalax microphthalmus **c**
Red Squirrel *Sciurus vulgaris* **m**
Beaver *Castor fiber* **a**
Hazel Dormouse
  Muscardinus avellanarius **g**
Wood Mouse
  Apodemus sylvaticus **b**
Brown Rat *Rattus norvegicus* **h**
Norway Lemming
  Lemmus lemmus **f**
Harvest Mouse
  Micromys minutus **g**
Bank Vole
  Clethrionomys glareolus **k**
Field Vole *Microtus agrestis* **m**
Artiodactyls
Elk *Alces alces* **a**
Red Deer *Cervus elaphus* **b**
Roe Deer *Capreolus capreolus* **d**
Reindeer *Rangifer rangifer* **c**
Mouflon *Ovis musimon* **f**
Wild Boar *Sus scrofa* **e**

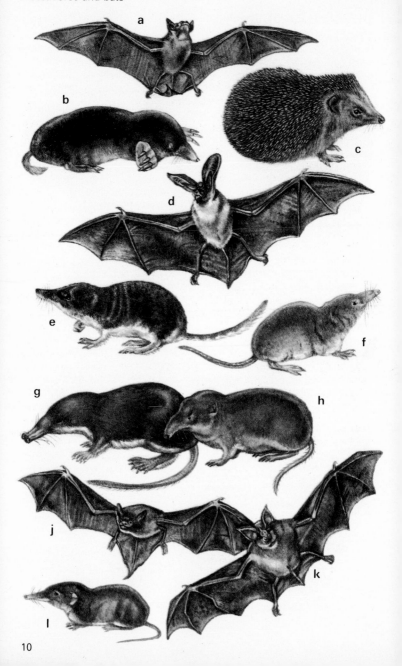

Tracks and trails

When an animal moves across a soft surface it leaves foot impressions known as *tracks*. A sequence of such tracks, together with any accessory marks such as tail or feather drag, forms a *trail*. The layout of the trail and the form of the tracks can convey a great deal of information to the naturalist who knows how to interpret them: it is possible not only to identify species (often from a single isolated track), but to establish the age, sex and condition of the animal that made it and the speed at which it was moving. If recent enough a trail may lead to the animal itself – stalking deer is a well established practice, and many species of mammal and ground-living bird can be successfully tracked.

The best recording medium for the tracks of all but the smaller species is wet silt with no litter cover. Wet mud and deep snow both take bold track impressions, but these are generally distorted unless they are very tiny: small mammals and birds leave crisp tracks, but all others are greatly enlarged. Fresh shallow snow on an otherwise solid surface is an excellent material for recording track form accurately; a drawback is that it is not suitable for making plaster casts (see page 276).

For the purposes of this section of the book a system of categorizing tracks according to their *form* and *size* has been adopted in preference to the more orthodox taxonomic system. Track form depends on the structural adaptation of the limb. Examples of the ways in which it can vary are given for the major animal groups – mammals, birds, amphibians and reptiles – treated separately in this section on tracks and trails. The size categories developed for use in the book are the same for all animal tracks, and are as follows:

Enormous more than 15cm long

Large 10–15cm long

Medium 7–10cm long

Small 2.5–7cm long

Minute less than 2.5cm long

Note: all scale bars, regardless of their colour and the size at which they are reproduced, invariably represent a measurement of 5 centimetres.

Size does of course vary with the age of the animal, and there are often size differences (and, indeed, considerable morphological variations) between fore and hind feet. There are also size differences between the tracks of different sexes in many species. Because of these variations some species appear in more than one category, in which case a combination of two scale bars of different colours is used.

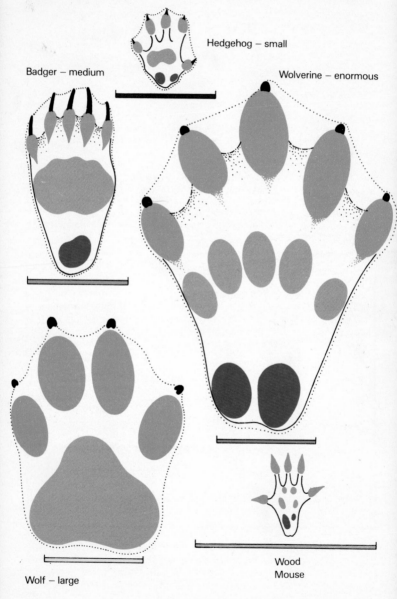

Hedgehog – small

Badger – medium

Wolverine – enormous

Wolf – large

Wood Mouse

Mammal track morphology

Mammals walk on the flat of their feet (*plantigrade*), up on their toes (*digitigrade*) or on the extreme tips of one or two toes (*unguligrade*). This progression usually relates to modification for speed. Plantigrade and digitigrade limbs give tracks with pads, while unguligrade limbs give tracks with cleaves, or slots. In both tracks with pads and tracks with cleaves there are constant features which often make species identification possible even from distorted and imperfect tracks.

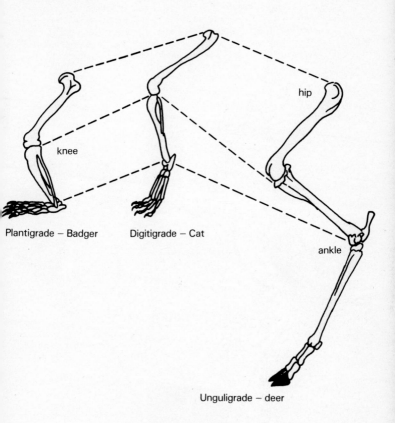

Plantigrade – Badger   Digitigrade – Cat

Unguligrade – deer

TRACKS WITH PADS

This shows a theoretical five-toed track in which all the possible elements are present. In almost all tracks the *digital pads* (toe pads) and *claws*, if present, are represented. The toes are numbered I to V away from the body. In most species some element of the *interdigital pads* (pads on the front of the palms or soles), which may be fused or separate, is present. One or two *proximal pads* (pads on the heel or the back of the hand) may show if the track is deeply impressed into the ground or if the species is heavily plantigrade; these are also sometimes known as the metatarsal pads. Some tracks show partial or complete *webbing*, which may be located in a proximal, mesial or distal position. In species where the pads are small, or where the ground is very soft, the entire outline of the fingers or toes and palm may be completely present giving a *hand impression*. Finally, *hair impressions* may be present between pads and around the edge of the track. The variations in these features often combine to make species identification possible from tracks.

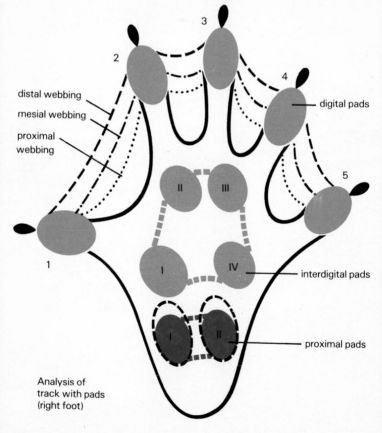

distal webbing

mesial webbing

proximal webbing

digital pads

interdigital pads

proximal pads

Analysis of track with pads (right foot)

Tracks with pads

Foot of Badger clearly showing the large interdigital pad, long claws and proximal or heels pads.

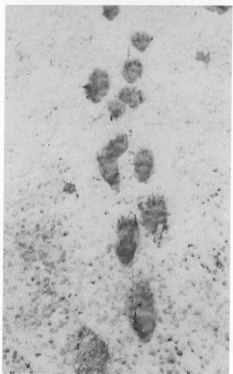

Badger trail in snow showing the whole track outlines and pad details. The tracks are splayed and there is some registration.

Mammal track morphology

Variations in the morphology of tracks with pads
Variations between species

The diagrams below demonstrate how the number of pads present and their arrangement on the track can vary. The most fundamental distinction lies in whether there are five digital pads (toes) or four. Some animals appear in both categories in the examples given: this is because a five-toed foot can, in some conditions, produce a track in which only four toes are evident.

Tracks with five toes

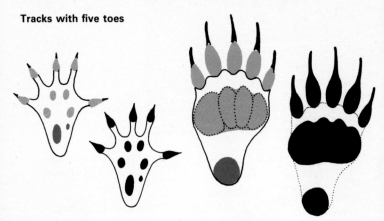

Four small separate interdigital pads; two proximal, one elongated; hand outline present (Rat)

Long attached claws; very large fused interdigital pads; one large proximal; hand outline indistinct (Badger)

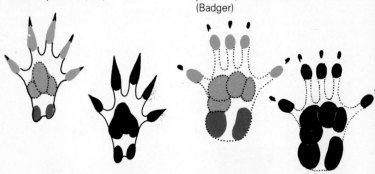

Large fused triangular interdigital pads; two oval symmetrical proximals at back of track; hand outline present (Hedgehog)

Long separate claws; four round, partly fused interdigital pads in an L-shape, one merging with one of two large proximal pads; hand outline indistinct (Edible Dormouse)

Six palm pads of near equal size; four interdigitals; two proximals which are small and symmetrical; hand outline present (Shrew)

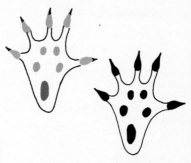

Four small separate interdigital pads; one large elongated proximal pad; hand outline present (Water Vole)

Digital I reduced; three rounded, medium-sized, partly fused interdigital pads; two fused asymmetrical proximals; hand outline present (Coypu – fore)

Digital I greatly reduced; four partly fused interdigitals; two elongated proximals; hand outline present (Dormouse)

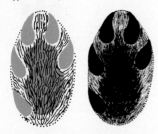

Digital pads only; fur on palm; diffuse outline (Rabbit, Hare)

Three rounded, partly fused interdigital pads; two asymmetrical proximals; hand outline present (Hedgehog – fore)

21

Tracks with four toes

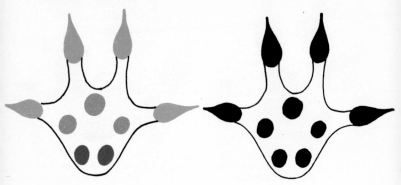

Three small interdigital pads; two
similar sized proximals – all separate;
hand outline present (Rat)

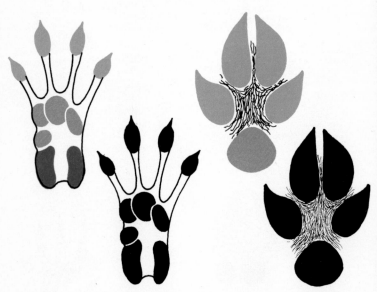

Three partly fused interdigitals in a
line, with a fourth set back and partly
fused with one of two very long proximals; hand outline present
(Dormouse)

Small rounded interdigital; hair
between pads; no hand outline (Fox)

Large triangular fused interdigitals;
no hand outline (Dog)

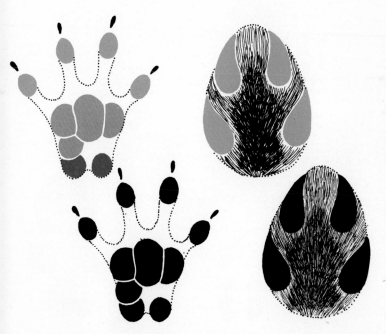

Long detached claws; four partly
fused interdigitals, one fused with
one of two small symmetrical
proximal pads; central interdigital
large; hand outline diffuse (Edible
Dormouse)

Digital pads only; diffuse outline with
large quantities of fur marks (Rabbit,
Hare)

23

Mammal track morphology

Variations due to age and sex of animal

The Badger (*Meles meles*) provides a good illustration of the variation in track form and size at different stages of maturity and between the sexes in a single species. It is important to find near complete tracks if they are to be used for definitive ageing and sexing purposes since large juveniles can be confused with small adults.

In all cases mature male tracks are wider than female (approximately 6cm against 5cm). In tracks with interdigitals only the overall length is greater in males, mainly because of the longer, heavier claw impressions. In entire tracks the width and length are much greater in the male. A characteristic of both cub and juvenile tracks is that the lobing on the front of the interdigital pads, obvious in adults, is less prominent or absent altogether. Another important diagnostic feature of young tracks is the width to length ratio, which is greater than 1:1 when measured from the back of the interdigital pads to the tip of the digitals or claws (if present). Cub tracks are easily recognized by their small size and completely absent or very small claws, which only become more prominent as the animal matures.

Adult male, interdigital and
digital pads only

Adult male, complete track

Adult female, interdigital
and digital pads only

Adult female, complete track

24

Cub, interdigital and digital pads only

Cub, complete track

Above: Registered Badger tracks in mud. Claws, interdigital and digital pads are clearly defined. The rear track lies at an angle to the fore suggesting either a deformity or that this is not true registration with the rear track being impressed from a later crossing at a slightly different angle.

Juvenile, interdigital and digital pads only

Juvenile, complete track

Analyzing incomplete or distorted tracks

Despite variations in size and quality, the tracks of many species have consistent structural features which can be used even in partial tracks to give positive identification. The Otter and the Coypu provide useful examples.

Incomplete or distorted tracks – example 1: Otter

The Otter (*Lutra lutra*) has five toes on fore and hind feet. The tracks below range from a complete one showing all the elements likely to be found in a mammalian track with pads to a rudimentary outline with few details. The feature which is consistent throughout is that *toes I and V are not aligned*. Many species show this lack of alignment, but *coupled with the known size range of otter tracks* it is diagnostic for the species.

The interdigital pads vary considerably: in some cases four fused pads are apparent, although the geometry is different, while in other cases three pads are apparent, the apex being formed from pads 2/3; sometimes only the apex of pads 2/3 may be visible.

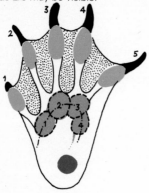 

Five digital pads, I and V not aligned; four fused interdigitals; one proximal pad; claw marks on all toes; webbing present between all digits; hand impression and outline present

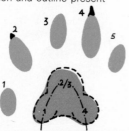 

Five digital pads, I and V not aligned; three fused interdigitals (1, 2/3 and 4); proximal pads, webbing and hand impression absent

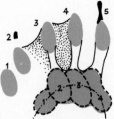 

Five digital pads, I and V not aligned; four fused interdigitals; proximal pads absent; claw mark on digital V only; partial webbing between digits II, III and IV; partial hand impression on digits III, IV and V

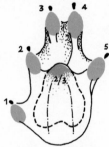 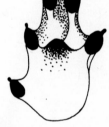

Five digital pads, I and V not aligned; apex of interdigitals 2/3 only; proximal pads absent; claw marks present on all digits; webbing present between all digits; incomplete hand impression

Five digital pads, I and V not aligned; four fused interdigitals; one proximal pad; claw mark on digital V only; webbing present between all digits; hand impression and outline present

Incomplete or distorted tracks – example 2: Coypu

The Coypu (*Myocastor coypus*) has five-toed fore and hind tracks which are different in both size and shape. Consistent diagnostic features are as follows. Hind track: *there are four interdigital pads forming an acute arc and rounded digital pads on all toes.* Fore track: *there are rounded digital pads on all toes and webbing is absent.* (Webbing is present between toes II to V only on the hind foot.)

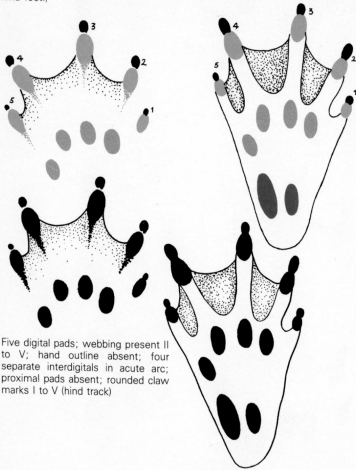

Five digital pads; webbing present II to V; hand outline absent; four separate interdigitals in acute arc; proximal pads absent; rounded claw marks I to V (hind track)

Five digital pads; webbing present II to V; hand outline complete; four separate interdigitals in acute arc; two asymmetrical unfused proximal pads; claw marks I to V (hind track)

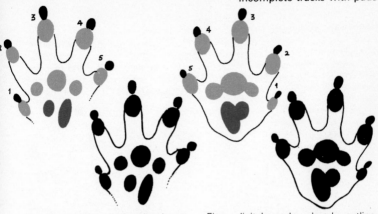

Five digital pads; hand outline incomplete; three unfused interdigital pads; two unfused proximal pads; claw marks I to V (fore track)

Five digital pads; hand outline complete; three partially fused interdigital pads; two asymmetrical fused proximal pads; claw marks I to V (fore track)

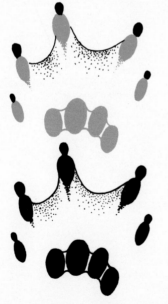

Five digital pads; webbing present II to IV only; hand outline absent; four partially fused interdigitals in an acute arc; proximal pads absent; claw marks I to V (hind track)

Five digital pads; webbing present II to V; hand outline incomplete; four fused interdigitals in an acute arc; two fused proximal pads; claw marks I to V (hind track)

29

Mammal track morphology

Registered tracks

Registration occurs when the hind foot is placed in more or less the same position as the preceding fore foot. The result may be complete elimination of the fore track, but more commonly it is partial obliteration leading to a complex combination of two tracks. The variations in registration, which mainly relate to the speed at which an animal is moving, are illustrated in the section on trail morphology (pages 45–46) and under the individual species. The analysis of registered tracks can be complicated but a series of examples showing different types of registration should help to simplify the process. In interpreting registration it is important to identify fore and hind before looking at the overall structure. The tracks illustrated are those of the Badger.

Complete lateral displacement: fore and hind tracks lie side by side, the two tracks barely touching laterally; this form of displacement is unusual and suggests misalignment due to injury or disease in one of the limbs

Slight lateral displacement: one track lies slightly to the left or right of the other – this is not uncommon, especially in young animals. This track also shows vertically normal registration: an uncommon pattern in which there is exact vertical matching of fore and hind tracks

Varying degrees of sub or pre-registration in adult animals: tracks of varying qualities show the hind placed slightly behind the preceding fore

Pre-registration (or sub-registration) in a juvenile: pre-registered tracks show large complex interdigital relationships and often a double row of digitals or claws

Post or over-registration: hind track placed partly ahead of the preceding fore. This situation can be so extreme that the hind interdigitals obliterate the preceding fore digitals.

Above: Muntjac path up a muddy stream bank. The slots are deep and there is much evidence of slipping.

TRACKS WITH CLEAVES

An idealized deer track is shown below. The impressions of the cleaves are called *slots*. There are two main slots (digits III and IV), sometimes with *dew claw* impressions from higher on the limb. These are the reduced digits II and V, and their height relative to III and IV is such that in some species they will show under any circumstances (e.g. in Reindeer, Musk Ox and Wild Boar), in others only when the ground is soft (e.g. Muntjac) and in some not at all (e.g. Bison). The main elements of the slots are the *walls*, the *sole* and the *toe pads*, and although these are fairly simple they can vary in shape and in their proportions. The overall shape and size of the tracks can also vary.

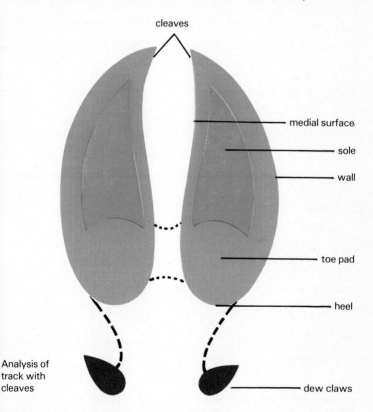

cleaves

medial surface

sole

wall

toe pad

heel

Analysis of track with cleaves

dew claws

Size categories All tracks with cleaves can be allocated to one of the five size categories listed on page 15 in the same way as tracks with pads. An example in each category is given here, although the majority of tracks with cleaves fall into the small and medium categories; even the broad rounded cow track normally only falls into the large category.

Mammal track morphology

The diagrams below show perfect tracks, but the majority found in field situations tend to be slipped or distorted in some way and normally appear larger. For this reason it is important to look at morphological features as well as size in identifying species from tracks.

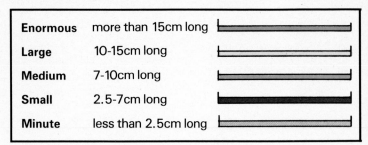

Enormous	more than 15cm long	
Large	10-15cm long	
Medium	7-10cm long	
Small	2.5-7cm long	
Minute	less than 2.5cm long	

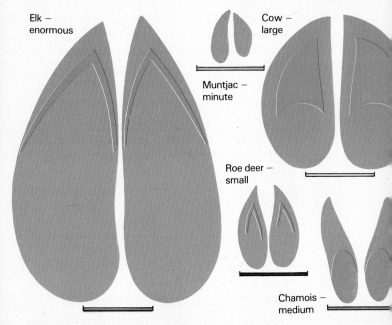

Elk – enormous

Cow – large

Muntjac – minute

Roe deer – small

Chamois – medium

Running tracks with cleaves Running tracks may show *dew claw impressions*, which are often lacking in normally impressed tracks, and some degree of *splay*, controlled by the amount of connective tissue between the toes. This varies between species and, in the deer at least, the cleaves on the fore foot are always more prone to splaying than on the hind. The positioning and size of dew claws is again characteristic of species. The illustrations on page 35 show decreasing splay related to structure. In each case the measurement is from dew claw to tip.

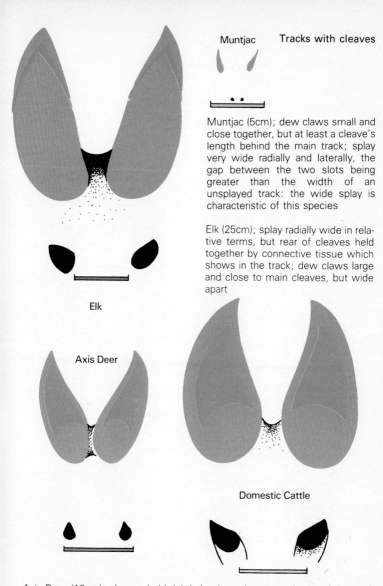

Tracks with cleaves

Muntjac

Muntjac (5cm); dew claws small and close together, but at least a cleave's length behind the main track; splay very wide radially and laterally, the gap between the two slots being greater than the width of an unsplayed track: the wide splay is characteristic of this species

Elk (25cm); splay radially wide in relative terms, but rear of cleaves held together by connective tissue which shows in the track; dew claws large and close to main cleaves, but wide apart

Elk

Axis Deer

Domestic Cattle

Axis Deer (13cm); cleaves held tightly by tissue in a central area of the track so that the heels show free; splay restricted to a limited radial form; dew claws small and set far behind main cleaves, distance between them large relative to track size

Domestic Cattle (18.5cm); dew claws rare, very large, close to main cleaves, widely spaced when present; cleaves held tightly by ligament at back, so open laterally rather than splaying at the tips

Variations in the morphology of tracks with cleaves
Variations between species

Tracks with cleaves do not show as much variety in form as tracks with pads. However, when the tracks are well impressed it is possible to categorize them, as the illustrations below show.

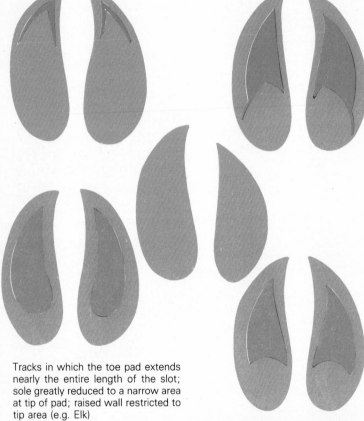

Tracks in which the toe pad extends nearly the entire length of the slot; sole greatly reduced to a narrow area at tip of pad; raised wall restricted to tip area (e.g. Elk)

Tracks with toe pad half or less of track length; sole prominent, more than half of track length; toe pads convex and lance-shaped (e.g. Wild Boar, Roe Deer)

Tracks with no obvious differentiation of features (e.g. Muntjac)

Tracks with toe pad reduced to less than half length of track, concave; sole very large, walls pronounced (e.g. Reindeer)

Tracks with toe pad reduced to half or less of track length, convex and rounded; sole prominent (e.g. Axis Deer)

Variations due to age of animal – example: Elk
The main change in Elk tracks as the animal matures is a reduction in the width to length ratio: the track becomes increasingly elongated and overall size increases. The proportions of the walls and toe pads also change.

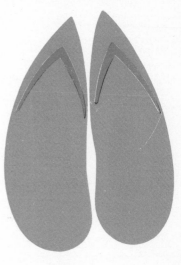

Calf track: overall size is much smaller than adult; shape broader and more rounded; cleaves with concave nick on front of medial wall

Entire adult track

Juvenile track: shows many of the adult qualities but heels are not so full; distinct concavity still present on front of medial walls

Juvenile (left) and calf (above) running tracks showing splay and dew claws. (Splaying does occur in adults but is less pronounced and dew claws are not seen so often.)

37

Mammal track morphology

Incomplete or distorted tracks

Tracks with cleaves show consistent structural features even though the quality of individual tracks can vary considerably, as it can with pads.

Example 1: Muntjac

The Muntjac (*Muntiacus reevesi*) is a good example since a consistent feature is that its tracks *always show one cleave longer than the other*, despite a wide range of track type related to surface conditions, gait, sex, age and condition of the animal. The cleave differential may be apical or proximal and the cleaves themselves may be offset.

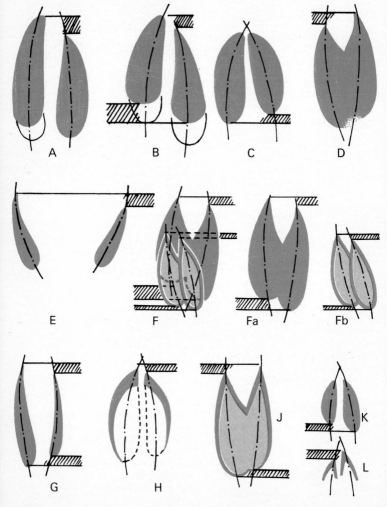

Imcomplete tracks with cleaves

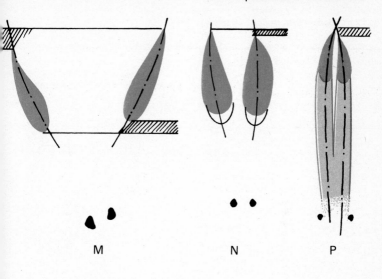

M

N

P

A Entire adult track on soft ground: cleaves parallel, slight slipping on left cleave; differential apical
B Entire adult track on soft ground: slight apical convergence, and slipping on both cleaves; differential apical and proximal
C Entire sub-adult track on soft ground: track wide; differential proximal
D Entire adult track on soft ground: cleaves fused, splay very slight; differential apical
E Adult running track on hard ground, showing walls and part of soles; splay very wide; differential apical
F Complex track involving two specimens at different times and showing partial registration; (a) older track of adult when ground was soft: cleaves entire, differential proximal; (b) newer track of sub-adult when ground had dried: walls and medial surface only, differential apical and proximal

G Adult track on hard ground, walls and medial surface only; differential apical and proximal
H Sub-adult track on hard ground, walls and medial surface only; differential apical
J Entire adult track on soft ground: cleaves fused with slight apical divergence; differential apical and proximal
K Entire juvenile track on soft ground: differential proximal
L Juvenile track on hard ground: tips of cleaves only; differential apical
M Almost entire adult track showing very wide splay and dew claws; differential apical and proximal
N Entire adult running track with slight apical divergence; dew claws present; slippage on both cleaves; differential apical
P Entire adult track on soft ground, slipped but not splayed: dew claws present; differential not apparent but small size diagnostic of species

Example 2: various deer species

This shows tracks of a number of different species of deer. These are all complicated and distorted, but with careful observation the underlying track morphology can be detected.

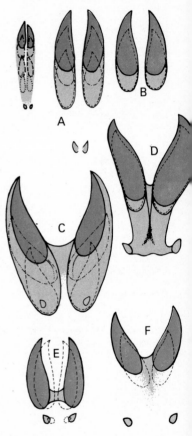

A Sika Deer: track is soft substrate showing small dew claws close together; the parallel cleaves have then slid forward to give an elongated track. Lack of splay and closeness of dew claws show that the animal was moving slowly on soft slippey ground.

B Axis Deer: track slightly elongated, slots parallel, dew claws absent; track on damp ground showing slight slide forward with no splay. Animal walking slowly on wet (and/or sloping) ground.

C Fallow Deer: track greatly enlarged, slipped and splayed; dew claws splayed; web between slots. Animal moving over soft ground at high speed.

D White-tailed Deer: track splayed and slipped, showing widely spaced dew claws and much of heel; some deformity in slots due to slipping. Deer moving at high speed on very soft ground

E Roe Deer: cleaves parallel and with dew claws; track extended laterally and showing web; separation of cleaves caused by lateral slipping or distortion.

F Red Deer: slightly slipped and widely splayed cleaves with dew claws and web between slots. Deer moving over fairly firm ground at high speed.

Mammal trail morphology

There are several general elements in the structure of a trail. The tracks may be *simple* or *compound*; there are additional body markings such as *tail drag*, *feather markings* or *body drag*. Between the tracks from the left and right side of the animal is an imaginary centre line of the trail called the *median line*. The distance between the left and right tracks is known as the *straddle*. The *angle* that tracks form with the median line gives information about the gait, as does the length of the *stride* – the distance between two tracks made by the same foot.

TRAIL CLASSIFICATION

Trails fall into groups related to the gait of the animal. The main gaits are *walking, trotting or running, galloping* and *bounding and hopping.* There is some overlap between the different types of trail, and these categories are introduced for ease of explanation. The illustrations here cover the range of commonly occurring trails; special gaits such as 'flopping' in seals and bat 'walking' are discussed in the context of the individual species only.

Walking trails

The walking gait involves the movement of only one limb from the ground at any one time. The stride is relatively short and the hind feet are placed very close to the fore, giving good registration (if registration occurs in the species concerned at all). In some of the rodents and insectivores the body is carried low to the ground so that body and tail marks are common. The walking trail indicates that the animal has been moving at leisure and perhaps grazing or browsing as it goes.

Trotting and running trails

As pace increases, alternate opposite limbs are lifted from the ground at the same time (e.g. right fore and left hind); length of stride increases and registration becomes less perfect, with over-registration becoming more common. Straddle decreases in many groups, but track splay increases in the hoofed species; body drag and tail marks become less prominent or disappear; the tracks are more heavily impressed (ground permitting); there is increased distortion and slipping; and in tracks with cleaves dew claws become more common. The trotting gait is the normal pace for some carnivores and the run is normal in many insectivores and rodents.

Galloping trails

At the gallop the animal is moving at high speed and all four feet are off the ground together at some point in the stride. The tracks are not registered and occur in irregular groups of four with a variable distance between them. Often the hind tracks appear almost opposite, with the fore tracks in a line either ahead of or behind them. In the galloping gait the bulk of the impetus for take-off is derived from the fore legs. Tracks are deeply impressed and show considerable detail.

Bounding and hopping trails

Although these two gaits mark extremes in terms of speed they have certain common characteristics. In the bounding gait the whole body is lifted from the ground by the impetus of the hind legs. In hopping the impetus is from either fore or hind. The weasels bound at varying speeds, the tracks appearing neatly in groups of four in opposite pairs (i.e. the two hind and two fore tracks directly opposite each other across the median line). Sometimes the tracks may be so closely grouped that partial registration takes place, and because the weasels arch their bodies tail drag may be present. The hopping gait of the lagomorphs (hares and rabbits) leaves closely grouped tracks which become more deeply impressed as speed increases.

Examples of the variation in all main features of mammal trails are given on pages 46–49 and illustrated in diagrammatic form together with an actual example found in the field in each case.

Mammal trail morphology

Examples of gaits

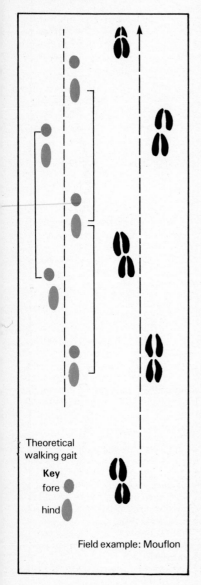

Theoretical
walking gait

Key
fore
hind

Field example: Mouflon

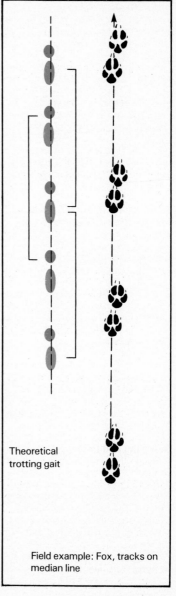

Theoretical
trotting gait

Field example: Fox, tracks on
median line

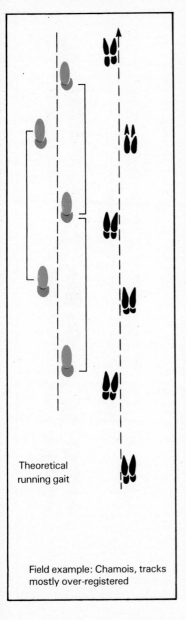

Theoretical
running gait

Field example: Chamois, tracks
mostly over-registered

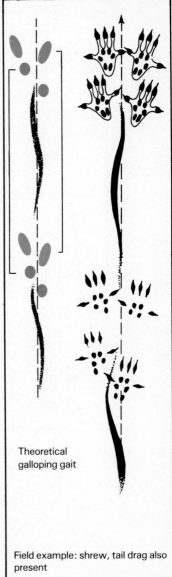

Theoretical
galloping gait

Field example: shrew, tail drag also
present

Mammal trail morphology

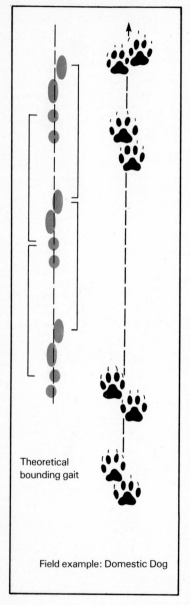

Theoretical
bounding gait

Field example: Domestic Dog

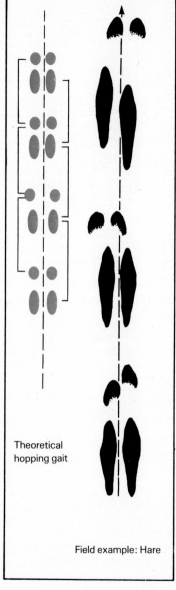

Theoretical
hopping gait

Field example: Hare

Registration

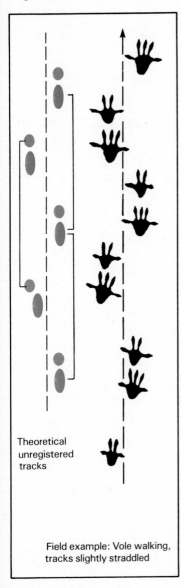

Theoretical
unregistered
tracks

Field example: Vole walking,
tracks slightly straddled

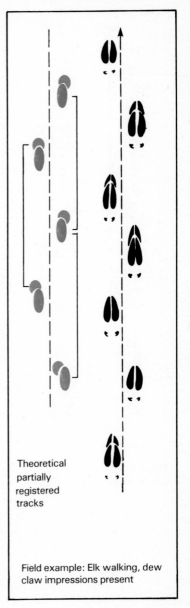

Theoretical
partially
registered
tracks

Field example: Elk walking, dew
claw impressions present

45

Mammal trail morphology

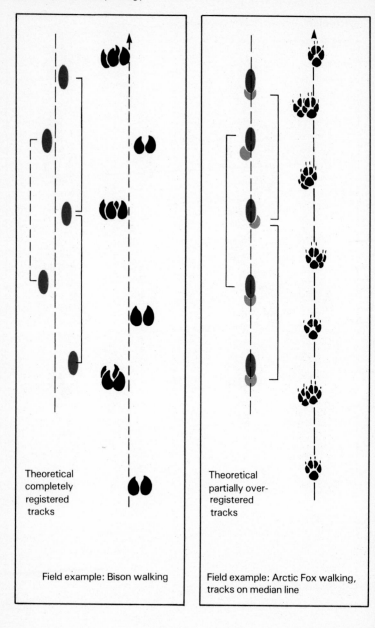

Theoretical completely registered tracks

Field example: Bison walking

Theoretical partially over-registered tracks

Field example: Arctic Fox walking, tracks on median line

Straddle

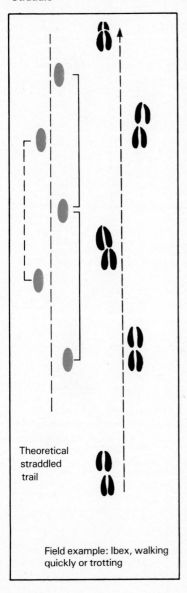

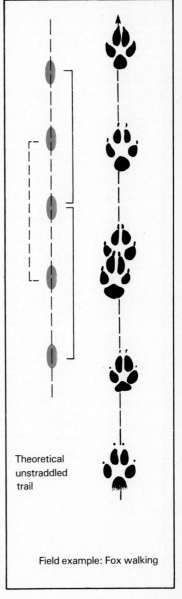

Theoretical straddled trail

Theoretical unstraddled trail

Field example: Ibex, walking quickly or trotting

Field example: Fox walking

47

Track angle with median line

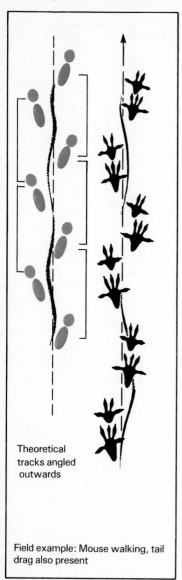

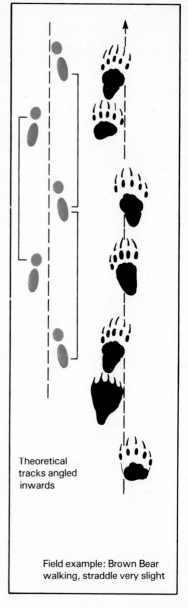

Theoretical
tracks angled
outwards

Theoretical
tracks angled
inwards

Field example: Mouse walking, tail
drag also present

Field example: Brown Bear
walking, straddle very slight

Tail drag

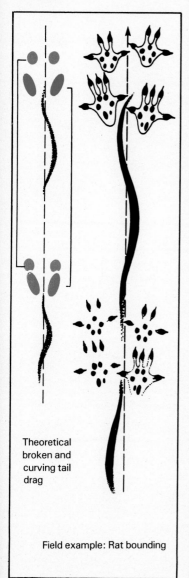

Theoretical
broken and
curving tail
drag

Field example: Rat bounding

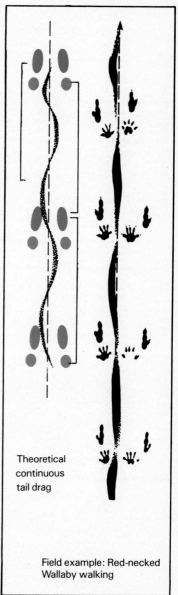

Theoretical
continuous
tail drag

Field example: Red-necked
Wallaby walking

The mammal tracks of Europe

The pages that follow contain full descriptions of the tracks and trails of individual mammal species. They are not arranged taxonomically in the traditional way (i.e. in Orders); instead they are arranged according to the size and shape of the hind track. (Fortunately, although there may be size differences between fore and hind tracks, there are relatively few species in which they are totally dissimilar.)

For the purposes of this book mammal tracks have been divided into three broad morphological groups and five size categories. The morphological groups are (i) five- and four-toed tracks with pads; (ii) four-toed tracks with pads and (iii) tracks with cleaves. The size categories and their colour-coded scale bars have already been described and illustrated on pages 16 and 34. This arrangement makes it easier to use the book as a practical field guide to tracks.

Within each morphological group, descriptions start with the largest hind track and work down towards the smallest. Of course animal track sizes are not absolute, and so when a track is seen the inexperienced observer may need to compare it with a number of the descriptions and illustrations given here in order to make an identification. Full track and trail analyses are given, together with information about the animal's behaviour, habitat and distribution, which should help to confirm that the identification made is correct. Obviously the situation occurs when only a single fore track or just a few partial tracks are found, and then it is a matter of finding the approximate location; with patience and experience it will often prove possible to identify such tracks.

Key to mammal tracks

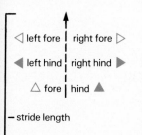

A slipped track
B splayed track
C distorted by disease or obstruction on the ground

- ● complete track
- ◗ incomplete track
- ○ track in hard ground (e.g. digital pads and claws only)
- ◑ track in intermediate ground (e.g. claws, digital and interdigital pads; sometimes proximal pads)
- ● tracks in very soft ground or snow (e.g. claws, pads, track outline, webbing, etc.)
- ◗ perfect or near perfect registration
- (◗ lateral registration (side by side)
- ◗ pre (under) registration (fore before hind)
- ◗ post (over) registration (hind before fore)
- ✳ registered tracks with features missing

Brown Bear *Ursus arctos*

The adult Brown Bear is very large (up to 2.5m) and heavily built, with short rounded ears which just project above the outline of the head. There is an angle between muzzle and forehead; tail is absent. **Behaviour** solitary, generally nocturnal, more active by day in remote areas. Hibernates; young born in hibernating den (normally a cave or rock crevice). **Habitat** deciduous and coniferous forests, extending into tundra and high-mountain areas. **Distribution** N, S, SF, SU; more rarely in remote upland areas of A, AL, BG, CH, CS, E, F, GR, H, I, P, PL, YU.

Track enormous; fore 23–30 × 17cm, hind 25–30 × 17cm (including the very long claws); fur marks may be present, giving entire hand print. Tracks are 5-toed and very broad, the large unlobed interdigital pad forming a kidney shape with the digitals in a slight curve in front of it. The combined areas of the 5 digitals fit within the interdigital area. A single proximal pad sometimes shows, particularly on the fore track.

Trail normal gait is a walk in which the tracks, especially the fore, point inwards towards the median line; registration does not normally occur; stride usually 80–100cm. Faster walk shows hind track in front of the preceding fore; galloping gait shows closer registration with bounds of up to 150cm.

Brown Bear

European Brown Bear eating the bottom of rush stems, which are being held delicately between the toes.

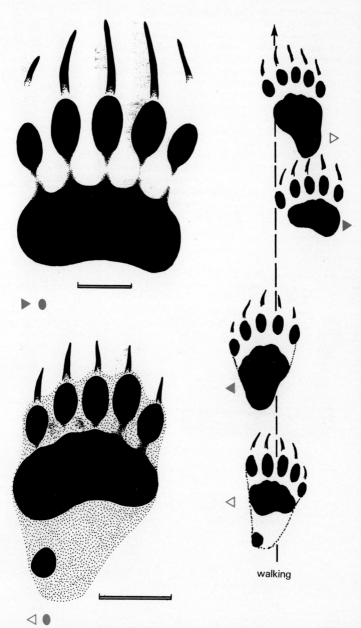

walking

Polar Bear *Thalarctos maritimus*

Similar in size to the Brown Bear, but the ears do not protrude above the head outline and there is no angle between muzzle and forehead. Coat is always a whitish colour. **Behaviour** solitary and diurnal, travelling over great distances. Female only hibernates, giving birth to young in snow den. Much time spent in sea. **Habitat** Arctic coastal area. **Distribution** Spitzbergen; occasionally reaching north N and IS on drift ice.

Track enormous, often more than 30 × 17cm. Similar to Brown Bear track but claw marks are short and blunt. The heavy covering of fur frequently shows, as does a single proximal pad.

Trail normal gait is a walk with slightly inturned tracks which sometimes register; strides of about 100cm are common. Tracks are grouped in the galloping gait, with up to 200cm between each group.

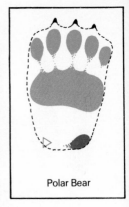

Polar Bear

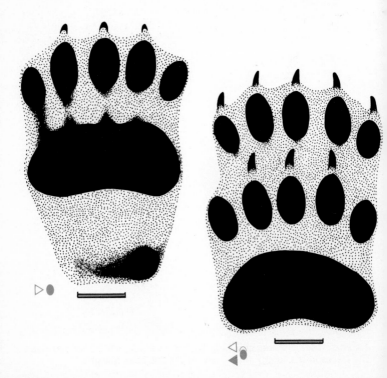

A complex set of tracks showing the site of a 'seal kill' by a Polar Bear. The tracks in the foreground show where the bear charged.

Wolverine *Gulo gulo*

Largest of the mustelids: body up to 80cm, tail to 25cm. Diagnostic features are size, relatively long legs, bushy tail and the pale areas between the eye and ear along the flank. **Behaviour** solitary, mainly nocturnal, active throughout the year; ground-living but able to climb well. Lair built in rocks, under tree roots or in a snow hole. **Habitat** boreal forests and tundra. **Distribution** restricted to the Arctic areas of N, S, SF and SU.

Track hind enormous (15 × 12cm); fore large (12 × 11cm). The interdigital pad has 5 lobes; digital pads may appear single or fused according to digitigrade or plantigrade walk. Claw marks short, blunt, attached to the digital pads; hand impression and mesially connected web often

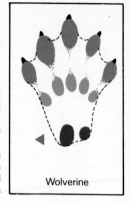

Wolverine

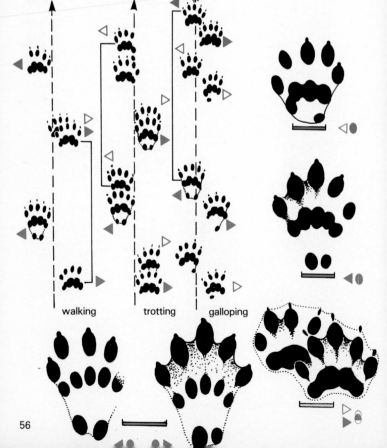

walking   trotting   galloping

present. The long broad tracks with distinctive webbing and fine features in the interdigital pads are unique to this species, even in juveniles.

Trail changes in gait are frequent. Almost complete registration is common in walking; stride 15–60cm. Trotting gives paired tracks, partially registered; stride 35–50cm. The gallop gives tracks in groups of four with at least 90cm between each group.

Red-necked Wallaby *Macropus rufigriseus*

Small marsupial; distinguished by bipedal stance, small forelegs, very large rear legs and long thick tail. **Behaviour** solitary or in small groups; active throughout the year. **Habitat** scrub woodland and moorland. **Distribution** restricted to two small areas in GB.

Track fore medium (7 × 7cm); hind large, (12 × 5cm). Three toes on hind track, one very large, 2nd smaller and 3rd vestigial; if the animal is resting the full length of the foot to the heel (up to 25cm) will show.

Trail walking gait shows fore tracks with the long hind tracks ahead in groups of 4; tail drag distinct; stride about 50cm. In the (more normal) hopping gait only the hind tracks show; tail drag marks absent; stride 45–60cm, occasionally over 100cm.

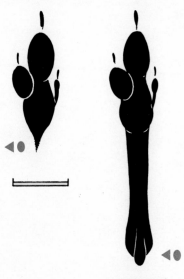

hopping

Beaver *Castor fiber*

Largest European rodent: body up to 100cm, tail to 40cm. Easily confused with the Otter when in water; in the absence of a land sighting, when its large, laterally flattened scaly tail is unmistakable, the Beaver is best identified by signs. **Behaviour** gregarious, living in family groups; nocturnal, although may be diurnal if undisturbed; active throughout the year. Highly adapted to an aquatic existence: produces elaborate dam, bank tunnel and 'lodge' systems in which to rest and breed. **Habitat** lakes and rivers in deciduous woodlands (aspen, birch, willows, elms, poplars). **Distribution** highly fragmented, augmented by introduction of the identical *C. canadensis* and re-introduction of the native species in recent years. Colonies in A, CH, D, DDR, F, N, PL, R, S, SF and SU.

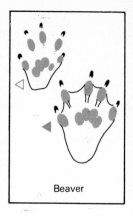

Beaver

Track hind large (up to 15 × 9.5cm); fore medium (up to 9 × 8cm). Five toes on fore and hind feet. Fore tracks show 5 digital pads, sometimes with blunt rounded discrete claw marks; interdigital pad has 4 small, partially fused lobes; toes I and V set back against interdigital. Heel outline sometimes shows, but there is no webbing.

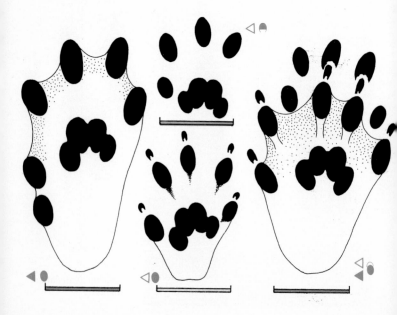

Hind track has 5 large digital pads; claw marks rare. Digital pad V is at the back of, or even behind, the small interdigital pad, which has 4 small, partially fused lobes. There are distal web marks between all toes and sometimes a full heel outline and a single proximal pad.

Trail normal land trail is from a walk: tracks turn inwards towards median line; registration almost complete; tail drag shows as a prominent zig-zag depression between tracks on alternate sides. Stride about 30cm. Running tracks become more widely spaced and less perfectly registered. When carrying young or food the Beaver may walk on its hind feet only: this shows as alternate hind tracks and tail drag marks; stride short, shuffling, no more than 15cm.

Birch tree partially gnawed through by a Beaver. The very large incisor marks may be clearly seen.

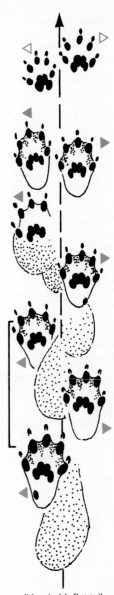

walking (with flat tail marks)

59

Coypu *Myocastor coypus*

A large animal (body up to 60cm, tail to 45cm) resembling the Beaver but distinguishable on land by its long cylindrical tail and in the water by a smaller slower-moving head profile. **Behaviour** gregarious, often abundant; nocturnal and crepuscular; active all year. Breeds and rests in waterside burrow systems which may be extensive. **Habitat** fresh water; brackish channels and marshes. **Distribution** GB, F; smaller colonies in D, I, L, N, PL and SU.

Track hind large (up to 15 × 8cm); fore small to medium (6 × 6cm); both very variable. Five toes on both feet; on the fore digital pad I very small, and I and V not level. Digitals prominent with large rounded claws. The interdigital has 3 fused lobes; 2 proximal pads, partially fused. There is no webbing and a hand outline is common. Hind track shows 5 digital pads, 4 small separate interdigitals and 2 partially fused proximal pads. Hand outline common; complete distal webbing between digital pads II and V only: this feature is unique in European tracks.

Trail generally the trail shows tracks which almost straddle the median line; partially registered; a broad tail drag swings from side to side.

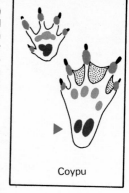

Coypu

Coypu floating in open water. The tail is cylindrical and the external ears are larger than those of the Beaver.

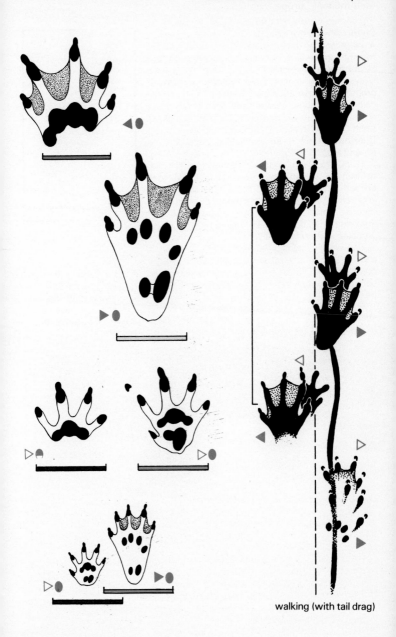

walking (with tail drag)

Porcupine *Hystrix cristata*
Large rodent (up to 75cm): easily distinguished by large black and white spines. **Behaviour** living in small groups; completely nocturnal; active all year. Shelters and breeds in caves or burrows. **Habitat** open woodland and Mediterranean scrubland. **Distribution** southern I and Sicily.

Track medium; 5-toed. Fore foot has 5 digital pads with claws; interdigital pad has 3 almost completely fused lobes. In a fully impressed track 2 proximal pads show. Hind track normally only shows 4 digital pads; interdigital pad with 3 partially fused lobes; 2 unequal proximal pads.

Trail normal gait is a walk. Partial registration occurs and the tracks point straight forward; stride about 30cm; drag marks occur in soft conditions.

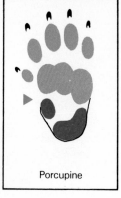

Porcupine

Himalayan Porcupine *Hystrix hodgsoni*
Similar to *H. cristata*, but slightly smaller and without the pronounced bristle crest. **Behaviour and habitat** similar to *H. cristata*. **Distribution** zoo escape in various countries.

Track medium; 5-toed. Fore track shows 4 large digital pads, 4-lobed interdigital and 2 unequal proximals; proximal web is distinct in soft conditions. Hind track has 5 digital pads; wide interdigital pad; very large proximal pads; proximal web.

Trail similar to *H. cristata*.

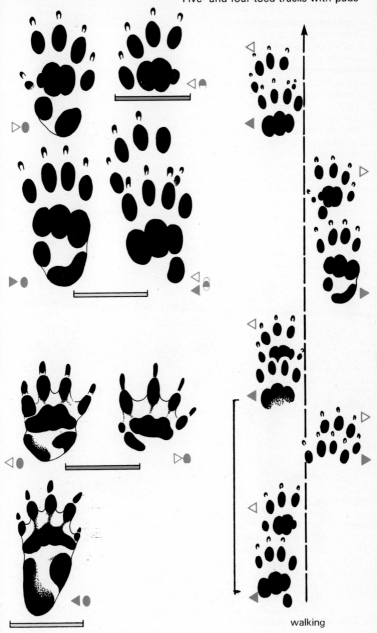

walking

Raccoon *Procyon lotor*
Medium-sized carnivore (body up to 60cm, tail to
25cm), distinguished by large ears, black face mask
and short thick banded tail. **Behaviour** solitary and
nocturnal; long periods of inactivity in the winter.
Spends much time on the ground, but is an agile
climber and a good swimmer. Rests and breeds in
high tree holes or rock crevices. **Habitat** woodlands, mainly deciduous, close to water. **Distribution** present DDR, D and spreading into B and NL.

   Track medium: hind up to 8.5 × 6.5cm, fore 7.5
× 6.5cm. Five digital pads show on each track,
normally with a toe outline. Short sharp claw marks
are common as is a complete hand outline.

   Trail normal gait is a walk. The tracks are slightly
registered and straddle the median line with a tendency to point outwards; stride about 35cm.

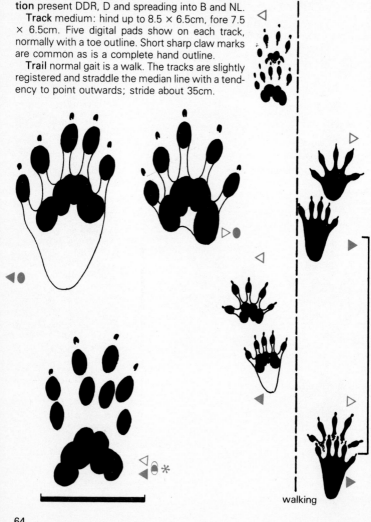

walking

Pine Marten *Martes martes*

The Pine Marten is a large mustelid (body up to 55cm, tail to 27cm). Ears are larger, legs longer, tails longer and more bushy than in polecats and mink. Diagnostic feature is a large dull orange–yellow patch on the neck, the fur otherwise being uniform and dark. **Behaviour** solitary, crepuscular and nocturnal; active all year. Spends much time on the ground, but is adapted to an arboreal existence. Nests in hollow trees and rock crevices. **Habitat** coniferous and deciduous woodlands, cliffs and rocky places. **Distribution** widespread over much of Europe; restricted in E and GB, absent from GR, IS and P.

Track medium: hind 8.5 × 6cm; fore 8 × 6cm. Interdigital pad may show as a heavy square block or as 4 or 5 small, partly fused lobes. Five digital pads normally show with short blunt claw marks; deeply impressed tracks show elongated double proximal pads on the hind feet and a single large proximal pad on the fore feet. Proximal webbing and fur impressions are sometimes present and complete hand outlines are common.

Trail at a walking gait the tracks are unregistered and tend to be randomly placed with an irregular stride of about 50cm. The normal mustelid bounding trail with the tracks in groups of 4 does occur, but the bound frequently gives equidistant and alternate pairs of fore and hind tracks about 60–90cm apart. Tail drag rare.

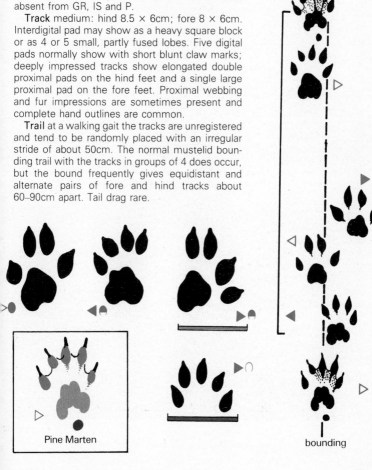

Pine Marten

bounding

65

Pine Marten den in a
well sheltered crevice.

Beech Marten *Martes foina*

A large mustelid (body up to 48cm, tail to 26cm). Diagnostic feature is the white bib on the throat which is often divided or reduced to a small patch. **Behaviour** solitary, crepuscular and nocturnal; active all year. Adept climber, frequently building dens in house roofs as well as trees or rock crevices. **Habitat** deciduous woodlands, open hillside and human habitations. **Distribution** throughout Europe except GB, IRL, IS, N, S, SU and northern SF.

Track small to medium, slightly smaller than Pine Marten: hind 5.5–6 × 5–6cm; fore 5 × 4.5cm. Interdigital pad shows as a heavy square or as 4 or 5 small, partly fused lobes; 1 proximal pad. The 5 digital pad impressions carry long slender claw marks rather than the blunt marks of Pine Marten; overall track impression is more distinct and less hairy.

Trail the walking gait gives pairs of unregistered or slightly registered tracks; stride about 30cm. Normal gait on the ground is the arched-back mustelid bound, giving tracks in groups of 4 with 40–60cm between each group.

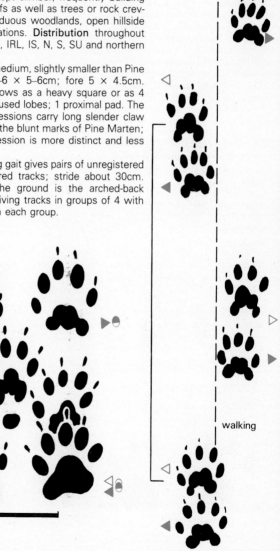

walking

Otter *Lutra lutra*

The Otter is a large mustelid (body up to 80cm, tail to 45cm). Recognized on land by long pointed tail, white chin and bib. In water, where often only the head is visible, distinguished from Coypu and Beaver by its speed. **Behaviour** solitary and nocturnal; active throughout the year. The Otter spends much time in water, for which the species is adapted, but is capable of moving quickly over land. Spends day in 'holt', often located under river-bank tree roots, in rocky banks or in reed beds. **Habitat** rivers, marshy areas, lakes and the sea coast. **Distribution** widespread over the whole of Europe except central D, DDR, Balkan area of SU, south GR and all of IS. Numbers declining drastically in many countries.

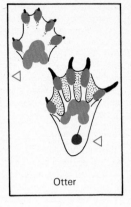

Otter

Track medium: hind 8.5 × 6cm; fore 6.5 × 6cm. Tracks are square with a 3 or 4-lobed interdigital pad; 5 digital pads are normal on fore and hind, but sometimes only 4 show. In deep impressions a single proximal pad is present. Short blunt claw marks, continuous with digital pads, often show clearly and the distal web, which is present between all 5 toes on fore and hind, is frequently impressed. Complete hand impressions are uncommon except in very soft ground.

Trail walking trail shows near perfect registration of hind over fore; stride over 35cm. The galloping gait gives loose groupings of 4 unregistered tracks with a stride of 50cm or more. The characteristic weasel bound gives 4 neatly grouped tracks with at least 80cm between each group. Trails in the snow show much variety: the bounding trail shows the tracks in groups of 4 with body marks but no tail drag. Walking trail shows body drag and tail marks; sliding trail shows all these elements and claw marks as well. See also pages 26–27.

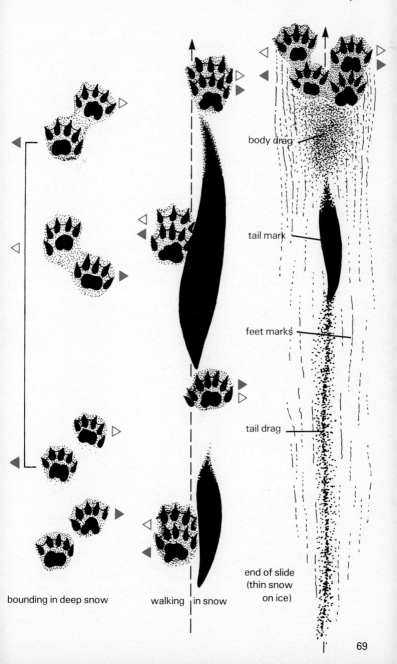

Five- and four-toed tracks with pads

body drag

tail mark

feet marks

tail drag

bounding in deep snow

walking in snow

end of slide
(thin snow
on ice)

69

Muskrat *Ondatra zibethica*

A large vole (body up to 40cm, tail to 27cm). Smaller than Coypu and Beaver, recognized by long, vertically flattened tail. **Behaviour** solitary or in small groups; active day and night throughout the year. Excellent swimmer and diver. Makes extensive burrow systems in banks and 'lodges' in reed beds. **Habitat** always by freshwater bodies and marshes. **Distribution** introduced into two main ares: in central Europe in B, BG, CH, CS, D, DDR, DK, F, H, L, NL, PL, R and YU; in northern Europe in S, SF and SU.

Track small; hind 6 × 6.5cm; fore 3.5 × 3.5cm. Five toes on fore and hind. Fore foot shows 5 small rounded digital pads, digital I often not showing in tracks; claws are long, slender and discrete. Three interdigital pads, just fused; 2 slightly unequal proximal pads. Full hand impression is common. Hind track shows 5 small oval digital pads with long slender discrete claws; 4 equal interdigital pads, oval, partially fused or unfused; 2 asymmetrical proximal pads. Hand outline is common. The small digital and interdigital pads and the distance between them are diagnostic of this species.

Trail walking trail shows tracks in pairs, partially registered and close to the median line; tail drag shows strongly; stride about 10cm. Bounding trail shows tracks in groups of 4, with hind appearing ahead of fore and tail drag showing between groups. There is about 15cm between each group at slow speed, but stride increases with pace to over 40cm.

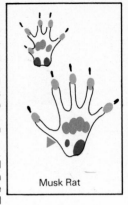

Musk Rat

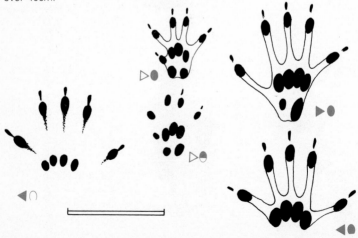

Muskrat lodge: these breeding lodges are smaller and more flimsy than those of the Beaver and tend to stand as isolated structures in open water.

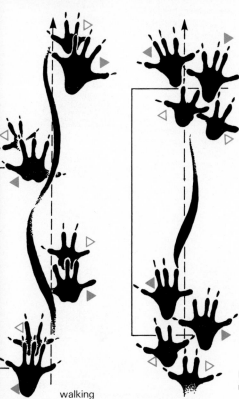

walking

bounding (over registration may occur)

Badger *Meles meles*

The Badger is a large mustelid (body up to 80cm, tail to 19cm), distinguished by black and white face pattern, grey back, black underside and short tail. **Behaviour** gregarious, mainly nocturnal; reduced winter activity. Breeds and spends most of daylight hours in extensive underground tunnel systems known as setts. **Habitat** deciduous and coniferous woods, grassland and arable land. **Distribution** throughout Europe except IS; absent from high mountain and Arctic areas of N, S, SF and SU.

Track small to medium: hind 6 × 5cm; fore 6 × 5.5cm (both including very long claws). The tracks are broad in relation to length and the fore is larger than the hind. Most solid of all weasel family tracks, with a very large, broadly kidney-shaped interdigital pad. Unlike other mustelid tracks the 5 digital pads all lie in front of the interdigital pad in a shallow arc. Very long slender claw marks, normally separated from the digital pads, are often present and in rare cases a single proximal pad may show. Rarely, a partial hand outline shows in soft ground with a suggestion of a mesial web. See also pages 24–25.

Trail the walking trail shows almost completely registered tracks, frequently turned in towards the median line, with a variable stride of 15cm or more. At a slow walk the body is carried close to the ground and hair traces may show. Trotting trail shows imperfectly registered tracks which are 20cm or more apart. Galloping trail gives pairs of almost perfectly registered tracks; bounding trail gives the characteristic weasel grouping of 4 tracks with at least 40cm between each group.

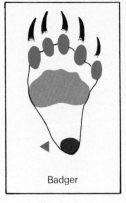

Badger

damaged interdigital pad and very long claws indicate damage to foot

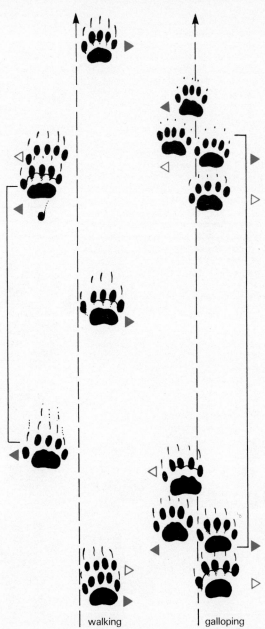

walking

galloping

Alpine Marmot *Marmota marmota*

Large and squirrel-like (body up to 58cm, tail to 19cm), the Alpine Marmot is easily identified by its size, short but well haired tail and restricted habitat preference. **Behaviour** gregarious, living in small family groups; diurnal; true hibernation October to April. Lives and breeds in deep burrows. **Habitat** high Alpine pastures, although may extend further if tree cover is absent. **Distribution** mountainous areas in A, CH, CS, E, F, H?, I, PL and YU.

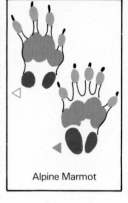

Alpine Marmot

Track small: hind 5.5 × 4cm; fore 5 × 3.5cm; an entire hind track may be 8.5cm long. Four toes on fore, 5 on hind. Digital pads are small and oval with short detached claws. The interdigital pad on the fore foot is large, 4-lobed, almost completely fused and irregular. Hind foot also has a large 4-lobed interdigital pad which tends to be more regular and frequently not so completely fused. One or two proximal pads; one is extremely large and merges with the interdigital pads: this is a diagnostic feature in marmot tracks. Complete hand impressions rare, but slender toe outlines sometimes show.

Trail in the normal walking trail most of the track components are present; registration near complete. The tracks lie close to the median line in alternate pairs and point straight forward; stride about 20cm. Bounding trail shows the tracks in groups of 4 with the 2 hind tracks in front of the fore. The tracks point straight forward and lie close to the median line; stride up to 50cm.

unusual track showing all palm pads as separate also complete heel mark

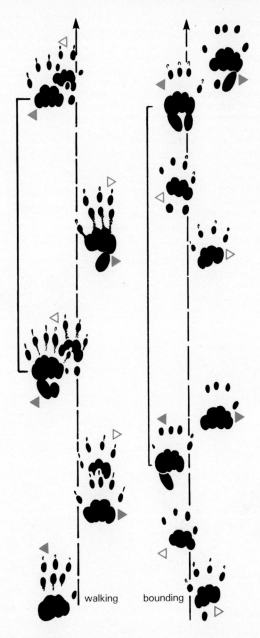

walking   bounding

Red Squirrel *Sciurus vulgaris*

Both squirrels have a very long bushy tail. The Red Squirrel is the smaller of the two (body up to 25cm, tail to 20cm) and has distinct ear tufts. Colour varies from red to black, or even grey. **Behaviour** generally solitary; diurnal but especially active at dusk and dawn; reduced winter activity. Spends much time in trees and is a very agile climber and jumper. Breeds and shelters in nests built in tree forks, known as dreys. **Habitat** coniferous and deciduous forests. **Distribution** all countries except IS, P and Mediterranean islands; largely absent from E and much of England, where *S. carolinensis* advanced earlier this century.

Track small (hind 4.5 × 3.5cm wide; fore 3.5 × 2.5cm. Four toes on fore, 5 on hind. Four digital pads on fore track; large, almost completely fused 3-lobed interdigital pad. Toe marks long and fine with integral or separate claw marks; single or symmetrical double proximal pad may be present. Hind track shows 5 digital pads; interdigital pad large with 4 almost totally fused lobes. Partial hand

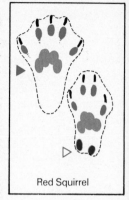

Red Squirrel

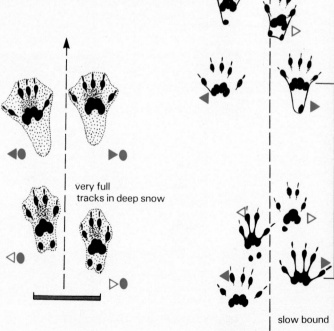

very full
tracks in deep snow

slow bound

outlines and a single oblong proximal pad are sometimes present.

Trail normally a series of bounds; tracks show in sets of 4, slightly straddled, with strides of up to 1m. Browsing pace shows strides of up to 45cm as the animal hops; registration is very rare and the tail is held clear of the ground. Very long leaps (more than 3m) are sometimes taken.

Grey Squirrel *Sciurus carolinensis*
Body to 30cm, tail to 24cm. Never has ear tufts, is generally grey and often has a whitish fringe to the tail. **Behaviour** broadly similar to Red Squirrel. **Habitat** mainly deciduous woodlands; has adapted well to coniferous plantations. **Distribution** restricted to GB and IRL.

Tracks and trail very similar to Red Squirrel but full hand impressions are more common; interdigital pads frequently much heavier; stride tends to be greater than in Red Squirrel but the actual tracks are smaller so it is difficult to distinguish the two species on track and trail evidence alone.

Above: Group of four tracks from a leaping Grey Squirrel. The hand outline of the hind tracks is distinct, as are the three central toes of equal length and the large interdigital pad on the fore.

Polecat *Mustela putorius*

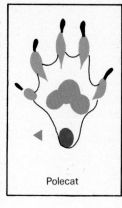

Polecat

The Polecat is a medium-sized mustelid (body to 44cm; tail to 18cm); uniform dark coat. Diagnostic features are white muzzle and a white band behind the eye. **Behaviour** solitary and nocturnal; active all year. Rarely climbs or swims. Nests on or close to the ground. **Habitat** deciduous and coniferous woodlands, farmland and marshland. **Distribution** widespread in A, B, BG, CH, CS, CY, D, DDR, DK, E, F, H, I, L, M, NL, P, PL, R and SU; more restricted in AL, GB (Wales), N, S, SF and YU.

Track small; fore 3.5 × 3.5cm; hind 4.5 × 4cm. Five digital pads on each foot, arched around a fused 4-lobed interdigital pad. Digitals I and V are set back against the interdigitals. Claw marks long, blunt, continuous with the digitals. One small proximal pad; hand impression and mesial web may show in a deep track.

Trail bounding gait is normal with tracks in groups of 4, up to 60cm between each group. Walking gait gives slightly registered tracks; stride about 25cm. In soft conditions tail drag may show, particularly when the animal is bounding. Tracks are more widely separated in galloping than in the bounding trail.

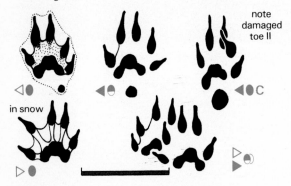

note damaged toe II

in snow

Steppe Polecat *Mustela eversmanni*

Similar to Polecat, but characterized by more sandy-coloured coat. **Behaviour** solitary and diurnal; active all year. Frequently lives in burrows. **Habitat** grassland and farmland. **Distribution** BG, CS, H, PL, R, SU and YU.

Track and trail similar to Polecat.

Marbled Polecat *Vormela peregusna*

Slightly smaller than other polecats, with a long tail

Opposite: Polecat track in soft ground. Note the relatively small interdigital pad with five radiating digital pads and long claw marks.

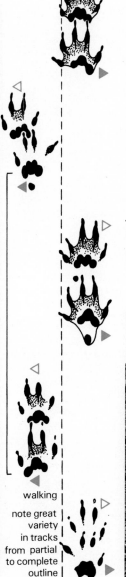

(body up to 38cm, tail to 20cm). The bold mottled coat pattern on the back and tail is diagnostic. **Behaviour** solitary and diurnal; active all year, often in underground burrows. **Habitat** open woodland and grassland. **Distribution** very restricted distribution in BG, GR, R, SU and TR.

Track and trail similar to Polecat.

Domestic Ferret *Mustela furo*

Similar in size and markings to Polecat but with a lighter coloured coat. **Behaviour** specimens living wild show similar patterns to Polecat, from which the species is derived. **Habitat** feral specimens favour woodland with good ground cover. **Distribution** widespread, normally associated with man.

Track and trail generally similar to Polecat, except that the interdigital pad and proximal pad (when present) tend to be heavier.

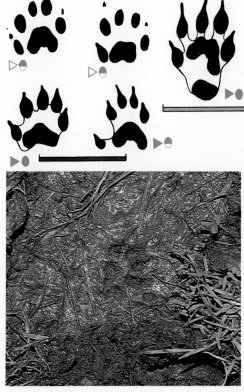

walking

note great variety in tracks from partial to complete outline

79

American Mink *Mustela vison*
Medium-sized mustelid (body to 40cm, tail to
14cm). Many uniform fur colours occur; diagnostic
feature is white fur on lower lip only. **Behaviour**
mainly solitary and nocturnal; active all year.
Spends much time in water; shelters and breeds
in riverside burrows. **Habitat** marshes, lakes and
rivers, especially close to woodland. **Distribution**
present in B, DK, E, F, GB, IRL, IS, L, N, NL, S, SF
and SU; spreading in many locations.

Track small: fore 3 × 4cm; hind 4.5 × 3.5cm.
Both tracks have a fused 4-lobed interdigital pad
with 2 large central lobes; 5 digital pads arched
around the interdigital; claw marks long and may
be continuous or discrete. Distal web between all
toes frequently shows in tracks; 1 very small
proximal pad shows often in the hind. Track size is
similar to Stoat but can always be distinguished by
the large interdigital pads.

Trail normal gait is an arched-back gallop with
near perfect registration of tracks; stride 30–40cm.
An ambling gait gives rise to imperfectly registered
tracks in groups of 4. The fast bound gives unregistered tracks in groups of 4 with at least 40cm
between each group. Tail drag may be present in
soft mud or snow. Galloping trail gives tracks in
groups of 4, less tightly bunched than in bounding
trail.

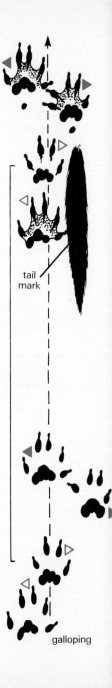

tail
mark

galloping

note small twig under
digital I

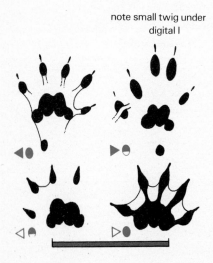

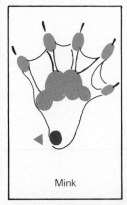

Mink

Both the introduced American and native European Mink live close to water and are extremely able swimmers.

European Mink *Mustela lutreola*
Similar in all respects to the American Mink, except that the range in coat colour is less and the colour is always dark. **Behaviour** generally solitary but sometimes gregarious; crepuscular or nocturnal; active all year. Spends much time in the water, but like the American Mink is not fully aquatic. Young born below ground in bankside nests. **Habitat** marshes, lakes and river banks. **Distribution** main range in R, SF and SU with an isolated population in western F.

Track and trail identical to American Mink.

ambling

Western Hedgehog *Erinaceus europaeus*

The hedgehogs are distinguished by size (20–27.5cm according to species), sharp pointed snout and body covering of over 5,000 spines of uniform length. The Western Hedgehog is identified by the uniformly dark fur on its underside. **Behaviour** solitary, nocturnal, with varying degrees of reduced winter activity. Strictly terrestrial. Breeding nests on ground, hibernating nests often under tree roots or in compost heaps. **Habitat** deciduous woodlands, Mediterranean scrubland, arable land and human habitation. **Distribution** A, B, CH, D, DDR, DK, E, F, GB, I, IRL, L, N, NL, P, S, SF, SU and YU; little geographical overlap with other species of hedgehog.

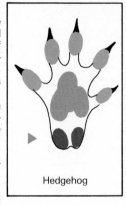

Hedgehog

Track small: hind 4.5 × 2.5cm; fore 4 × 2.5cm. Five toes on fore and hind. Claw marks are long and show as a continuation of the deeply impressed, rounded digital pads. Three fused asymmetrical interdigital pads; 2 unequal proximal pads. Hand outline common.

Trail normal gait is a shuffling walk, giving partial registration with feet turned slightly outwards from median line; drag from spines may be present; stride about 15cm. When alarmed the animal runs with the body held clear of the ground: there is no spine drag, stride increases to about 20cm and greater registration occurs. Proximal pads are absent in running tracks.

Eastern Hedgehog *Erinaceus concolor*

Similar to Western Hedgehog, but the underfur shows a light coloured breast and a darker abdomen. **Behaviour and habitat** similar to Western Hedgehog. **Distribution** AL, BG, CS, DDR, GR, I, PL, R, SU, TR and YU; overlaps with Western Hedgehog from P to I.

Track and trail identical to Western Hedgehog.

Algerian Hedgehog *Erinaceus algirus*

Algerian Hedgehog tends to be smaller than the other species (body maximum 25cm). Underfur is uniformly pale and there is a spine-free area on the crown. **Behaviour** solitary and nocturnal; no noticeable winter reduction of activity; frequently rests in burrows. **Habitat** agricultural land, scrub woodland and Mediterranean scrubland. **Distribution** restricted to the extreme south of E and F with a population in the Dordogne of F.

Track and trail as for Western Hedgehog.

walking

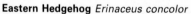

Hedgehog tracks showing elongated digital pads and claws in the mud.

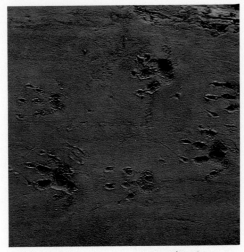

running

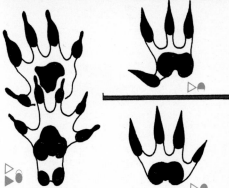

Pyrenean Desman *Galemys pyrenaicus*
A medium-sized insectivore (body to 13.5cm, tail to 14cm), the Pyrenean Desman is distinguished by very long tail, large webbed feet and an elongated, flat and spatulate muzzle. **Behaviour** solitary and diurnal; active all year. Spends much time in water, nesting in bankside holes, rock crevices or under tree roots. **Habitat** mountain streams and unpolluted upland canals and rivers. **Distribution** restricted to mountainous areas in north E and P and the Pyrenees in E and F.

    Track and trail rare and minute. Fore and hind tracks with 5 toes; similar to Water Shrew; webbing present.

Garden Dormouse *Eliomys quercinus*

A large dormouse (body to 17cm, tail to 12cm), distinguished by large ears, black mask and furry tail with a tufted black and white tip. **Behaviour** generally solitary and nocturnal, although may be active at dusk. Agile climber but often seen on ground. Hibernates, but may become active in warm spells. Nests in tree holes, rock crevices, piles of rocks and sometimes house lofts. Vocal, making chattering calls. **Habitat** mainly deciduous and coniferous woodland, but also scrubland, parks, gardens and orchards as well as human habitations. **Distribution** throughout A, CH, E, F, I, L, P and western Mediterranean islands and in parts of B, CS, D, DDR, NL, PL, R, SF and SU.

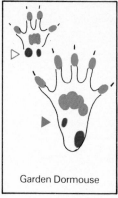

Garden Dormouse

Track small: hind 4 × 3cm; fore 3 × 3cm. Similar in size to Red Squirrel but more slender. Four toes on fore, 5 on hind. Four small digital pads on fore foot; claw marks slender; interdigital pad is 3-lobed; 2 proximal pads are normally obscured by registration. Hind track shows 5 digital pads, often with complete long slender toe marks; 4 equal, partially fused oval lobes on the interdigital pad; 2 proximal pads. Entire hand outlines or just pads may show, but the tracks of this species are distinguished by their size and slender nature.

Trail walking trail shows alternate pairs of tracks across median line; stride about 10cm; tracks turn slightly outwards and partial registration occurs. Bounding trail shows tracks in groups of 4 with about 15cm between each group. Tail drag is not always present.

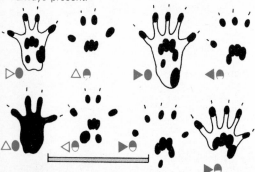

Forest Dormouse *Dryomys nitedula*

Medium-sized dormouse (body to 13cm, tail to 9.5cm), distinguished from other species by size, presence of a black mask, short ears and an untipped tail. **Behaviour** solitary, nocturnal; hiber-

walking

nates in nests built around tree and shrub branches; agile climber. **Habitat** deciduous woodland with thick shrub layer, sometimes well into the foothills of mountains. **Distribution** A, AL, BG, CH, CS, GR, H, tip of I, PL, R, SU, TR and YU.

Track and trail similar to Edible Dormouse but slightly smaller.

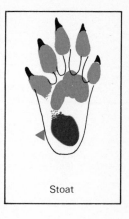

Stoat

Stoat *Mustela erminea*

Small and slender (body up to 30cm, tail to 12cm). Black tip on tail is diagnostic; coat varies from rich red-brown to white. **Behaviour** may be solitary or gregarious; diurnal and active throughout the year. Burrows and crevices in rocks are common breeding and sheltering places. **Habitat** near universal, wherever there is cover. **Distribution** throughout Europe except AL, GR, I and IS; also generally absent from Mediterranean areas.

Track fore minute: 2 × 2.2cm; hind small: 4 × 2.5cm. Fore track has 3-lobed interdigital which is generally delicate and distinct, although it may join with the 5 radiating digital pads; claw marks small, sharp, joined to digitals. Hind track has a main 4-lobed fused interdigital pad and sometimes a small separate pad below toe V; digital prints 5, radiating, with short sharp claws; one single proximal pad. Short mesial web may be present in both tracks. Hind tracks particularly may have a hand outline.

Trail normal gait is a slow gallop with arched back: this gives almost complete registration, tracks occurring in twos about 20cm apart. High-speed bound gives tracks in groups of 4 with 30–50cm between each group. Also moves at slow speeds stopping frequently to look around, and sitting on hind feet before dropping down: this gives groups of irregularly spaced tracks.

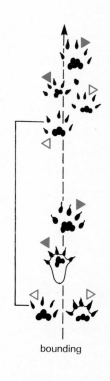

bounding

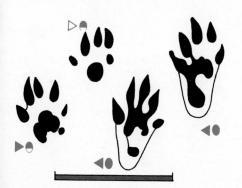

Flying Squirrel *Pteromys volans*

Small grey squirrel (body to 20cm, tail to 14cm); membrane between legs used in gliding is unique, but shows only as a fold of skin when the animal is running. **Behaviour** solitary and nocturnal, rarely seen in daylight; reduced winter activity, but does not hibernate. Spends most of time in trees, but does come to the ground. Rests and breeds in hollows in trees. **Habitat** mixed forests, especially with birch, aspen and alder; sometimes gardens and parks. **Distribution** most of SF and northern SU.

Track hind small: 2.5–3.5 × 2.5cm; fore minute: 1.5–2 × 2.3cm. Four toes on fore, 5 on hind. Digital pads on fore feet small, round; interdigital pads slightly fused, 3-lobed; claw marks very fine, long, separate. Hand outline with very fine toes, very small detached 4th interdigital pad and 2 large fused proximal pads with the outline of the anterior membrane may show in soft ground. Digital pads on the hind tracks very fine; interdigital pad slightly fused, distinctly 4-lobed; in full track a small detached interdigital pad and large proximal may be present. Hand outline common in soft conditions; pads very delicate.

Trail hopping trail shows fore tracks in front of hind; stride about 10cm. The bound gives tracks in groups of 4 with strides over 15cm. The impression of the animal landing in snow from a jump is quite distinctive and may show the full outline of the membrane. Body drag may show in very soft conditions.

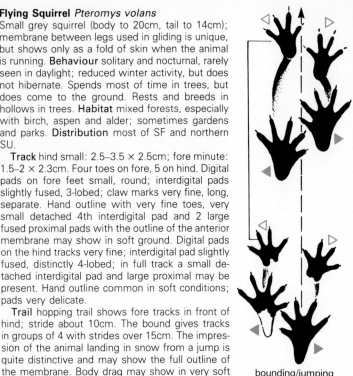

bounding/jumping

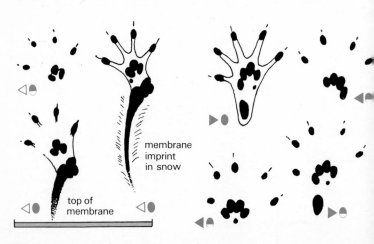

membrane imprint in snow

top of membrane

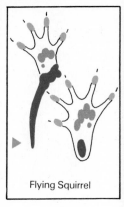

Flying Squirrel

Above right: Flying Squirrel. The gliding membrane (skin fold) is clear even when the animal is at rest. The large eyes are an advantage to this largely nocturnal species.

Right: The Siberian Chipmunk is a small squirrel which is identified by its striped coat.

Siberian Chipmunk *Tamias sibiricus*
Small (body to 22cm, tail to 14cm). Distinguished from all other European squirrels by 5 dark stripes running the length of the back. **Behaviour** solitary, diurnal; greatly reduced in winter. Mainly a ground-living squirrel, but capable of climbing small trees and bushes with agility. **Habitat** mixed forests with dense undergrowth. **Distribution** native to SU; colonies in A, BL, D, F and SF.

Track and trail similar to a small squirrel.

87

Brown Rat *Rattus norvegicus*

Large rat (body to 26cm, tail to 23cm, hind foot to 4.5cm, ear to 2.2cm). Identified by short ears and tail shorter than body. **Behaviour** gregarious, sometimes in very large colonies; mainly nocturnal; active all year. Strong burrower and swimmer; climbs well, but not as often as *R. rattus*. **Habitat** associated with all types of human habitation, especially warehouses and farms. Frequents coastal areas and estuaries. **Distribution** widespread, except in the extreme north of N, S and SU.

Track hind small: 3.3 × 2.8cm; fore minute: 1.8 × 2.5cm. Four toes on fore, 5 on hind. Four deeply impressed digital pads on fore track, 5 palm pads; hand outline. Hind track has 5 digital pads; 6 palm pads; one greatly elongated proximal pad (as in *R. rattus*). There is a long heel area on the hind track.

Trail in the running trail there is partial registration; tracks are widely spaced from the median line, rarely with tail drag; stride 14–15cm. In the bounding trail the tracks are in groups of 4 about 60cm apart. Tail drag absent even in the slow walking trail where the stride is about 15cm.

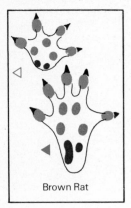

Brown Rat

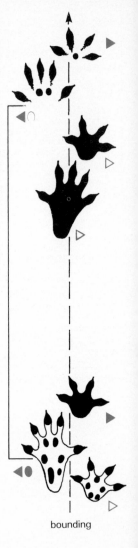

bounding

Water Vole *Arvicola terrestris*

Large vole (body to 19cm, tail to 10cm in north; body to 16cm, tail to 8cm in south). Distinguished from other voles by size, relatively long tail and dark coloration. **Behaviour** solitary or in small groups; active all year. **Habitat** mainly freshwater banksides in well covered habitats; occurs away from water in grassland in the south. **Distribution** widespread; totally absent from IRL, IS, P and much of F and GR.

Track hind small: 3 × 3.1cm; fore minute: 1.8 × 2.3cm. Four digital pads with short integral claws on fore track; 3 interdigital and 2 proximal pads, all equal; hand outline common. Hind track has 5 digital pads with integral claws and only 5 palm pads, a distinguishing feature; one proximal pad is elongated and the heel is short; hand outline common.

Trail fast walk or running trail shows partially registered tracks; stride about 10cm; tail drag absent. Bounding trail shows tracks in groups of 4; no tail drag; about 30cm between groups.

Southwestern Water Vole *Arvicola sapidus*

Difficult to distinguish from *A. terrestris*, except it is much larger (body to 20cm, tail to 13cm) and darker than local races of that species. Tail also relatively longer. **Behaviour** similar to aquatic forms of *A. terrestris*. **Habitat** always by freshwater bodies and marshes where there is good ground cover. **Distribution** confined to E, western F and P.

Track and trail as for *A. terrestris*.

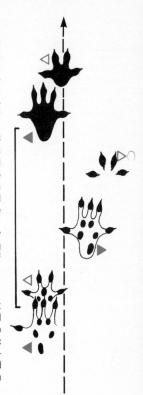

bounding

Rat tracks showing the star like appearance of the toes, small palm pads and evidence of tail drag.

Edible Dormouse *Glis glis*

Largest dormouse (body to 19cm, tail to 15cm); grey with a very bushy tail. Resembles the Flying Squirrel but there is little overlap in range and the tracks are diagnostic. **Behaviour** mainly solitary and nocturnal, sometimes in small colonies; hibernates for up to 7 months. Agile climber but spends much time on ground. Summer nests high in trees, hibernating nests in tree holes, underground or in buildings. Vocal in nests. **Habitat** mature deciduous woodland; extends into foothills; frequents lofts and outbuildings. **Distribution** A, AL, BG, CH, CS, D, DDR, E, F, GB (introduced), GR, H, I, PL, SU, TR and YU.

Edible Dormouse

Track hind small: 3 × 2.5cm; fore minute: 2 × 2cm. Four toes on fore, 5 toes on hind. Digital pads on fore feet very small; interdigital pad may show as a rectangular block amalgamated with the proximal pads or as 4 small discrete interdigital lobes and 2 variable proximal pads; outline of whole track may be present. Hind track shows 5 tiny digital pads and often complete toe prints, rarely a complete hand outline; 4-lobed interdigital pad frequently fused with 2 proximal pads. All tracks are distinguished by small interdigital pads, minute or completely absent claw marks and complex interdigital-proximal pad relationships.

Trail walking trail shows tracks turning outward from median line; partial registration; tracks widely splayed across median line; distinct bushy tail drag; stride about 8cm. Running trail shows greatly increased stride. Bounding trail shows tracks in groups of 4 with about 30cm between groups; tail drag marks immediately behind each group.

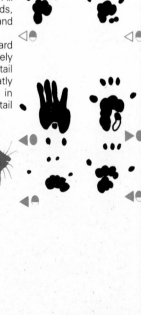

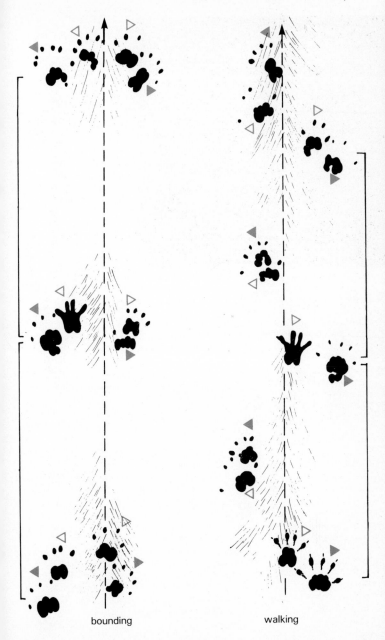

bounding

walking

Complex of Black Rat tracks in very soft mud. The long heel impression distinguishes rat tracks from those of Water Vole.

Black Rat *Rattus rattus*

Small rat (body to 23cm, tail to 25cm, hind foot to 4cm, ears to 2.7cm). Identified by having tail longer than body and large ears. **Behaviour** gregarious; primarily nocturnal but diurnal if not disturbed; active all year. Extensive burrower, but nests in any suitable building cavity. Agile climber and good swimmer. Rather secretive. **Habitat** mainly human habitation, disturbed land and farms. Leaves many signs of activity. **Distribution** widespread; restricted in DK, GB, IRL and S; absent from IS, N, SF and much of northern SU.

Track minute: hind 2.5 × 2.5cm; fore 1.5 × 2cm. Four toes on fore, 5 on hind. Fore track has 4 digital pads with deeply impressed integral claws; 3 interdigital, 2 proximal pads, all equal; hand outlines common. Hind track has 5 small delicate digital pads; 4 interdigital pads, and 2 proximals, one elongated; hand outline common.

Trail running trail shows partially registered tracks close to median line; heavy, continuous tail drag – a diagnostic feature of this species; stride about 10cm. Bounding trail shows the tracks in groups of 4 with up to 50cm between each group. In the hopping trail only hind tracks and tail drag are seen.

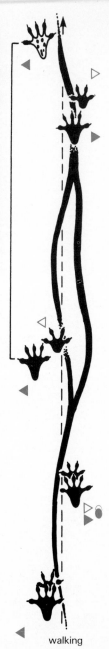

walking

Black Rat

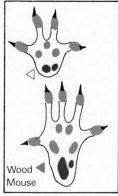

Wood Mouse

running

Wood Mouse *Apodemus sylvaticus*

Medium-sized mouse (body to 11cm, tail to 11.5cm, hind foot to 2.4cm). Back is yellow-brown, underside silvery-grey, often with a single yellow streak. **Behaviour** solitary or in small groups; mainly nocturnal but showing intense crepuscular activity, especially in winter; active all year. Ground-living, but an agile climber. May create complex tunnel systems with entrances often under tree roots; has regular runs and territory. **Habitat** mainly deciduous woodland, but also verges, coastal areas, cultivated land and human habitation. **Distribution** widespread, frequently the most common mouse; present everywhere except in SF, northern N, S and SU.

Track minute: hind 2.2 × 1.8cm; fore 1.3 × 1.5cm. Four toes on fore, 5 on hind. Tracks frequently show as a complete outline with the detail obscured. Fore track has 5 digital pads with long integral claws; 3 small interdigital, 2 proximal pads. Hind has 5 digital pads with claws, 4 small interdigitals, 2 proximal pads, one long, the other small and circular.

Trail walking trail has alternate pairs of tracks close to, but pointing out from the median line. Partial over-registration may occur; no tail drag; stride about 8cm. In the running trail stride is about 10cm; hind tracks appear ahead of preceding fore. Hand impressions not common; no tail drag. Bounding trail shows tracks in groups of 4 with tail drag between; stride up to 15cm; individuals may jump more than 50cm.

93

Yellow-necked Field Mouse *Apodemus flavicollis*

Large mouse (body to 12cm, tail to 13.5cm, hind foot to 2.6cm). Usually with a large orange chest spot. **Behaviour** similar to *A. sylvaticus*, but appears to climb higher into trees and spend more time above ground. **Habitat** deciduous and coniferous woods, human habitations and less frequently in more open areas. **Distribution** A, AL, B, BG, CH, D, DDR, DK, E (part), F (part), GB (south), GR, H, I (part), L, N (south), P. (part), PL, R, S (south), SF (south), SU (south), TR and YU.

Track similar to *A. sylvaticus* but normally a little larger (hind 2.4 × 1.9cm; fore 1.6 × 1.8cm); tends to be impressed more heavily (this is not diagnostic).

Trail similar to *A. sylvaticus* but feet tend to splay more widely; again this is not diagnostic and the two species cannot reliably be split on the basis of track and trail.

Mouse trails in snow showing both foot and tail drag.

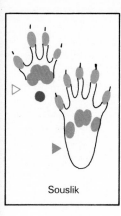

Souslik

European Souslik *Spermophilus citellus*

Small ground squirrel (body to 22cm, tail to 7cm); very short ears, large eyes; short hairy tail. **Behaviour** highly gregarious and diurnal; true hibernation lasting until March. Produces extensive underground burrow systems with many entrances. Surface feeding and highly vocal. **Habitat** dry grassland, pastures and arable land. **Distribution** BG, CS, H, PL, R, SU, TR and YU.

Track minute: hind 2 × 1.3cm; fore 1.8 × 1.2cm. Four toes on fore, 5 on hind. Digital pads small with long detached claw marks. Toes lie above the interdigital pads on both feet; a distinctive feature is interdigital pad on fore feet is 4-lobed, almost completely fused, square; rarely one central proximal pad shows; full hand prints frequent. The hind interdigital pad consists of 4 partially fused or unfused lobes; hand outline common; proximal pads absent.

Trail two common gaits: running trail gives alternate pairs of tracks parallel to the median line; stride about 10cm. Bounding trail shows tracks in groups of 4 with fore tracks close behind hind tracks; stride is about 15cm. All tracks point outwards from median line.

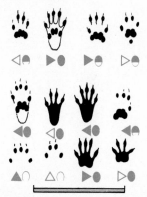

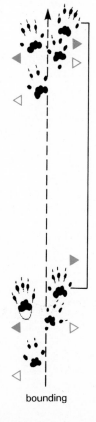

bounding

Spotted Souslik *Spermophilus suslicus*

May be slightly larger than *S. citellus* (body to 25cm), but tail is distinctly shorter (not more than 4cm); body spotted. **Behaviour and habitat** similar to *S. citellus*, but occurs more frequently on cultivated land, where it can be a serious pest causing damage to crops. **Distribution** PL, R and SU.

Track and trail as for *S. citellus*.

Norway Lemming *Lemmus lemmus*

Largest of the lemmings (body to 15cm, tail to 2cm). Marked dark back and yellow belly are diagnostic; very short ears and tail. **Behaviour** gregarious; diurnal and nocturnal; active all year. Burrows in soil in summer, under snow in winter. Migratory tendencies when population densities are high. **Habitat** tundra, Arctic zones, northern coniferous forests. **Distribution** upland and Arctic areas of N, S, SF and SU.

Track minute; 4 toes on fore, 5 on hind. Tracks similar in many details to other voles. Fore with 4 digital pads; 5 equal palm pads. Hind with 5 digital pads; 6 equal palm pads; hand outline often present; claw marks discrete or integral, very long, especially in winter (a valuable clue to species identity).

Trail unique among rodents: the median line oscillates from side to side, although the cycle may be 36m and may not be apparent over a short distance. The normal trail is a walk, with partial registration; stride about 8cm. The tracks are straddled and body marks are common.

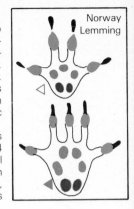

Norway Lemmings have large population peaks in good years. They are easily identified by their striped markings.

walking trail
showing
oscillating
median line

Balkan Snow Vole *Dinaromys bogdanovi*
Large vole (body to 14cm, tail to 11cm); pale in
colour. Distinguished from the Snow Vole by its
relatively long tail and large hind feet (more than
2.2cm). **Behaviour** probably more solitary than
other voles; diurnal; active all year. Does not climb;
rests in rock crevices or under stones. **Habitat**
mountain areas above the tree line. **Distribution**
eastern mountain areas of AL and YU only.

Track and trail similar to Norway Lemming.

Grain eaten by House
Mouse with
droppings.

House Mouse emerging from sacks of grain. Great damage may be done to stored food by this species.

Spiny Mouse: this mouse has coarse, spine-like hairs on its back.

House Mouse *Mus musculus*

Medium-sized mouse (body to 9.5cm, tail to 9.5cm, hind foot to 1.9cm); eyes, ears and feet smaller than in *Apodemus*. Tail prominently ringed. Dark grey forms distinct, lighter colours more easily confused with *Apodemus*. **Behaviour** generally solitary and nocturnal in open country; more sociable and diurnal near human habitation. Active all year. Extensive burrow systems in the open, regular runs and tunnels in buildings. **Habitat** most common in buildings and farmyards, but near universal where there is cover. **Distribution** absent only from the extreme north of N, S and SU.

Track minute: hind 1.8 × 1.8cm; fore 1 × 1.3cm. Four toes on fore, 5 on hind. Digital pads fine, with integral claws; hand outline common. Fore track has 3 interdigital pads, 2 proximals, all small and round. Hind track has 4 interdigital pads, 2 proximals; interdigitals and one proximal small and round; the other proximal pad large and oval.

Trail walking trail shows unregistered tracks which point slightly outwards. Undulating tail drag is diagnostic of this species at this gait; stride about 5cm. Running trail shows partial over-registration, tail drag and a stride of about 7cm. Jumping trail shows tracks in groups of 4 with about 10cm between each group, but jumps of up to 50cm are not uncommon.

Steppe Mouse *Mus hortulanus*
Similar to *M. spretus* (below), but does not overlap with it. Differential diagnosis on dentition. **Behaviour** similar to other members of the genus, but more colonial; extensive tunnel systems, often with food stores above the ground. **Habitat** grassland and arable land. **Distribution** AL, BG, CS, GR, H, R, SU, TR and YU.
   Track and trail as for *M. musculus*.

Algerian Mouse *Mus spretus*
Small mouse (body to 8.5cm, tail to 7cm, hind foot to 1.7cm). Light colour and short tail help with identification, but positive differentiation depends on dentition. **Behaviour** as for *M. musculus*. **Habitat** wetter areas of open woodland, scrub, *arable land and gardens*. **Distribution** E, P and *southern F*.
   Track and trail as for *M. musculus*.

Cretan Spiny Mouse *Acomys cahirinus*
Large mouse (body to 12cm, tail to 12cm). Similar to *Apodemus* from a distance; but in the hand the covering of stiff spiny hairs on the back is unique. **Behaviour** social, diurnal; active all year. Makes burrows or lives in crevices. **Habitat** Mediterranean scrub and human habitation. **Distribution** only in Crete.
   Track and trail as for *Apodemus sylvaticus*.

Rock Mouse *Apodemus mystacinus*
Largest member of genus (body to 13cm, tail to 14cm, hind foot to 2.8cm). Grey coat. **Behaviour** as for *A. sylvaticus*. **Habitat** dry Mediterranean woodland and open rocky hillsides with scrub cover. **Distribution** AL, GR, YU and Crete.
   Track and trail as for *A. sylvaticus* (page 93).

Cretan Spiny Mouse

Pygmy Field Mouse *Apodemus microps*
Small mouse (body to 9.5cm, tail to 9.5cm, hind foot 2cm). Relatively long hind feet distinguish this from other mice of similar size. **Behaviour** as for *A. sylvaticus*. **Habitat** scrubland, grassland and arable land. **Distribution** confined to inland areas of BG, CS, H, PL, R, SU and YU.

Track and trail similar to other members of genus, but slightly smaller (size not diagnostic).

Striped Field Mouse *Apodemus agrarius*
Medium size (body to 11.5cm, tail to 8.5cm, hind foot to 2.1cm). Single dark stripe on back. Overlaps with Birch Mice but is larger, has a relatively short tail and long ears. **Behaviour** similar to *A. sylvaticus* but less nocturnal. **Habitat** edges of deciduous woodland, scrubland and hedges. **Distribution** A, BG, CH, CS, D, DDR, DK, H, PL, R, SF, SU, TR and YU.

Track and trail similar to other members of the genus, but tends to be smaller.

Sicista species
Two species, distinguished from other mice by having a tail longer than the body, a dark stripe on the back and small ears.

Northern Birch Mouse *Sicista betulina*
Body to 7cm, tail to 10.5cm. Distinguished by very long tail and median dark stripe running down an otherwise uniformly coloured back. **Behaviour** mainly solitary and nocturnal; hibernates. Active mainly on ground but very agile in trees and bushes. Excavates burrows or lives in rotten tree stumps. **Habitat** wet woodland in the north, especially birch with dense undergrowth; more open hill areas in south. **Distribution** continuous in SF and SU; smaller populations in A, DK, DDR, N, R and S.

Track and trail similar to Harvest Mouse; long tail sometimes leaves impressions.

Southern Birch Mouse *Sicista subtilis*
Similar in size to *S. betulina* but tail slightly shorter (up to 8.5cm). Distinguished from *S. betulina* (with which there is little geographical overlap) by light stripes on either side of median dark stripe. **Behaviour** as for *S. betulina*, **Habitat** open woodland and scrub, grassland, and close to cultivated land. **Distribution** BG, R, SU and YU.

Track and trail as for Northern Birch Mouse.

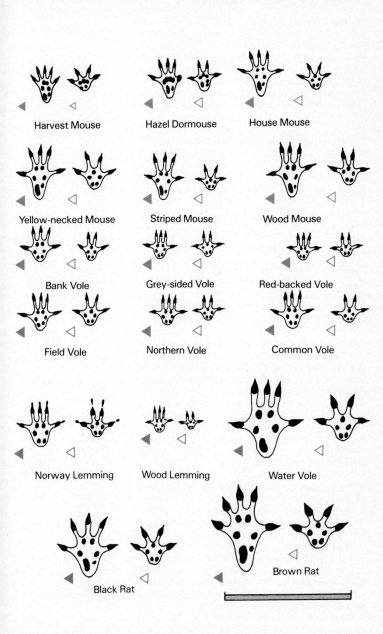

Harvest Mouse

Hazel Dormouse

House Mouse

Yellow-necked Mouse

Striped Mouse

Wood Mouse

Bank Vole

Grey-sided Vole

Red-backed Vole

Field Vole

Northern Vole

Common Vole

Norway Lemming

Wood Lemming

Water Vole

Black Rat

Brown Rat

Weasel *Mustela nivalis*
Weasel is very small and slender (body up to 23cm,
tail to 6cm) with a short tail which has no black tip.
Male larger than female. **Habitat** near universal;
requires very little cover. **Distribution** common
throughout Europe except IRL and IS.

Track minute: fore 1.3 × 1cm; hind 1.5 ×
1.3cm. Three-lobed delicate interdigital pad on both
tracks; 5 digital pads with sharp attached claws;
digitals radiate. Mesial webbing sometimes
present, although proximal pads and full hand
impressions are not common in tracks of this small
light carnivore.

Trail normal gait is the mustelid arch-back
gallop; almost complete registration; stride
25–30cm. The high-speed bound gives groups of
4 tracks with more than 30cm between them. May
(like Stoat) walk slowly if frightened or stalking:
individual tracks show clearly, without registration;
stride about 10cm only.

Northern Mole *Talpa europaea*
The three species of European mole are medium-
sized insectivores (body 10–15cm according to
species). They have turned-out, highly modified
front feet and a dark coat. In the hand the Northern
Mole is distinguished by having eyes that can be
opened. **Behaviour** solitary and diurnal; active all
year. Mature individuals spend almost their entire
life in a subsurface tunnel system. **Habitat** near
universal, wherever there is a sufficient depth of
unfrozen, non-waterlogged, neutral to basic soil
with a food supply. **Distribution** common in A, B,
BG, CH, D, DDR, DK, much of E, F, GB, part of Gr,
H, north I, L. NL, PL, SU and TR; present in north
P, YU, south S and SF, absent AL, IRL, IS, N and
much of I and P.

Track minute: about 1.5 × 1cm. Hind track is an
unmodified hand shape with 5 digital pads; short
attached claws; no interdigital or proximal pad
detail. Fore foot totally different: highly modified
so that the animal walks on the side of the feet;
generally only the digital pads show in an L-shape;
little or no detail of other pads.

Trail tracks and trail are both rare. If a trail is
found the hind tracks widely straddle the median
line with the fore tracks lying inside. Underside of
body is dragged across the ground leaving extensive scuff marks. At higher speed the gait remains
similar, but stride increases to 5–10cm.

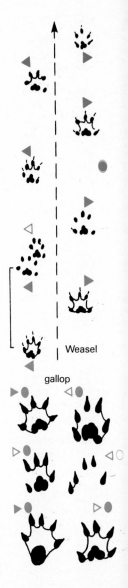

Weasel

gallop

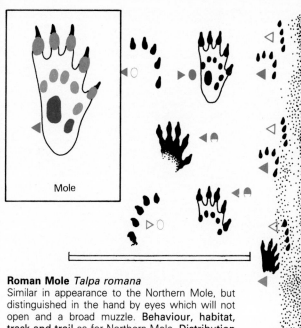

Mole

Roman Mole *Talpa romana*
Similar in appearance to the Northern Mole, but distinguished in the hand by eyes which will not open and a broad muzzle. **Behaviour, habitat, track and trail** as for Northern Mole. **Distribution** parts of AL, GR, I and YU; does not overlap with Northern Mole.

Blind Mole *Talpa caeca*
Generally similar to other two species (body to 13cm). In hand has permanently closed eyes; hind foot less than 1.7cm whereas it is at least 1.75cm in the other species. **Behaviour, habitat, track and trail** as for other moles. **Distribution** whole of E and P, parts of AL, GR, I and YU.

Greater Mole-rat *Spalax microphthalmus*
Both species of mole-rat completely lack external eyes, ears or tail. There is a line of stiff bristles on either side of the head and the incisors are very prominent. *S. microphthalmus* is up to 31cm long and the hind feet are over 2.5cm long. **Behaviour** solitary, each animal normally occupying a single burrow system; nocturnal; active all year. Adapted to an almost totally subterranean existence. **Habitat** grassland and arable land. **Distribution** BG, GR, R and SU.

    Track and trail rare and minute; similar to rat but with no tail drag; feet not modified for digging.

Mole

Fast walk

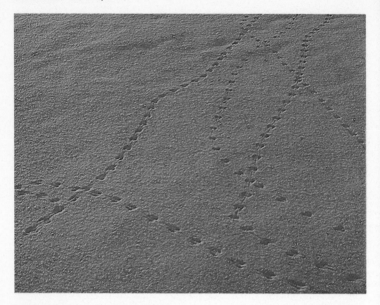

Lesser Mole-rat *Spalax leucodon*
Very similar to *S. microphthalmus* and there is
some geographical overlap. Generally smaller, with
body to 26cm and hind feet less than 2.5cm in
length. **Behaviour and habitat** as for *S. microphthalmus*. **Distribution** BG, GR, R, TR and YU.
   Track and trail as for Greater Mole-rat.

Complex of Bank Vole
trails in the snow as
the animal, or animals,
have ranged around
looking for food.

Hazel Dormouse *Muscardinus avellanarius*
Small dormouse (body to 9cm, tail to 7.5cm);
orange-brown to chestnut colour. Distinguished
from other small rodents by hairy tail. **Behaviour**
solitary and mainly nocturnal; hibernates. Extremely agile climber, spending most of time in trees
and bushes. Summer nests often in vegetation,
hibernating nests in stone walls, under tree roots or
even in burrows. Nest boxes sometimes adopted
throughout the year. **Habitat** deciduous woodland
with dense shrub cover. **Distribution** A, AL, B, BG,
CH, CS, D, DDR, F, GB, GR, I, L, NL, PL, R, south
S, SU, TR and YU.

Hazel Dormouse

   Track minute: hind 1.5 × 1.1cm; fore 1 ×
0.8cm. Feet highly prehensile with distinctive pad
development. Fore foot has 4 digital pads; claws
slender, attached; 6 distinct palm pads (4 interdigital, 2 proximal) in a circular pattern. Hand outline
common. Hind foot shows 5 digital pads, digital I

is short, stubby, clawless and set back against the interdigital. This has 4 small round lobes, barely fused and in a line; 2 elongated proximal pads may merge with the interdigitals. Hand outline common.

Trail normally a walking trail: tracks turn distinctly outwards, with partial registration. There are pairs of tracks close to the median line with long linear tail drag marks weaving in between; stride up to 7cm. Running trail shows increased stride; bounding trail has tracks grouped in fours with up to 15cm between groups.

Mouse-tailed Dormouse *Myonimus roachi*

Small (body to 11cm, tail to 8cm); grey colour; distinguished from other dormice by tail with short hairs. Distinguished from mice and voles by combination of grey-coloured coat, short ears and large eyes. **Behaviour** little known, but seems to spend a great deal of time underground. **Habitat** dry deciduous woodland and scrub. **Distribution** only reported from BG and eastern GR.

Track and trail similar to Hazel Dormouse.

Mouse-tailed
Dormouse

Bank Vole *Clethrionomys glareolus*

The three *Clethrionomys* species have a russet coat, a moderately long tail and more prominent ears than Grass or Pine Voles. *C. glareolus* has a body up to 11cm, tail to 6.5cm; distinguished by longer tail and very wide distribution. **Behaviour** gregarious, active by day and night, throughout the year. Makes extensive surface runways and burrows. May climb quite high into bushes and young trees; high densities sometimes occur. **Habitat** near universal wherever there is suitable ground cover, although best adapted to woodland habitats; extends into foothills of mountains. **Distribution** widespread; absent from IS, GR, P, much of E, IRL, I, TK, YU and northern N, S, SF and SU.

Track minute: hind 1.5 × 1.7cm; fore 1.1 × 1.3cm. Typical vole tracks. Four toes on fore, 5 on hind. Four digital pads and 5 palm pads on fore; 5 digital pads and 6 palm pads on hind. Hand outline common, but integral claw marks are short and do not always show. Track not diagnostic.

Trail running trail shows unregistered tracks, stride about 6.5cm; tail drag is absent; tracks are close to the median line and point straight ahead. Bounding trail shows tracks in groups of 4 with about 15cm between each group.

Common Hamster *Cricetus cricetus*

Largest hamster (body to 30cm, tail to 6cm): recognized by very short tail, dark brown coloration, distinct white patches and black underside. **Behaviour** solitary and nocturnal; hibernates, but may be disturbed. Extensive deep burrow systems may contain underground food stores. **Habitat** grasslands and the edge of arable land. **Distribution** continuous in BG, DDR, PL, R, SU and YU; other populations B, CS, D, H, L, NL and R.

Track and trail large and vole-like; hind track up to 3.5cm long.

Rumanian Hamster *Mesocricetus newtoni*

Smaller hamster (body to 18cm, tail to 2cm). Markings similar to Common Hamster, but less black on the underside. **Behaviour** as for Common Hamster. **Habitat** grassland and arable areas. **Distribution** small areas of BG, R and SU.

Track minute: hind 1.4 × 1.4cm; fore 1 × 1cm. Four toes on fore, 5 on hind. Fore track has 4 digital pads with short integral claws and 5 palm pads. Hind track has 5 digital pads with claw marks and 6 palm pads, 5 of similar size and one a much smaller proximal pad. Track not diagnostic.

Trail walking trail normal, with a tendency to lateral registration; stride about 8.5cm.

Golden Hamster *Mesocricetus auratus*

Similar to *M. newtoni*, but specimens from domestic stock have much less distinct coloration. **Behaviour and habitat** as for *M. newtoni*. **Distribution** wild populations of escaped specimens.

Track and trail as for *M. newtoni*.

Grey Hamster *Cricetulus migratorius*

Small (body to 11cm, tail to 2.8cm); no distinct markings; distinguished from voles by having large eyes and ears and a short tail. **Behaviour** similar to Common Hamster. **Habitat** grassland and open woodland. **Distribution** small areas in BG, GR and TR.

Track and trail as for smaller voles (see pages 114–116).

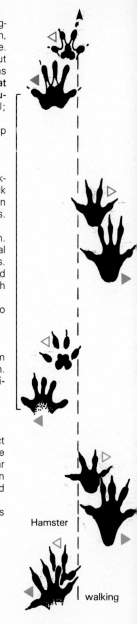

Hamster

walking

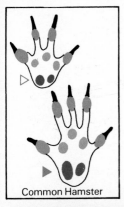

Common Hamster

Common Hamster eating grain.

Water Shrew *Neomys fodiens*

Largest of the shrews (body to 9cm, tail to 7cm, hind feet to 2cm). Black on top, light underside. Whole length of tail has a fringe of hairs as do the hind feet. Teeth are red-tipped (see page 284). **Behaviour** solitary and diurnal; active all year. Mostly in water; on land makes runways in dense vegetation and tunnels in riverbanks. **Habitat** wherever there is water and cover, including seashores. **Distribution** widespread and common except in much of B and GR, the Mediterranean islands and northern Scandinavia.

Track minute: hind 1.4 × 1cm; fore 1.2 × 1cm. Similar to other shrew tracks with 5 digital pads, 3 pointing ahead and 2 set back opposite each other; 4 interdigital and 2 proximal pads. In very moist conditions the fringe of hairs will show; complete hand outline nearly always present.

Trail running trail is normal, with the tracks splayed; imperfect registration; stride 4.5cm or more; fairly broad tail drag often present.

Miller's Water Shrew *Neomys anomalus*

Similar to *N. fodiens*, but tends to be slightly smaller and fringe of hairs on tail is absent or confined to the distal end; hind feet less hairy. **Behaviour** similar to *N. fodiens*. **Habitat** as for *N.*

bounding

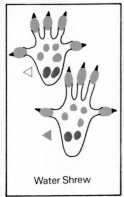

Water Shrew

Opposite: Water Shrew eating an earthworm. Note the dark coloured back and light underside of the shrew.

Above right: Harvest Mouse climbing a corn stalk and showing its very long tail.

fodiens, but extends into higher mountain areas and damp grasslands and deciduous woodlands away from water. **Distribution** continuous in B, GR, PL, SU, YU and mountains of A, AL, CH, CS, D, DDR, E, F, H, I and P; often overlaps with *N. fodiens*.

Track and trail as for *N. fodiens*; in perfect tracks the lack of hairs on the hind feet may be diagnostic.

Harvest Mouse *Micromys minutus*
Smallest European mouse (body to 7.5cm, tail to 7cm); identified by long tail, very short ears and deep orange-brown coat. **Behaviour** solitary , probably active 24 hours; reduced winter activity. Extremely good climber with prehensile tail. Breeding nest in low vegetation, winter nests at or below ground level, sometimes in burrows (see page 253). **Habitat** scrubland, road verges, some arable land with cereal crops, marshes, river banks and edges of reed beds. **Distribution** generally widespread; completely absent from IRL, IS, N, P, S, and much of A, AL, CH, E, GR, I and YU as well as Scotland.

Track minute: hind 1.3 × 1cm; fore 0.8 × 0.8cm. Fore foot with 5 toes, hind with 5. Fore track has 4 digital pads, distinct integral claw marks; 3 separate interdigital pads; 2 proximals. Hand outline distinct. Hind track shows 5 digital pads, long distinct integral claw marks; 4 small circular interdigital pads; 2 small proximals. Hand outline common.

Trail running trail normal with over-registration; pairs of tracks straddle the median line and point straight forward; tail drag shows as a thin wavy line and weaves between the tracks; stride about 4cm. Bounding trail shows the tracks in groups of 4 with about 8cm between each group.

Microtus species

The external morphology of the grass voles is very similar and many species can only be reliably differentiated on dentition (see page 303).

Field Vole *Microtus agrestis*

Body to 13cm, tail to 4.5cm. Dark grey-coloured coat, may be long in winter; tail dark above, light below. **Behaviour** gregarious, with cycles in population density; active day and night, all year. Extensive burrow and tunnel systems in surface vegetation, litter and just below ground; each system inhabited by one individual. **Habitat** all grassland habitats where the vegetation provides cover; extends into foothills and uplands. **Distribution** widespread in northern Europe; absent from AL, BG, GR, I, IRL, IS, much of E, P, R, TR, YU and parts of F.

Track minute: hind 1.5 × 1.8cm; fore 1.2 × 1.5cm. Star-shaped arrangement typical of vole tracks. Fore track has 4 digital pads with very short attached claws; 3 interdigital pads; 2 proximals of similar size; hand outline present. Hind has 5 digital

Field Vole: the short tail is a distinguishing characteristic.

pads, very short attached claws; 4 interdigitals; 2 proximals of similar size; hand outline present.

Trail normal gait is a run with body held close to ground; scuff marks rarely show. Tracks are in pairs, splayed wide across the median line; registration uncommon; tracks tend to turn outwards slightly, stride 5.5–6cm.

Common Vole *Microtus arvalis*
Body to 12cm, tail to 4.5cm; coat pale with short hair; ears less hairy than in *M. agrestis*. **Behaviour** similar to *M. agrestis* but burrows more and needs less cover; greater night-time activity. **Habitat** grassland, including pastures. **Distribution** widespread; absent from GB (except islands), IRL, IS, N, P and S, and from much of AL, E, F, GR, I, SF and YU.

Track and trail typical of genus.

Root Vole *Microtus oeconomus*
Slightly larger than other members of genus (body to 15cm, tail to 6.5cm). **Behaviour** gregarious, active day and night, all year. Burrows extensively, but may make nests and stores on surface of wet ground (see page 251). Swims and dives well. **Habitat** wet grassland, marsh and sedge areas. **Distribution** continuous in DDR, PL, R, north SF and SU; populations in B, H, NL, N, S and SF.

Track minute: hind 1.2 × 1.6cm; fore 1 × 1.3cm; typical of genus.

Trail normal trail is a walk: tracks appear in pairs, almost unregistered; tail drag present; stride about 4.5cm.

Snow Vole *Microtus nivalis*
Body to 14cm, tail to 7.5cm. Distinguished by relatively long tail and pale coloration. **Behaviour** more diurnal than other members of genus; spends more time in the open. **Habitat** high mountains, scrubland and dry hill woodland. **Distribution** locally in high mountains in A, AL, BG, CH, CS, E, F, GR, H, I, P, PL, SU and YU.

Track and trail typical of genus but with prominent tail drag.

Gunther's Vole *Microtus guentheri*
Body to 12cm, tail to 3cm. Distinguished by very short tail, light coloured feet and tail. **Behaviour** as for other *Microtus* species. **Habitat** grassland and arable land. **Distribution** BG, GR, TR and YU.

Track and trail typical of genus.

Cabrera's Vole *Microtus cabrerae*
Very like *M. arvalis* but long protruding hairs on
hind quarters may help identification. **Behaviour**
similar to *M. arvalis*. **Habitat** ranges over marshland to hill scrub woodland. **Distribution** E and P
only.
Track and trail as for other *Microtus* species.

Genus *Pitymys*
Pine voles are characterized by very small eyes and
ears and only 5 palm pads on the hind feet.

Common Pine Vole *Pitymys subterraneus*
Body to 10cm, tail to 4cm, hind feet less than
1.5cm. Like other pine voles the eyes and ears
are very small. Species identified by dentition (see
page 302). **Behaviour** normally solitary and
nocturnal; high densities may occur. **Habitat**
grassland, including short pasture, and open woodland. **Distribution** AL, B, BG, CS, D, DDR, F, GR,
H, L, NL, PL, R, SU and YU.
Track and trail as for Field Vole.

The following species are almost identical to *P.
subterraneus*.

Alpine Pine Vole *Pitymys multiplex*
Slightly larger than *P. subterraneus*; hind foot over
1.5cm. **Behaviour** more diurnal than *P. subterraneus*, otherwise similar. **Distribution** Juras and
Alps. **Habitat, track and trail** as for *P.
subterraneus*.

Tatra Pine Vole *Pitymys tatricus*
Larger and darker than *P. subterraneus*. **Distribution** Tatra Mountains in CS and PL.

Mediterranean Pine Vole *Pitymys
duodecimcostatus*
Body to 10.5cm, tail to 3cm, hind feet to 1.8cm.
Very short tail, fur yellow above, silver below,
dense and soft. **Behaviour and habitat** as for *P.
subterraneus*. **Distribution** southern E, F, GR, P
and YU.

Savi's Pine Vole *Pitymys savii*
Similar in all respects to *P. subterraneus*. **Distribution** E, F, I, GR and YU.

Grey-sided Vole *Clethrionomys rufocanus*
Large vole (body to 12cm, tail to 4cm). Distingui-

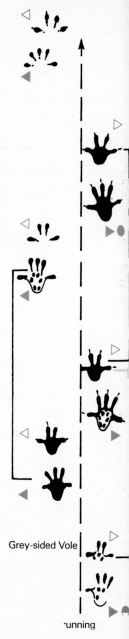

Grey-sided Vole

running

shed by narrow russet band on back. **Behaviour** similar to other members of the genus, but less shy and climbs more; highly active under snow. **Habitat** Arctic scrub, woodland heath and moorland to almost open tundra. **Distribution** Arctic and high mountain areas of N, S, SF and northern SU.

Track minute: hind 1.1 × 1.4cm; fore 1 × 1.4cm; similar to other vole tracks.

Trail normal gait is a scurry: tracks occur in pairs across the median line with a horizontal gap between tracks; stride about 6cm.

Wood Lemming *Myopus schisticolor*

Body to 9.5cm, tail to 2cm. Coloration unique: dark slaty-grey with a subdued rush streak on lower back. **Behaviour** gregarious, mainly nocturnal; active all year. Tunnels and runs made in the moss layer, upon which the species feeds almost exclusively (see page 204). Population fluctuations occur, but not as extreme as in *L. lemmus*. Vocal and rather quarrelsome. **Habitat** wet coniferous forests, especially with a densely mossy floor; riverside areas. **Distribution** N, S, SF and SU.

Track minute: hind 1 × 1.1cm; fore 0.8 × 1cm. Four toes on fore, 5 on hind. Similar to *Lemmus lemmus* (page 100) but very small and claw marks less distinct.

Trail characteristic oscillating trail is more apparent, partly due to the small size of the animal. Fast walking trail common: stride 4cm, partial registration; tail drag absent.

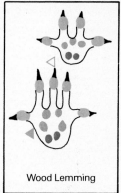

Wood Lemming

Wood Lemming

fast walk

Wood Lemming feeding on forest floor mosses.

Northern Red-backed Vole *Clethrionomys rutilus*

Body to 10cm, tail to 3.5cm. Lighter and more brightly coloured than *C. glareolus* with a shorter, densely tufted tail. **Behaviour** similar to *C. glareolus* but more inclined to enter houses and farm buildings in winter. Very active beneath the snow. **Habitat** open pine, birch and willow scrub areas of the Arctic; also human habitations. **Distribution** Arctic areas of N, S, SF and northern SU.

Track minute: hind 1 × 1.4cm; fore 0.9 × 1.4cm. Similar in all respects to other vole tracks.

Trail normal gait is a fast run or scurry; tracks not registered; stride about 8cm.

Greater White-toothed Shrew *Crocidura russula*

Medium-sized shrew (body to 8.5cm, tail to 5cm, hind feet to 1.3cm). Similar to Common Shrew, but tail is bristly and coat grey-brown. Outline of external ear is distinct in all white-toothed shrews. In hand, 3 white unicuspid teeth (see page 285). **Behaviour** solitary, diurnal and crepuscular, burrows and keeps to cover. **Habitat** deciduous woodlands, grasslands, arable land and human habitation; extends to lower slopes of mountains. **Distribution** A, AL, B, CH, CS, D, DDR, E, F, GR, H, I, L, NL, P, YU and Mediterranean islands.

Track and trail as for *Sorex* species (see page 119).

Lesser White-toothed Shrew *Crocidura suaveolens*

Similar to *C. russula* but smaller (body to 7.7cm, tail to 4cm, hind feet to 1.2cm). Critical identification by dentition (see page 285). **Behaviour and habitat** as for *C. russula*; also found in coastal areas. **Distribution** A, AL, B?, BG, CH, CS, E, F, GB (Scilly Isles), GR, H, I, L?, P, PL, SU, TR and YU.

Track and trail similar to other shrews but slightly smaller in detail than *C. russula* and *Sorex araneus*.

Bicoloured White-toothed Shrew *Crocidura leucodon*

Similar size to *C. russula* (body to 8.5cm, tail to 4.5cm, hind feet to 1.3cm). Clear demarcation between dark grey back and light underside; tail bristly. **Behaviour and habitat** as for other members of genus. **Distribution** continuous in A, AL, B, BG, CH, CS, D, DDR, F, H, L, NL, PL, R,

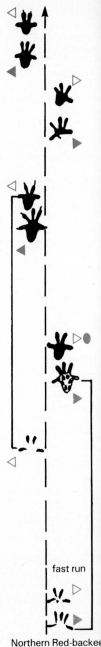

fast run

Northern Red-backed Vole

SU, TR and YU, part of GR, with a separate population in south I.

Track and trail as for *C. russula* and *Sorex araneus*.

Common Shrew *Sorex araneus*

The six *Sorex* species all have red-tipped teeth. The body of Common Shrew is up to 8.5cm, the hind foot 1.2–1.3cm; flank fur colour different to both back and belly. Critical identification on dentition (see page 285). **Behaviour** solitary and diurnal; active all year. Lives in dense ground cover, frequently nesting under logs, roots or vegetation tussocks. **Habitat** near universal, wherever there is ground cover. **Distribution** throughout Europe except IRL, IS, P, much of E and parts of AL, GR and YU.

Track minute: hind 1 × 1cm; fore 0.8 × 0.9cm. There are 6 distinct palm pads, 4 interdigital and 2 proximal. All tracks 5-toed; distinct digital pads with small sharp attached claws; hand outline normally complete, although shrews are so small and light that it is rare to find tracks in the field. Sometimes only 2 interdigital pads show if the animal is moving at speed. Toes I and V are always opposite each other.

Trail almost continuous fine tail drag occurs in all gaits. Normal gait is a run with feet straddled across the median line; partial registration; stride about 4cm. In the bounding gait feet are bunched together to give 4 distinct tracks with about 5cm between groups.

Alpine Shrew *Sorex alpinus*

Similar to *S. araneus* (body to 7.5cm) with large feet (up to 1.6cm); but tail is as long as head and body; colouring dark grey. Critical identification on dentition (see page 284). **Behaviour** typical of genus but probably also a strong swimmer. **Habitat** coniferous forests, especially close to water. **Distribution** mountainous areas of A, AL, CH, CS, D, F, GR, H, I, PL and YU.

Track and trail typical of genus.

Pygmy White-toothed Shrew *Suncus etruscus*

Tiny shrew (body to 4.5cm, tail to 3cm, hind feet to 0.8cm). Feet small in proportion to body; tail bristly; muzzle with long whiskers or 'vibrissae'. In hand, 4 white unicuspid teeth. **Behaviour** appears to be solitary and nocturnal; active throughout the year; surface-living. **Habitat** Mediterranean scrub,

bounding

Common Shrew

grassland and even human habitation; occurs in foothills. **Distribution** Mediterranean areas of AL, E, F, GR, I, P, YU and the Mediterranean islands except Crete; extends into Aquitaine in F.

Track and trail tracks extremely small and rare, often only 0.6 × 0.5cm, but typical of shrews. Tail drag present; stride about 3cm.

Pygmy Shrew *Sorex minutus*
Small (body to 6cm, hind feet to 1.2cm). Two-coloured coat. Critical identification on dentition (see page 284). **Behaviour** solitary and diurnal; active all year. Active in litter layers, but tunnels less than Common Shrew and is an agile climber. **Habitat** near universal, tolerant of exposed situations with little cover. **Distribution** common and widespread except in the extreme north of N and S, much of E, the whole of IS, P; absent from the Mediterranean islands.

Track and trail like *S. araneus* but tracks only 0.4–0.5cm long; stride only 2–3cm.

Laxmann's Shrew *Sorex caecutiens*
Intermediate between *S. araneus* and *S. minutus* (body to 7cm, hind feet to 1.2cm); two-coloured coat. Critical identification on dentition. **Behaviour** solitary and diurnal, active all year; ground-nesting.

bounding
Pygmy Shrew

Habitat deciduous and coniferous woodlands, high mountains and tundra. **Distribution** north N and S, east PL, much of SF and SU. Never very common.

Track and trail similar to *S. araneus* but slightly smaller.

Least Shrew *Sorex minutissimus*
Smallest of northern shrews (body to 4.5cm, hind feet to 0.9cm); tiny feet are distinctive. **Behaviour** solitary and diurnal; active all year; ground-nesting. **Habitat** Arctic areas and wetter boreal forests. **Distribution** small areas of N and S; continuous in SF and north SU.

Track and trail extremely small and rare. Tracks are frequently only 0.6 × 0.6cm; tail drag fine but continuous. Groups of tracks in bounding gait may be 6cm apart, despite small size of animal.

Opposite: Lesser White-toothed Shrew in a seashore habitat.

Dusky Shrew *Sorex sinalis*
Similar size to *S. araneus* (body to 8cm), but feet much larger (up to 1.5cm). Belly fur is dark. **Behaviour** similar to other *Sorex* species. **Habitat** mainly wet coniferous forests. **Distribution** small areas of S, much of SF and SU.

Track and trail similar to other *Sorex* species, but tracks larger (hind 1.5 × 1.2cm; fore 1 × 1cm). Stride up to 10cm in bounding trail.

Below: Dead Pygmy Shrew. As is so often the case with this species, there is no apparent cause of death.

Four-toed tracks with pads

Domestic Dog *Canis familiaris*

Behaviour follows human patterns; if allowed the freedom spends much time wandering at random with frequent stops and deviations to investigate scents and food and, particularly in males, to urinate. **Distribution** throughout Europe.

Track there is great variation in size between breeds. Tracks normally 4-toed; interdigital pad triangular, lobed, much larger than the 4 digital pads; these are arched around the interdigital; claw marks common. Fox and dog tracks of comparable size can be distinguished by the wide spread of toes around a large interdigital pad in the dog; fox toe formation is tighter and neater in front of smaller interdigital pad.

Domestic Dog

Trail walking gait leaves unregistered tracks located at random on either side of, but diagonal to, the median line: this feature is due to the 'crab walk' (in which the hind quarters are carried slightly to one side of the fore even though the animal is moving straight forward) which distinguishes domestic dogs from their wild cousins. Registration occurs in trotting and tracks are more widely spaced. Walking and trotting trails are frequently meandering. Bounding gait give widely spaced groups of 4 tracks asymmetrical about the median line.

Fox and Dog prints together on a muddy woodland path. The smaller registered Fox prints are to the left, the Dog print to the right. The small interdigital pad of the Fox is clearly visible.

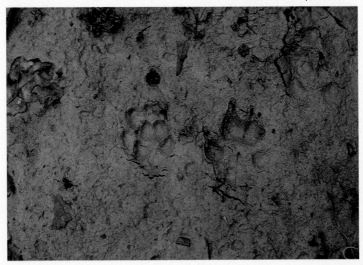

Four-toed tracks with pads

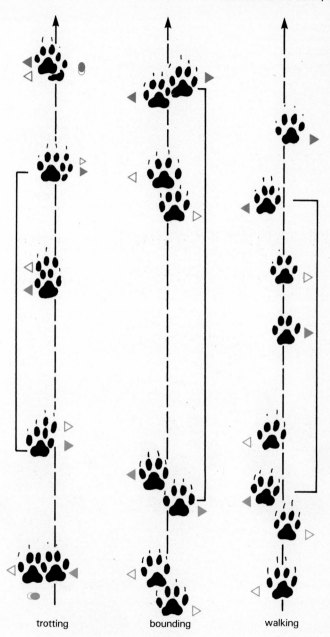

trotting

bounding

walking

119

Wolf *Canis lupus*

Large Alsatian-like animal (body to 130cm, tail to 50cm) but with broad head, short rounded ears, shallower chest and uniform coat colour; head carried low. **Behaviour** gregarious; mainly nocturnal but may be diurnal in remote areas; active all winter, when groups may amalgamate to hunt in packs. Breeds in underground dens. **Habitat** tundra, high mountains, boreal and deciduous forests. **Distribution** AL, BG, E, GR, I, N, P, PL, R, S, SF, SU and YU. Widespread in remote areas of eastern Europe; numbers small and groups isolated in west.

Track large, from 10 × 7.5cm to 11 × 9.5cm in adults. Fore track slightly larger than hind; 4 toes in both. Digital pads clearly impressed, often with short blunt claw marks; interdigital pad strongly lobed, triangular and large; faint hair marks may be present between pads. Narrow and more slender in detail than large dog tracks.

Trail normal gait is a trot or lope with tracks in partially registered pairs either side of the median line; stride up to 120cm; crab-wise tendency of large domestic dog trail not apparent. Running and bounding trails show discrete groups of 4 tracks. In running the tracks are spread slightly along the median line; strides up to 180cm. In bounding they are bunched tightly together; stride up to 200cm.

Wolf

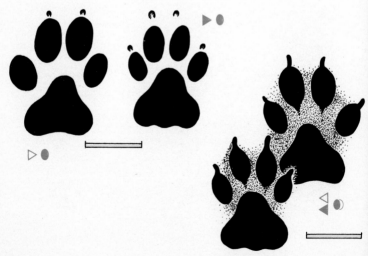

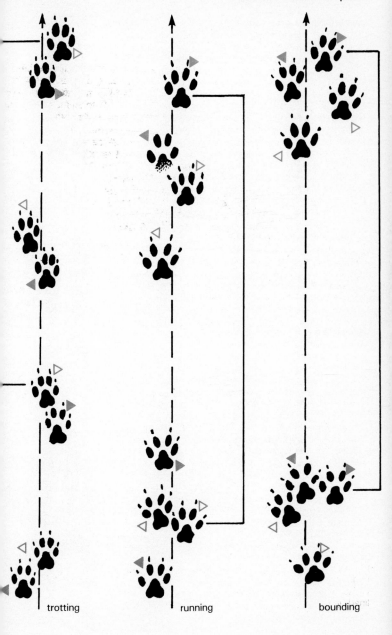

Four-toed tracks with pads

trotting

running

bounding

Brown Hare *Lepus capensis*

Body up to 65cm. The Brown Hare is identified by very long black-tipped ears (up to 10.5cm), long legs and black and white tail. **Behaviour** mainly solitary, active at dusk or night, although sometimes seen in the day, especially in spring. Active all year. Breeds and shelters in shallow surface depressions known as forms. **Habitat** mainly farmland (especially arable), open woodland and moorland areas. **Distribution** widespread except in IS, much of N, S, SF, northern SU and high in the Alps.

Track hind large (up to 15 × 4.5cm); fore small (about 4 × 4cm). Distinguished from rabbit by size, the structural components – 4 digital pads, no interdigital or proximal pads – being the same. Full hind track is slipper-shaped and often shows a 5th toe. Hair marks are generally present on all but the hardest ground; the outline of the fore track is often completely circular.

Trail slow hop shows hind tracks close behind the fore with a stride of about 25cm. Bounding gait gives hind tracks close to and opposite the median line with the fore tracks behind them. The high-speed bound gives a similar track but with greater splaying and separation; stride may exceed 2.5m.

Mountain Hare *Lepus timidus*

Like the Brown Hare but smaller (body up to 60cm) with shorter ears (up to 8cm) and lacking black fur on the tail. In winter the fur may be wholly white or transitional. **Behaviour** mainly solitary, but may form small groups. Generally crepuscular or nocturnal but will feed by day in bad weather; active all year. Excavates shallow shelters; sometimes also digs short breeding burrows. **Habitat** upland moors and heaths, tundra and Arctic Alpine areas; also open woodland and cultivated areas in uplands. **Distribution** restricted to northern and upland areas in A, CH, CS, F, GB and SU, throughout IRL, N, S, SF and YU.

Track hind large (up to 13 × 3cm); fore small (3.5 × 3cm). Similar to other lagomorphs; often delicate with only the extreme tips of the digital pads showing. A distinctive feature is the very thick hair covering, which may distort the positioning of the digital pads.

Trail hopping gait gives hind tracks in opposite pairs close to the median line, with fore tracks behind; stride about 25cm. Bounding gait shows typical lagomorph splay with hind feet paired, fore lined up behind; stride up to 2m.

bounding

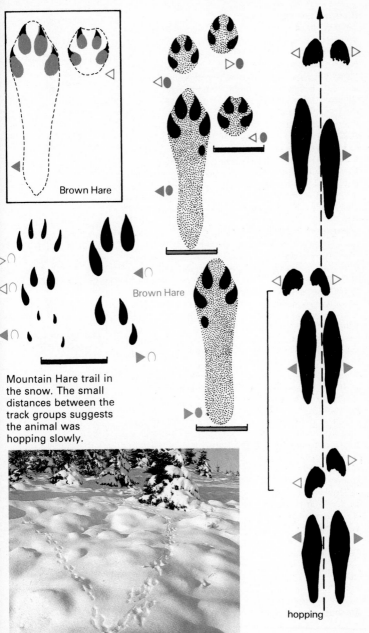

Four-toed tracks with pads

Brown Hare

Brown Hare

Mountain Hare trail in the snow. The small distances between the track groups suggests the animal was hopping slowly.

hopping

Rabbit *Oryctolagus cuniculus*

The Rabbit body grows to 45cm, ears to 7cm with no black tip. Legs are not long enough to hold body completely clear of the ground as they do in the hares. **Behaviour** gregarious, generally crepuscular, but may be diurnal; active all year. Rabbits live and breed in extensive underground tunnel systems known as warrens. **Habitat** wide range, including woodland, cultivated land, scrubland and dune area. **Distribution** A, B, CH, CS, D, DDR, DK, E, F, GB, H, I, IRL, L, NL, P, PL, south S and a small area of SU.

   Track small to medium: hind 6 × 2.5cm; fore 3.5 × 2.5cm. Rabbit and hare species show common characteristics: no interdigital or proximal pads: frequently a complete covering of hair between the digital pads. Four oblong digital pads with short integral claws normally show on fore and hind tracks; sometimes only claw marks show. The hind track is often a slipper-shaped impression: there is a toe V but this is very small and rarely shows even in a complete print. In hare tracks toe V is seen more frequently.

   Trail as in hare species, registration does not occur at any normal gait. The hopping trail shows the fore tracks in pairs with the hind tracks positioned close behind. Stride about 20cm. The running trail shows tracks in loose groups of four. The trail from a high speed bound shows the hind feet opposite to each other across the median line with the fore feet placed one in front of the other on the median line. This trail is characteristic of all the lagomorphs and shows strides of up to 80cm in the Rabbit.

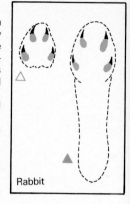

Rabbit

Opposite: Trail of Rabbit hopping in the snow. Typical track grouping with the hind side by side and the fore in line ahead.

unusual complex of registered tracks showing digitals only

the deep impression of the tracks suggests a larger more complex animal track at first sight

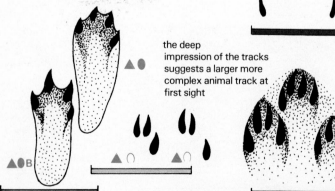

Four-toed tracks with pads

slow hop moving from
hard to soft ground

125

Lynx *Felis lynx*

Large cat (body to 125cm, including 15cm tail). Intensity of marking varies with race, but long legs, short tail, long ear tufts and short mane are diagnostic. **Behaviour** solitary and nocturnal; active all year. Terrestrial, but an excellent climber. Breeds and rests in dens amongst rocks or in hollow trees. **Habitat** coniferous woodlands in north, Mediterranean scrub in south. **Distribution** continuous but thin in SF and SU; secondary centres in N and S; relict populations in E and P; occasional reports from A, BG, CH, F, GR, H, I, PL, YU but many of these are unlikely and the species is in decline everywhere.

Track medium: 7–8 × 8.5–9.5 cm. Large 3-lobed triangular interdigital pad with 4 digital pads arched around it. Claws rarely show except in snow; fur marks may be seen between pads on soft ground.

Trail similar to other cats: normal gait is a walk, when tracks tend to show in single file; partial or complete registration common; sets of double tracks frequent. Walking stride is about 40cm, increasing to 250cm in fast run.

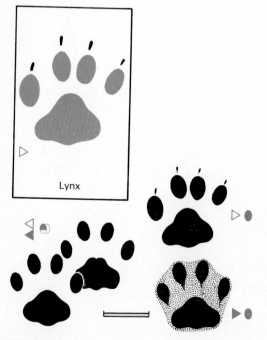

Lynx

walking

Wild Cat *Felis sylvestris*

Size of large Domestic Cat (body to 65cm); distinguished by thick bushy tail with discrete rings and striped body markings. **Behaviour** solitary, generally nocturnal; active all year. Terrestrial but an excellent climber. Rests and breeds in subsurface shelters such as rock dens or upturned tree roots. **Habitat** deciduous and coniferous forests, Mediterranean scrub, open hill and mountain areas. **Distribution** widespread in AL, B, E, GR, I, P, R and YU; present in mountainous areas of A, CH, D, F, GB (Scotland) and TR; possibly in B, L and NL.

Track small: about 6 × 5cm. Large 3-lobed triangular or lozenge-shaped interdigital pad with 4 digital pads normally present on fore and hind tracks. Claw marks, a fifth digital pad (I) and a single proximal pad may show if the animal jumps on to very soft ground so that the whole wrist structure impresses; complete hand outline may then also be present.

Trail walking gait shows paired, unregistered tracks; stride 30cm or more. Gallop gives partial registration; stride about 60cm. Tracks always close to median line with little splaying.

Lynx in the snow. Such a view is more likely than the perfect profile. The bob tail and pointed ears are obvious even so.

Wild Cat

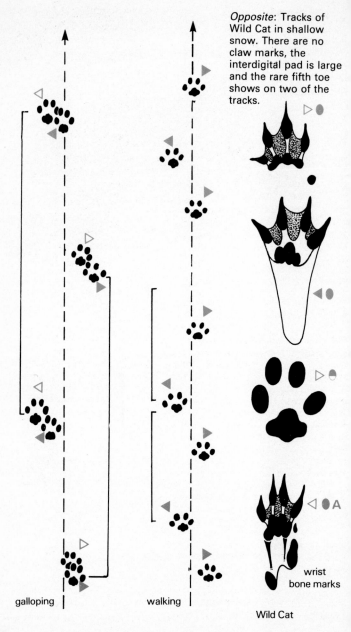

Opposite: Tracks of Wild Cat in shallow snow. There are no claw marks, the interdigital pad is large and the rare fifth toe shows on two of the tracks.

galloping | walking | Wild Cat

wrist bone marks

128

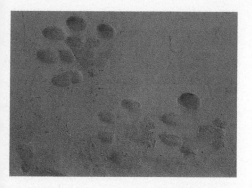

Raccoon Dog *Nyctereutes procyonoides*

Small, heavily built dog with short legs (body to 65cm, tail to 20cm). Ears very short and rounded; tail short and uniformly coloured; black face mask. **Behaviour** solitary and nocturnal; hibernates in north of range, male sometimes with female. In south reduced winter activity (unusual in dogs) is sustained by fat reserves. Rests and breeds in underground dens. **Habitat** woodlands, especially close to rivers and marshes. **Distribution** PL, R, SF, SU; spreading into A, BG, CH, CS, N and S; smaller colonies in other countries.

Track small: fore (5 × 4.5cm) larger than hind (4.5 × 3.5cm). Tracks 4-toed, although toe I sometimes shows on fore track; interdigital pad distinctly triangular, lobed, larger than digital pads. Claw marks normally present. These are slender and do not point inwards.

Trail walking trail shows tracks close to and parallel with median line; partial registration; stride about 25cm in adults. Bounding trail shows tracks in groups of 4 with about 50cm between each group.

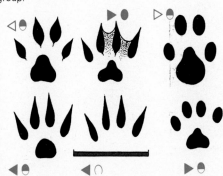

Raccoon Dog bounding

129

Red Fox *Vulpes vulpes*

Red Fox is about the size of a medium dog (body to 75cm, tail to 45cm). Distinguished by long narrow muzzle, large pointed ears and a bushy tail which is frequently white-tipped. Coat generally chestnut. **Behaviour** solitary and generally nocturnal, but diurnal in some areas; active all year. Breeds in burrows or now in other shelter, including cellars and outbuildings. **Habitat** near universal, even adapting to live in urban areas. **Distribution** common and widespread throughout Europe except Iceland.

Track small: 5 × 4.5cm; similar to Arctic Fox in form, but the triangular interdigital pad is normally relatively smaller (barely equal to one digital). Hair shows less frequently between pad impressions in *Vulpes* than in *Alopex*. Small interdigital pads are diagnostic of foxes.

Trail normal trotting gait leaves tracks which are evenly spaced on either side of the median line and rarely registered; stride about 45cm. The trotting trail is purposeful and straight, unlike that of domestic dogs. Stalking trail shows tracks close together, bunched into groups and partially registered. Bounding gait gives groups of 4 tracks 60cm or more apart.

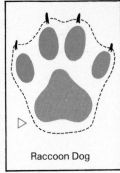

Raccoon Dog

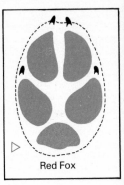

Red Fox

toes and interdigital pad
distorted by injury or
disease

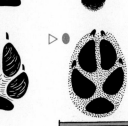

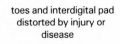

Four-toed tracks with pads

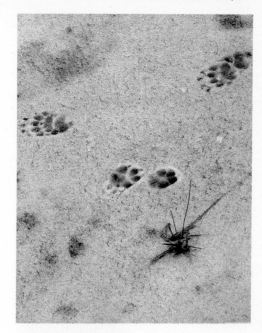

Tracks of trotting fox passing from left to right with registered boar badger tracks passing from right to left above.

Left: Fox foot showing interdigital pad of similar size to digital pads, small claws and hair between the pads.

walking

Arctic Fox *Alopex lagopus*

Smaller than Red Fox (body to 65cm, tail to 35cm), with shorter ears and muzzle. Fur uniform in colour, brown or blue-grey in summer, normally white in winter. **Behaviour** gregarious in small groups; active all year, 24 hours a day in summer months; hours of darkness only in winter. Terrestrial, but sometimes transported on ice floes. Breeds in burrows. **Habitat** tundra and high mountains; may move into forests in winter. **Distribution** IS, N, S, SF and SU; frequently ranges over Arctic ice sheet in winter. Populations fluctuate with food availability.

Track small, about 5.5 × 5cm; fore track larger than hind. Normally 4 toes in all tracks, but rarely toe I and proximal pad will show on a fore track. Digital pads small and distinct; claw marks pointed and separated, pointing inwards on 2 central toes; interdigital pad lobed, triangular, only slightly larger than digital pads. Tracks show fur impressions between pads and on perimeter.

Trail walking trail shows a line of tracks close to median line with near perfect registration; stride 40cm. The tail or 'brush' may leave marks in soft ground. Running or trotting tails show tracks close to median line, the tracks paired and unregistered; stride about 80cm. Bounding trail gives groups of 4 tracks with 60–100cm between them.

Arctic Fox

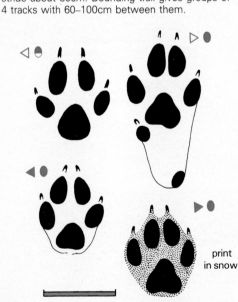

print in snow

bounding

Jackal *Canis aureus*
Larger than foxes but smaller than the Wolf (body to 100cm, tail to 40cm). Ears long and pointed; tail short and thick; coat colour uniform. **Behaviour** generally solitary and nocturnal; active all year. Normally breeds in burrows. Vocal animal, howling particularly at dusk. **Habitat** Mediterranean scrub, grasslands, arable land and pastures. **Distribution** AL, BG, GR, H, R, TR and YU; locally common and widespread.

Track and trail similar to a large dog.

Genet *Genetta genetta*
Cat-like (body to 60cm, tail to 45cm), but with pointed muzzle, prominent ears, short legs and a very long, ringed tail. **Behaviour** solitary and nocturnal; active all year. Mostly on ground, but an active climber; breeds and rests in dens in trees or rocky places. **Habitat** deciduous woodlands, Mediterranean scrubland and mountain grasslands. **Distribution** E, F, IL and P.

Tracks small (rarely more than 4 × 4cm). Interdigital pad frequently triangular, with 3 fused lobes; 4 digital pads on each foot. Digital pads small relative to interdigital; long claws frequently show.

Genet

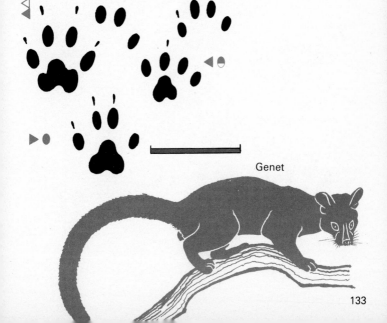

Genet

133

Domestic Cat *Felis cattus*
Behaviour similar to Wild Cat although modified by association with man. **Habitat** anywhere there is cover. **Distribution** widespread throughout Europe, normally associated with man. Feral populations resembling Wild Cat are common, but the two species do not appear to interbreed.

Track small: 3.5–4 × 3.5–4cm. Tracks square or wider than long. Interdigital pad large, 3-lobed and triangular or lozenge-shaped; 4 digital pads, rarely a fifth to the back of the interdigital. Claw marks very rare as claws are retracted in walking or running; fur marks may be present.

Trail many gaits are adopted. Stalking tracks are close together, frequently almost toe to heel. Walking gives widely spaced separate tracks. In trotting or running there is partial to complete registration and stride length increases. Bounding gait gives loose groups of 4 tracks which may be more than 90cm apart. Sometimes the cat leaps, taking off from exactly the same place as it lands: this gives tight groups of 4 tracks which may be close together or up to 2m apart.

Domestic Cat

Pheasant and Domestic Cat trails in the snow. Note also Fox tracks at the top and bottom.

additional toes are not uncommon as both these examples show

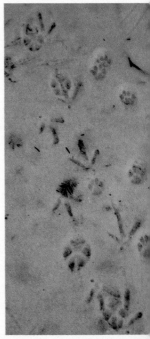

Egyptian Mongoose *Herpestes ichneumon*
Medium-sized carnivore (body to 55cm, tail to
45cm). Characterized by pointed muzzle, uniform
grizzled coat, short legs with very small feet and
long hairy tapering tail. **Behaviour** solitary, often
active 24 hours, all year round. Strictly terrestrial;
shelters and breeds in underground dens. **Habitat**
open deciduous woodland, Mediterranean scrubland and rocky hill area. **Distribution** southwest E
and P and an island off YU coast.

   Track small: hind 3.5 × 3cm; fore 3 × 3cm.
Interdigital pad asymmetrical, 3 or 4-lobed. Hind
interdigital has a lobe which extends back beyond
the body of the track. Fore tracks normally show
4 digital pads, hind show 5. Toe V is set far back
against the interdigital pad, a diagnostic feature in
conjunction with the extended lobe on the interdigital. Small sharp separate claw marks present.
Tracks very small relative to size of animal.

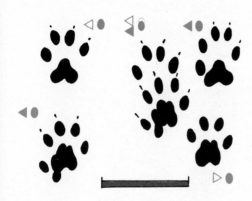

   Trail normal gaits are runs at various speeds
with tracks in groups of 2, partially registered, all
on the median line; stride at least 20cm, sometimes more than 50cm at higher speeds.

running

Indian Grey Mongoose *Herpestes edwardsi*
Slightly smaller than Egyptian Mongoose with tail
equal to length of body. **Behaviour and habitat**
as for Egyptian Mongoose. **Distribution** one small
area of I only.

   Track and trail as for Egyptian Mongoose.

Order Pinnipedia Seals

Eight species of this order occur regularly in European waters.

The body of seals is heavy and torpedo-shaped with a short neck. The limbs are adapted for an aquatic existence. The thigh bone is short and the shin bones proportionately longer. Five fully developed digits are present on the fore limb with I and V being the longest and II being shortest; the digits are connected by webs. The hind feet extend beyond the body to serve as a rudder in the water, but they are useless for movement on land. Most of the fore limb lies within the body and there is no collar bone, so the limb can move freely beneath the skin. The limbs lie out to the side of the body and are used to create a fulcrum so that the animal can over-balance forward and hence move on land.

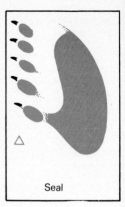

Seal

Although seals do not move easily on land, **tracks** are common on mud flats and sandy areas used for resting and breeding. The proportions of the tracks vary according to species, but the morphology is generally similar. The tracks are always enormous in adults (17 × 13cm). There are 5 distinct digital pads with well developed claw marks and the rest of the track shows as a large rounded palm area. The digital pads lie in a line parallel to the direction of movement.

The **trail** shows the front limb (flipper) marks in opposite pairs: these are widely spaced from the median line, the distance being dependent on body size. The distance between each track – the stride

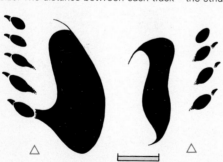

– varies according to speed and size, but is generally over 30cm. The other feature of the trail is the body drag which is always present between tracks. The tracks are not diagnostic for species and direct sightings are the only reliable means of identification.

Seal tracks in the sand leading down to the sea.

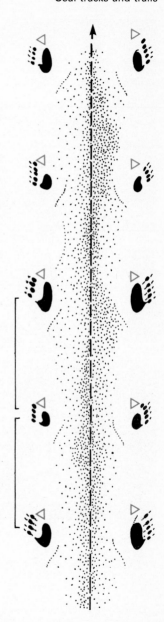

Atlantic Seal cow
suckling her young
pup by the water
edge.

Common Seal *Phoca vitulina*
Small (to 190cm). Muzzle short, break in profile of muzzle and forehead. Nostrils converge at bottom to form a V-shape. Colour variable; pups brown. **Distribution** breeding and non-breeding populations around the coasts of B, D, DK, GB, IRL, IS, N and the Baltic coast of PL and SU.

Grey Seal *Halichoerus grypus*
Large (male to 320cm, female to 250cm). Muzzle and forehead without break, muzzle long with widely separated nostrils. Dark background with darker markings; young are white. **Distribution** breeding and non-breeding populations on the coasts of D, DK, northern E, F, GB, IRL, IS, N, PL, S, SF and SU.

Monk Seal *Monachus monachus*
Medium (230–380cm). Coat brown in colour, pups initially black. **Distribution** restricted to Mediterranean (where it is the only seal), the Black Sea, Aegean and Adriatic.

Ringed Seal *Phoca hispida*
Small (to 115cm). Difficult to distinguish from *P. vitulina* but there is a distinct pattern of rings in the coat. **Distribution** Arctic coast of SU, Baltic S and SF, north coast of IS.

Harp Seal *Pagophilus groenlandicus*
Medium (to 200cm). Distinct black and white pattern, most marked in males. Pups white. **Distribution** restricted to north coast of IS, N and SU.

Bearded Seal *Erignathus barbatus*
Large (to 250cm). Uniform sandy colour, whiskers very long. Young initially greyish. **Distribution** north coasts of IS, N and SU; very rare.

Hooded Seal *Cystophora cristata*
Large (to 300cm in male, female slightly less). Similar to *Halichoerus grypus* but background to markings very light. Males have a large sack on the nose which can be inflated.

Walrus *Odobenus rosmarus*
The size, uniform grey colour, long whiskers and tusks make the animal distinctive. The fore flippers are much larger than in other seals and the hind flippers also come forward; this gives a track and trail unlike any other species of Pinnipedia, although Walrus rarely comes ashore on to a substrate which will show tracks.

Leisler's Bat in a walking position. The open mouth shows the large canines and the gap between the upper incisors.

Order Chiroptera Bats

The bats are adapted to life on the wing and, when they are not in flight, they rest in roosts above the ground surface. Rarely some species do land and move across the ground, but the animals are light so tracks are uncommon. They may be found in very soft mud close to water and sometimes on cowpats. Other than size, there is little variation in track morphology between species. It is difficult to identify bats on the wing and so the general characteristics of the main groups are identified by silhouette and the in-hand identification characteristics are briefly listed for each species.

Tracks and trails On the ground bats move in the same way as other terrestrial mammals, ie. with fore and hind limbs moving as diagonally opposite pairs. Various gaits may be identified, but the fore track always shows as a single thumb mark or dot, while the hind tracks are 5-toed and usually display claw marks. Hind tracks point out at an angle from the median line reflecting the curved femur, which enables the legs to bend so that the bat can hang upside-down.

In the walking gait the tail tends to be pressed to the ground to give stability. The fore and hind tracks are close to each other in this trail. The

Bat-running in restricted space

running trail shows a considerable distance between fore and hind tracks and, if movement is unrestricted, the wingtip prints are very widely spaced; the tail is held clear of the ground and drag does not show. A rare gait is leapfrogging, when the bat moves both fore limbs forward as a pair and then brings the hind feet close behind. The pairs are parallel, close to the median line and equidistant. It is not clear if the tail plays a supporting role in this movement, but a faint impression does occur on the median line.

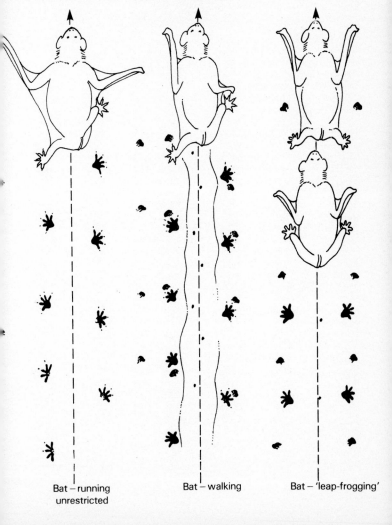

Bat – running unrestricted

Bat – walking

Bat – 'leap-frogging'

Two Lesser and one Greater Horseshoe Bats in a sleeping position. Many horseshoe bats wrap their wings around the body when they sleep, as the specimen on the left has done.

Horseshoe Bats

Characterized in the field by the complex lobes of skin around the nose from which the group takes its name, and the lack of a tragus in the ear. When hibernating most of the horseshoe bats almost completely enclose their body by folding their wings around it.

Greater Horseshoe Bat *Rhinolophus ferrum-equinum*

Largest horseshoe bat (body to 6.8cm, wing span to 39cm, forearm to 5.9cm). In hand, sella saddle-shaped with square angle in profile. **Behaviour** gregarious, large colonies in summer dispersing in winter; breeding colonies noisy; nocturnal, emerging late and flying throughout the night; flight butterfly-like. Hibernates, often in caves and mines. **Habitat** mainly wooded country, roosting in caves, mines and tunnels in winter; summer breeding colonies often found in roof spaces and barns. **Distribution** continuous in A, B, CH, CS, GB, H, NL, with smaller colonies in D, DDR, PL, and R.

Lesser Horseshoe Bat *Rhinolophus hipposideros*

Smallest horseshoe bat (body to 3.9cm, wingspan to 25cm, forearm less than 4.2cm). In hand, sella tapers upwards and shows a flat top angle in profile. **Behaviour** gregarious, forming large colonies in summer, smaller groups in winter. Mainly nocturnal, emerging shortly after sunset with erratic fluttering flight. Hibernates in caves, tunnels, even cellars. **Habitat** mainly wooded areas. Breeding colonies in roofs and farm buildings; winter roosts often below ground. **Distribution** A, AL, B, BG, CH, CS, D, DDR, E, F, GH, GR, H, I, IRL, L, NL, P, PL, R, SU, TR and YU.

Mediterranean Horseshoe Bat *Rhinolophus euryale*
Medium size (body to 4.5cm, wingspan to 33cm, forearm to 4.9cm). Wings not wrapped around body when hibernating. Can only be identified in the hand: parallel-sided sella with slender pointed upper angle in front view. **Behaviour** gregarious, often forming very large colonies in summer, smaller groups in winter. Generally similar to *R. hipposideros*. **Habitat** as for *R. hipposideros*. **Distribution** mainly southern Europe: AL, BG, E, F, GR, H, I, R, and YU.

Blasius's Horseshoe Bat *Rhinolophus blasii*
Medium size, very similar to *R. euryale*. Only positive means of identification is the sella, which is constricted in front view. **Behaviour** little known. **Distribution** restricted to areas of A, AL, BG, GR, I, R, TR and YU.

Mehely's Horseshoe Bat *Rhinolophus mehelyi*
Second largest horseshoe bat (body to 6.2cm, wing-span to 36cm, forearm to 5.5cm). Pale coloured with large ears. In hand, top of sella (lancet) tapers and ends in a long slender point. **Behaviour** little known. **Habitat** mainly cave-dwelling. **Distribution** mainly southern, present in parts of BG, E, F, GR, I, R, SU, TR and YU.

Rhinolophus – horseshoe bats

Vespertilionid bats
Characterized by the lack of complex skin folds around the nose and by the presence of a tragus in the ear.

European Free-tailed Bat *Tadarida teniotis*
Large grey bat (body to 8.7cm, wingspan to 45cm, forearm to 6.4cm). Identified by long tail extending well beyond short membrane. Ears large, rounded, joined, extending forward almost to the nose tip. **Behaviour** colonies generally small; crepuscular, flying high and direct; activity reduced in winter, but hibernation is brief. Roosts in caves, tunnels and rock crevices. **Habitat** mountain and hill areas, sea-cliffs and human habitations, including towns. **Distribution** mainly confined to Mediterranean areas of AL, CH, E, F, GR, I, P, YU and islands.
    Track and trail distinguished from all other species by persistent tail drag.

Myotis species
Characterized by a long pointed tragus (pages 144–146).

Daubenton's Bat *Myotis daubentoni*
Small (body to 5cm, wingspan to 27cm; forearm to 4cm). Large feet with long calcar. In hand, diagnostic feature is the scantily haired tail membrane. **Behaviour** large summer breeding colonies, which disperse in winter. Summer roosts in trees and buildings. Emerge after sunset and fly through the night. Hibernate normally in small crevices in caves and tunnels. Fly along regular 'beats' such as hedgerows or the edge of woods. **Habitat** woodland areas in general. **Distribution** absent from southeast and extreme north of Europe, otherwise present in A, B, CH, CS, D, DDR, DK, E, F, GB, H, I, IRL, N, NL, P, PL, R, S, SF, SU and YU.

Nathalina Bat *Myotis nathalinae*
Almost identical to *M. daubentoni*; microscopic identification necessary. **Behaviour and habitat** little known; appears to be a cave-dweller. **Distribution** only known from CH, E and F.

Long-fingered Bat *Myotis capaccinii*
Similar size to *M. daubentoni*, distinguished by very hairy tail membrane. **Behaviour** highly gregarious, frequently occurring in large colonies; night-flying; roosts in caves all year round. **Habitat** generally lives in caves and tunnels close to water. **Distribution** present over the whole of I and parts of AL, F, GR, R, SU, TR, YU and Mediterranean islands.

Pond Bat *Myotis dasycneme*
Medium size (body to 6.1cm, wingspan to 34cm, forearm to 4.8cm). Grey colour, distinguished by almost hairless tail membrane. **Behaviour** gregarious; breeding colonies in roofs. Winter roosts in caves, often solitary. May migrate long distances between summer and winter roosts. Flies at dusk, probably making a single flight. **Habitat** woodland areas near water. **Distribution** continuous in B, D, DDR, DK, L, NL, PL, S and SU; recorded in east F.

Brandt's Bat *Myotis brandti*
Small (body to 4.8cm, wingspan to 22.5cm, forearm to 3.8cm). Adult has a dark coloured upper coat. Tragus almost half length of conch. Distinguishable from *M. mystacinus* on dentition (see page 289). **Behaviour** gregarious; tends to be diurnal. Summer colonies in buildings, winter roosts in caves. Slow fluttering flight. **Habitat** caves and buildings in wooded country. **Distribu-

tion confirmed reports from B, D, DDR, DK, GB, NL and S, but may be confused with *M. mystacinus.*

Whiskered Bat *Myotis mystacinus*
Smallest *Myotis* (body to 4.8cm, wingspan to 24cm, forearm to 3.7cm). Easily confused with other members of genus, but has small feet and is very dark in colour. Tragus relatively long and pointed. **Behaviour** gregarious; summer colonies, often large, in buildings and trees; winter roosts in caves, more dispersed. Active from sunset onwards, may be active in day. Slow fluttering flight; may make long migrations. **Habitat** caves, buildings and trees in wooded and open country. **Distribution** widespread; absent only from IS, north GB, N, S and SF and southern E and P.

Geoffroy's Bat *Myotis emarginatus*
Small (body to 5cm, wingspan to 30cm, forearm to 4.2cm). Wing membrane joins foot at base of outer toe, as in the following four species. Distinguished by deep step in rear margin of ear and sparsely haired edge to tail membrane. **Behaviour** gregarious summer and winter. Roosts in trees and buildings in summer and caves in winter. **Habitat** buildings, trees and caves, mainly in wooded country. **Distribution** continuous in A, AL, BG, CH, CS, F, GR, H, I, L, PL, R, TR and YU; isolated population in P, also present in B and NL.

Myotis bats

Natterer's Bat *Myotis nattereri*
Medium (body to 5cm, wingspan to 30cm, forearm to 4.3cm). Female larger than male. Fringe of stiff hairs along the edge of the interfemoral membrane is conspicuous. **Behaviour** large summer breeding colonies; more solitary in winter. Roosts in trees and buildings in summer, often deep in caves and tunnels in winter. Emerges after sunset with periods of activity throughout the night. Flight slow-medium and low. **Habitat** open woodland and parkland, often close to water; hollow trees, caves and buildings. **Distribution** most of Europe; absent from AL, BG, GR, IS, N and YU, and from most of R, S, SF, northern SU and Scotland.

Bechstein's Bat *Myotis bechsteini*
Medium (body to 5cm, wingspan to 30cm, forearm to 4.5cm). Ears relatively very long and slender, extending about half their length beyond the muzzle if laid forward. Interfemoral membrane has no fringe of hairs. **Behaviour** small groups all year;

roosts mainly in hollow trees, although also uses houses and caves. Slow, low flight. Emerges shortly after sunset. **Habitat** essentially a forest species. **Distribution** continuous in A, B, BG, CH, CS, D, DDR, F, H, I, PL, R and parts of BG, E, GB and NL.

Mouse-eared Bat *Myotis myotis*
Very large (body to 8cm, wingspan to 45cm, forearm to 6.8cm). Diagnostic features are pointed tragus and the lack of a post calcarial lobe. **Behaviour** gregarious; large summer colonies, smaller groups in winter hibernation. Summer roosts in buildings or caves; in winter in caves, often hanging fully exposed. Emerges well after dark. Slow heavy flight at medium heights. **Habitat** buildings and caves in open, lightly wooded country. **Distribution** continuous in southern Europe; absent from DK, IRL, IS, N, S, SF and SU and much of GB.

Lesser Mouse-eared Bat *Myotis blythi*
Only slightly smaller than *M. myotis*, with which it may be confused, but tragus is narrower and muzzle more slender. **Behaviour and habitat** as for *M. myotis*. **Distribution** restricted mainly to south Europe in AL, E, F, GR, H, I, R, TR and YU and Mediterranean islands.

Nyctalus, Eptesicus and Vespertilio species
Distinguished by long slender wings with a relatively short fifth finger. Ears short and rounded with a short rounded tragus.

Noctule *Nyctalus noctula*
Large (body to 8.2cm, wingspan to 39cm, forearm to 5.5cm). Distinguished from all other species except *N. lasiopterus* (see below) by large size and rich golden-brown fur. **Behaviour** gregarious, summer roosts mainly in trees. Colonies may be noisy. Winter roosts in trees and buildings. Emerges before sunset; flies very high; may migrate long distances. **Habitat** woodland, mainly a tree-roosting species.

Track and trail recorded as running and leapfrogging; unrestricted stride about 5cm; up to 18cm from wingtip to wingtip imprint; tail mark absent.

Greater Noctule *Nyctalus lasiopterus*
Only distinguishable from *N. noctula* by large size (forearm over 6cm). **Behaviour and habitat** wood-

land species; very little else known. **Distribution** rare; recorded from BG, CS, E, F, GR, I, PL, SU and YU.

Leisler's Bat *Nyctalus leisleri*
Medium size (body to 6.4cm, wingspan to 34cm, forearm to 4.7cm). Like a small noctule, but fur is dark, especially towards the roots, rather than uniform golden-brown. **Behaviour** breeding colonies often very large, frequently in trees. Smaller groups hibernate in trees and buildings. High flying, sometimes on the wing in the day or early evening. **Habitat** woodland areas, roosting in trees or buildings. **Distribution** discontinuous in A, B, BG, CH, CS, D, DDR, E, F, GB, GR, I, IRL, PL, R, SU and YU.

Serotine *Eptesicus serotinus*
Large (body to 7.5cm, wingspan to 38cm, forearm to 5.5cm). Dark coloured, distinguished by tail tip which projects beyond the end of the membrane (as in *E. nilssoni*). Naked skin very dark; tragus short, rounded and narrow. **Behaviour** females in small breeding colonies, males solitary. Normally roosts in buildings and tree holes, rarely in caves. Known to land on trees and ground to catch insect prey. **Habitat** woodland, sometimes associated with settlements. **Distribution** widespread; absent from northern GB and SU and the whole of IRL, IS, N, S and SF.

Eptesicus bats

Northern Bat *Eptesicus nilssoni*
Smaller than the Serotine, with which it overlaps in places. Pale colour, protruding tail and short narrow tragus are characteristic. **Behaviour** small summer breeding colonies, normally in wooden buildings or trees; smaller groups in winter, normally in trees or buildings and rarely in caves. Emerges early, often even flying by day. **Habitat** forests and farm buildings, frequently well into mountains in central Europe. **Distribution** mainly northern, continuous in H, N, PL, S, SF and SU; smaller concentrations in central Europe in A, CH, D, DDR and YU.

Parti-coloured Bat *Vespertilio murinus*
Medium size (body to 6.4cm, wingspan to 33cm, forearm to 4.9cm). Recognized by very dark fur on back, light underside. Tail projects slightly beyond membrane; tragus broad and rounded. **Behaviour** large colonies of males form in summer, while females roost singly or in small groups. Buildings,

hollow trees and rock fissures are frequented in summer; caves, tunnels and cellars in winter. Night flying, migratory and vocal. **Habitat** arable land, grassland, human habitation and woodland. **Distribution** continuous in A, CH, CS, D, DDR, PL, R, SU and YU; also occurring in southern N, S and SF; populations in F, I and GR.

Pipistrellus species
Characterized by a post-calcarial lobe in the membrane, rounded ears and short blunt tragus.

Pipistrelle *Pipistrellus pipistrellus*
Very small (body to 4.5cm, wingspan to 25cm, forearm less than 3.5cm). Uniform in colour with slender wings, finger V being less than 4cm in length. Critical identification based on dentition (see page 288). **Behaviour** large summer breeding colonies, frequently in buildings. Male solitary. Hibernates in trees and buildings, although large groups have been found in caves. Very noisy when emerging from roosts. Night flying; flight may follow a regular path and tends to be high, jerky and fast. **Habitat** near universal; absent only from very exposed areas. **Distribution** widespread over most of Europe; absent from IS and SF, most of N, S and northern SU.

   Track and trail very small dimensions, but has been recorded both walking and running.

Pipistrelle bats emerging from their roost and moving down a wall prior to flying off.

Nathusius's Pipistrelle *Pipistrellus nathusii*
Small (body to 5.3cm, wingspan to 25cm, forearm
to 3.5cm). Generally not uniform in colour; wing
broad (finger V about 4.5cm long). **Behaviour** as
for *P. pipistrellus* but appears to be more migratory.
Habitat mainly woodland; also parks, orchards and
near buildings. **Distribution** widespread in eastern
Europe; continuous in A, AL, BG, CH, CS, D, DDR,
south F, GR, H, I, PL, R, SU, TR and YU; secondary
concentrations in B, north F and NL with isolated
populations in DK, E, GB, P and south S.

Kuhl's Pipistrelle *Pipistrellus kuhli*
Lighter in colour than other pipistrelles; wing
membrane has a white margin. Critical identification on dentition (see page 288). **Behaviour and
habitat** as for *P. pipistrellus*. **Distribution** mainly
Mediterranean in A, AL, CH, E, F, GR, I, P and YU;
also Mediterranean islands.

Pipistrellus bats

Savi's Pipistrelle *Pipistrellus savi*
Critical identification on dentition (see page 288),
but generally distinguishable from *P. kuhli* by
marked separation of dark upper and light underside. Also individual hairs have dark base and light
tip. **Behaviour and habitat** similar to other pipistrelles but tends to extend higher into mountains.
Distribution confined to Mediterranean areas of
AL, BG, E, F, GR, I, TR, YU and islands.

Plecotus species
Distinguished from other European genera by very
long ears (up to 3.8 cm) the bases of which meet
on top of the head. The ears are folded back at
rest but the traguses remain erect.

Brown (Common) Long-eared Bat *Plecotus
auritus*
Small bat (body to 4.8cm, wingspan to 28.5cm,
forearm to 4.8cm). Grey-brown coat. **Behaviour**
breeding colonies sometimes form in house roofs,
but normally in trees; rarely in caves. May roost in
crevices or hang free. Some evidence of migration.
Night flying, with slow fluttering flight; hunts
among trees. **Habitat** woodland, roosting in trees
and buildings throughout the year. **Distribution**
widespread; absent from E, IS, P and much of
northern N, S, SF and SU.

Plecotus – long-eared
bats

Grey Long-eared Bat *Plecotus austriacus*
Similar to *P. auritus* but tends to be darker grey,

149

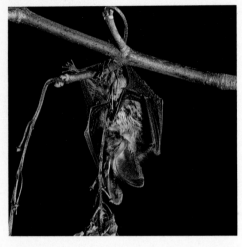

Long-eared Bat resting on a sycamore twig. The bat is wiping its muzzle after eating an insect.

with a wider tragus (0.6cm against 0.5cm); thumb less than 0.5cm long. **Behaviour and habitat** similar to *P. auritus* but more common around settlements. **Distribution** mainly southern Europe: A, AL, B, BG, CH, CS, southern D and DDR, E, F, extreme south of GB, H, I, southern NL, P, south PL, R, parts of SU and YU.

Barbastelle *Barbastella barbastellus*
Small (body to 5.2cm, wingspan to 28cm, forearm to 4.3cm). Distinguished in hand by short ears which meet on top of head, a compressed dark snout and very dark naked skin. **Behaviour** roosts in tree crevices in small numbers in summer. Often hibernates in large concentrations. Feeds over water. **Habitat** deciduous woodlands close to water, roosting in trees and sometimes buildings. **Distribution** A, B, BG, CH, CS, D, DDR, DK, E, F, GB, H, I, L, N, NL, PL, R, S, SU and YU.

Schreiber's Bat *Miniopterus schreibersi*
Medium size (body to 6cm, wingspan 32cm, forearm to 4.8cm). Ears very short, wings long and narrow at tips; subterminal segment of finger III is very long. **Behaviour** gregarious, with large breeding colonies forming in caves. Often emerges before darkness and may fly long distances. Flight fast and high. **Habitat** open country, roosting in caves and buildings. **Distribution** confined to southern Europe: A, AL, BG, CH, E, F, GR, H, I, P, R, TR and YU.

Tracks with cleaves

Order Perissodactyla

The two species of this order present in Europe are normally associated with man, although in some areas both the Domestic Horse (*Equus caballus*) and Domestic Donkey (*Equus asinus*) live in a semi-wild state. Both species are widely distributed, the semi-wild herds generally occurring in wilder remote uplands, on islands and in some woodlands and forests.

There are many breeds and sizes of *E. caballus*, but the general shape is similar. *E. asinus* differs from the smaller breeds of *E. caballus* in having longer ears, a narrow dark stripe on the back and shoulders, a short erect mane and a tail with short hairs at the base.

Track single toe mark large, almost circular; size varies greatly with age and breed, but unshod track is distinctive with blunt rounded front, flat sides and deep notch in dorsal surface. Sizes range from 12 × 12cm in a small pony to over 25 × 25cm in a Shire Horse. In shoed track only outline of shoe generally shows, in soft ground part of back of hoof will also show.

Trail extremely variable: walking trail shows tracks in 2s wide astride the median line. Stride increases in trotting and galloping trails; tracks may be partially registered.

Primitive Wild Horse.

Elk *Alces alces*

Elk is distinguished by very large size (body to 280cm, shoulder to 220cm) and long legs. Muzzle bulbous, overlaps mouth. Males with simple or palmate antlers, small relative to body. No tail. **Behaviour** mainly solitary or in small groups; small herds may form in winter. Active 24 hours and all year. Often feeds in lakes and marshes and on trees. Males vocal in rutting season. **Habitat** common in open forests, especially near to water, and in open areas not far from cover. **Distribution** widespread in N, S, SF and SU; just reaching into PL.

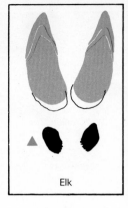

Elk

Track enormous in adults: 16.5 × 13cm. Cleaves very heavy, pointed; tips impress deeply. Medial walls are concave halfway down and diverge at anterior; dew claws may show in soft conditions: these are very large and may bring the overall track length up to 26cm. Cleaves may splay widely when the animal moves at speed. Tracks of young are broad and heavy and are concave at anterior of the medial wall. Slipping and slight splaying are common in young. Individual tracks from each of the 4 feet may be recognized, but the large size and heavy nature of the tracks is diagnostic.

Trail walking trail shows partially registered tracks, parallel and close to median line; stride about 90–100cm in adults. Registration imperfect or absent in trotting trail; stride about 150cm. Grouped tracks in galloping trail are up to 3m apart.

Tracks of Elk moving at speed in the snow. Note the splay in the cleaves.

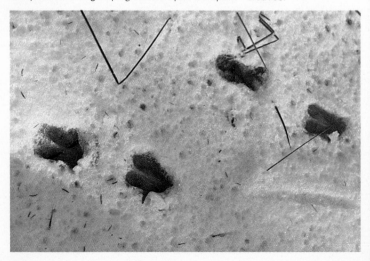

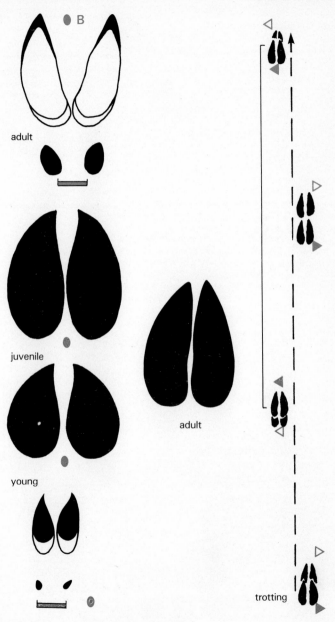

Tracks with cleaves

adult

juvenile

adult

young

trotting

153

Musk Ox *Ovibos moschatus*

Musk Ox is large (body to 240cm, up to 150cm at shoulder). Distinguished by long shaggy coat, and horns (in both sexes) which meet on the forehead and curve back around the head before pointing forward. **Behaviour** gregarious, small summer herds forming into larger herds in winter. Form circle of adults facing outwards for defence purposes. Move over large distances in search of grazing. **Habitat** tundra. **Distribution** introduced into 2 small fjell areas, one in S the other in N; also into Spitzbergen.

Track large to enormous: 14.5 × 12.5cm. Hind track broader than fore. Cleaves large, rounded and blunt. Concave in centre of medial surface, converging to dorsal and anterior ends. Cleaves do not spread even in soft snow. Dew claws very large, close to the back of the cleaves, almost always showing.

Trail normal gait is a slow walk: tracks in pairs, partial registration common; stride 150cm. Galloping trail shows unregistered tracks; stride up to 200cm. Hoof drag marks are common in snow. Able to move very quickly, even over deep snow.

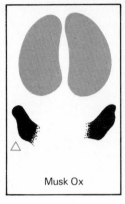

Musk Ox

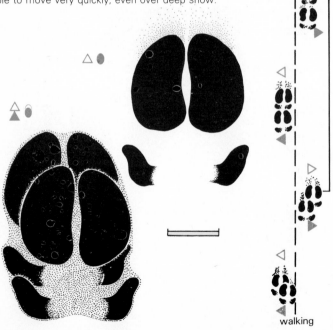

walking

154

Bison *Bison bonasus*
Large (body to 250cm, up to 190cm at the shoulder); distinguished by brown coloration and thick mane on the neck of both sexes. **Behaviour** bull solitary, female and young in small groups; diurnal; active all year. Browse and graze. **Habitat** deciduous woodland. **Distribution** restricted to a few small areas in PL, R and SU.

Track large: male 12.5 × 15cm; female 11 × 14cm, although there is great variation according to sex and age. Distinguished by great width in relation to length. Only 2 cleaves impress, as dew claws are set high. Each cleave is rounded, distinctly convex on outer and medial surfaces; deeply impressed sharp tips show slight concavity on medial surface. Cleaves slightly asymmetrical, coming close only between half to two-thirds of the way down. Convexity of the cleaves on both sides and the very broad track are diagnostic.

Trail in the walking trail tracks close to median line, lateral registration near perfect, vertical sometimes imperfect; stride very variable, about 90–100cm in adult female. Registration becomes less perfect and disappears altogether with increasing speed.

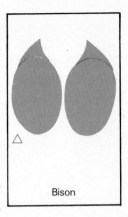

Bison

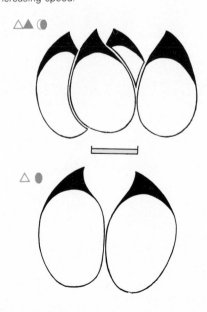

walking

155

Reindeer *Rangifer tarandus*

Large deer (body to 210cm, shoulder to 120cm). Male and female have antlers in which the brow line is branched, a feature unique to the species. Size and colour variable but feet always large and white rump distinctive; muzzle heavy, rounded above and below. **Behaviour** gregarious, young and females in large groups, adult male solitary; diurnal; active all year. Migrates variable distances in different seasons. Mainly a grazing species depending heavily on lichens in winter. **Habitat** mountains, tundra and open boreal forest. **Distribution** wild populations in N, SF and SU; partially controlled populations over much of Lapland in N, S and SF; introduced into IS and a small area of Scotland.

Track adult track variable but normally very large (14 × 13cm), broad, and always includes the large dew claws which are set very low. The whole area of each cleave shows: outer walls convex; medial walls concave and parallel to outer walls, giving each cleave a crescent moon appearance. Gap between cleaves is wide; cleaves rounded or pointed, spreading laterally but not splaying. Hair may show between cleaves and dew claws.

Trail walking trail shows near perfect registrations, except for dew claws; the tracks parallel to but straddled across the median line; stride 50–60cm. Stride decreases at the trot, tracks do not register. In galloping trail tracks are in groups of 4, spread; stride over 2m.

Reindeer in winter coat grazing on snow-covered fells.

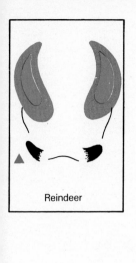

Reindeer

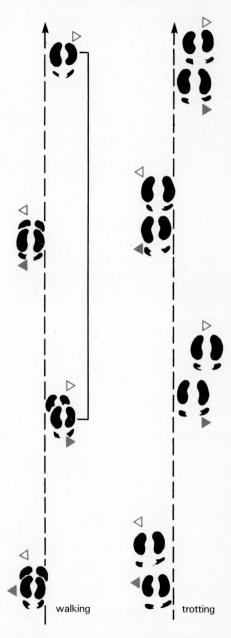

walking

trotting

Domestic Cow *Bos taurus*

There are many varieties kept in domestic situations or in a semi-wild state as with some hill cattle. The species is gregarious and spends much of the day grazing. Widespread over the whole of Europe.

Track large: 10 × 9.5cm. Cleaves rounded, medial surfaces almost parallel along much of their length, but with well marked concavity towards anterior end and convergence at posterior. Cleaves blunt, rounded at anterior, distinctly asymmetrical. Dew claws never show in normal animals.

Trail very variable but tracks normally wide of median line; virtually no registration. Outlines often blurred as feet are dragged. At slow walking pace the tracks just touch.

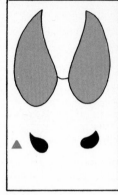

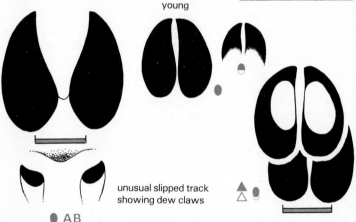

young

unusual slipped track
showing dew claws

A B

Water Buffalo *Bubalus bubalus*

Similar to Domestic Cattle, but distinguished by broad, flattened, backward-sloping horns and uniform grey/brown coat. **Distribution** southern Europe, especially Italy.

Track and trail as for Domestic Cattle.

Domestic Pig *Sus scrofa*

There are many varieties of the domestic Pig, all derived from Wild Boar stock. They vary in size, form and colour but all have a blunter, shorter snout. Generally kept in small groups domestically, unless in an intensive production unit. Semi-wild groups do occur in some areas. **Track and trail** similar to Wild Boar but with size variations according to breed, age, sex and condition.

Red Deer *Cervus elaphus*

Large deer (body to 260cm, up to 150cm at the shoulder). Distinguishing characteristic is a pale rump patch, never white. Antlers in male develop with age; 2 forward-pointing tynes on a full head. Both sexes develop darker, thicker coats in autumn/winter. Male has a distinct mane and antlers in early summer to late autumn. **Behaviour** gregarious, large herds in open country, small groups in woodland. Old stags solitary in winter, hinds and stag in separate groups. Diurnal; browsing and grazing. Hill herds range between upland pastures and valley woods or cultivated land in winter. **Habitat** open deciduous woods or cultivated land in winter. **Distribution** widespread in A, CH, CS, D, DDR, DK and parts of F, PL and Scotland; patchy in upland areas of B, BG, E, GB, H, IRL, L, N, NL, P, R, S and YU.

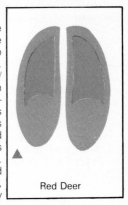

Red Deer

Track medium to large: 7.8 × 6cm. Cleaves fairly broad with well developed wall and distinct toe pads. Convex outer anterior cleaves with a straight or slightly concave medial surface. Cleaves generally parallel. In slipped tracks cleaves splay only slightly; rarely dew claws show; these are small and set far back.

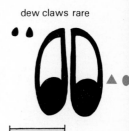

Trail in walking gait tracks are slightly straddled across the median line, imperfectly registered. Trotting trail shows tracks in a neat heel-to-toe arrangement on or close to median line. Galloping trail shows tracks in groups of 4, cleaves splayed, dew claws rarely present; 2–3m between each group.

dew claws rare

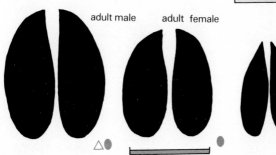

adult male   adult female   young

Wild Boar *Sus scrofa*

Large (body to 180cm, up to 100cm at shoulder) and similar to some domestic breeds, but with dense, coarse, dark coloured coat, very elongated snout and long tusks in the male. Young are striped. **Behaviour** generally solitary, males remaining alone except in the rut, females with young often from successive litters. Mainly nocturnal; active all year. Rests and breeds in shallow twig-lined lairs. **Habitat** deciduous woodlands, ranging into surrounding arable land and grassland; also marshy areas. **Distribution** A, AL, B, BG, CH, CS, D, DDR, DK, E, F, GR, H, I, L, NL, P, PL, R, SF, SU, TR and YU. Reintroduced into many of these countries for sporting purposes.

Track generally large in adults: 12cm to back of dew claws; 7cm across dew claws. Cleaves broad, rounded, with slightly concave medial surface at front and convex surface by sole. Soles and toe pads often show in track; dew claws invariably show in adults. A distinctive feature is that track is always broadest across dew claws.

Trail walking and trotting trails show tracks close to median line; registration almost complete although 2 sets of dew claws and slight anterior outward turn are seen; stride about 40cm. In young, stride shorter, tracks smaller, registration erratic. Galloping trail shows tracks in groups of 4 in line, unregistered; about 70cm between groups.

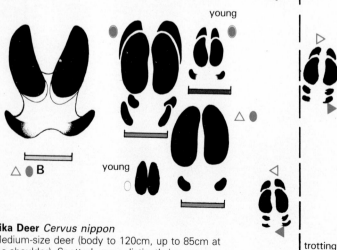

young

young

B

trotting

Sika Deer *Cervus nippon*

Medium-size deer (body to 120cm, up to 85cm at the shoulder). Spotted, more distinctly in summer;

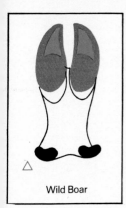

Wild Boar

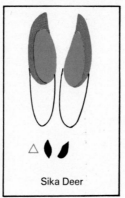

Sika Deer

coat darker in winter. Rump with white patch, a distinct black border; single forward tyne on antlers. **Behaviour** gregarious, living in small groups; mainly nocturnal, often lying up in day; sometimes diurnal in quiet areas; active all year. Follows regular routes within established territory. **Habitat** deciduous and coniferous woodlands, gorse scrub and adjacent cultivated land. **Distribution** introduced and escaped in B, CS, D, DDR, DK, F, GB, IRL and SU.

Track small – medium – large. Cleaves rounded, outer walls distinct and sometimes only part of track to show; slightly convex with pointed tips. Toe pads not distinct. Medial walls parallel or slightly concave. Dew claws close together, only showing in slipped track, when splaying may be present.

Trail walking trail shows tracks slightly straddled across median line; registration near perfect; stride about 100cm. Registration absent in trotting trail, tracks appearing heel-to-toe in pairs; stride about 125cm.

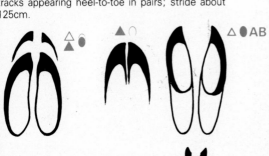

walking

Domestic Goat *Capra hircus*

Domestic Goat varies greatly in size and coloration. Both sexes have horns, variable in size but divergent and with a corkscrew pattern. **Behaviour** gregarious, normally in herds under the dominance of one male. Non-dominant males generally solitary. Mainly diurnal, grazing and browsing on trees and shrubs. **Habitat** farmland and open hill areas. **Distribution** widespread, both as domesticated, highly modified breeds and in wild form living an essentially unmodified existence.

Tracks small: 6 × 5cm, broader than in wild goats and Chamois. Track curved and rounded at ends. Cleaves tending to splay, often concave on the medial walls. In all goat tracks there is distinct divergence of the deeply impressed anterior section. Dew claws do not often show.

Trail varies with size and breed, but in walking and trotting trails the tracks lie side by side, not registered. Walking stride 60–65cm. Running trail shows tracks almost completely registered. Galloping trail shows tracks in groups of 4, pointing outwards, splayed.

Wild Goat *Capra aegagrus*

The Wild Goat has characteristics of both Ibex and Domestic Goat. Horns have a simple gentle curve with widely spaced transverse ridges. **Behaviour** gregarious, in small herds. Diurnal; browsing and grazing. **Habitat** open hillside. **Distribution** restricted to some Greek islands.

Track and trail as for Ibex and domestic Goat.

Alpine Ibex *Capra ibex*

Body to 150cm, shoulder to 80cm. Both sexes have horns, very large in the male. Horns curve backwards and have close-spaced ribs on front. **Behaviour** gregarious; females and young in small herds, male solitary for much of year. Diurnal; grazing and browsing. Extremely agile and able to negotiate steep rocky slopes. **Habitat** high mountains, always above the tree line. **Distribution** restricted to Alpine areas of A, CH, CS, D, F and H.

Track medium: 7.5 × 5cm. Cleaves slightly uneven, outer walls, heels and tips deeply impressed; touching at back, diverging at anterior. Medial wall concave towards the front. Dew claws do not show. Cleaves do not separate, however splayed, even in young. Posterior contact of cleaves is diagnostic of track.

Trail normal trails are walking, trotting or gallop-

walking

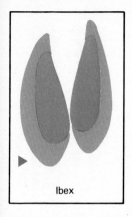

Ibex

ing. In trotting there is slight registration, which may show as over-registration; tracks parallel, close to median line; stride about 90cm. In young, registration is more complete in walking trail and posterior meeting of cleaves is marked.

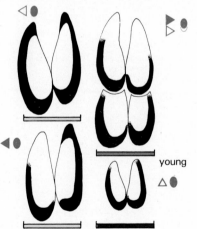

young

Spanish Ibex *Capra pyrenaica*

Similar to Alpine Ibex but horns spiral outwards and upwards as well as backwards; ribbing not prominent. Difficult to distinguish from some feral goat populations. **Behaviour and habitat** as for Alpine Ibex. **Distribution** isolated populations in mountainous areas of E and P.

Track and trail as for Alpine Ibex.

trotting

163

Mouflon *Ovis musimon*

Similar to Domestic Sheep, but wool concealed by normal hair. Male only with heavy curved horns; mature male has light patch on flank. Light rump and underside. **Behaviour** gregarious, females and young in separate flocks to males. Mainly nocturnal, resting in cover by day. Very fast and agile. Mainly grazing, feeding on grasses, sedges and heathers. Has defined territories and pathways. **Habitat** Mediterranean scrub close to the tree line; open woodlands and grasslands. **Distribution** A, B, CS, D, DDR, DK, E, F, H, I, Italian islands, NL and PL. Introduced into N, S and SF. Kept under semi-domestic conditions in some countries and may be confused with various primitive breeds of sheep.

Track small to medium: 6.5 × 5cm. Cleaves wide apart, tending to splay in parallel rather than radially, even at slow speeds. Medial walls vary between parallel and markedly concave. Tips of cleaves impress deeply; heel rounded; outer wall convex; front of cleaves pointed. Dew claws set a long way back, only showing at high speeds, in deep snow or when animal has jumped from a height.

Trail normally a walk or trot. Tracks barely register in trotting; splayed slightly across median line and pointing outwards; stride about 90cm. Registration almost perfect in walking trail. Tracks in groups of four at the gallop, often with more than 150cm between each group.

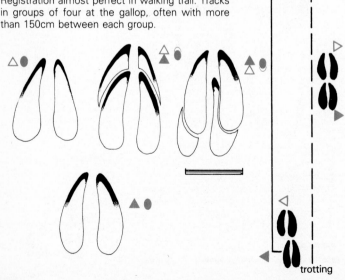

trotting

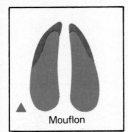

Mouflon

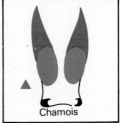

Chamois

Chamois *Rupicarpa rupicarpa*

Body to 130cm, shoulder height to 80cm. Both sexes have short hooked horns which are diagnostic. Coat dark in winter, light in summer; distinct dark bar and light areas on face. **Behaviour** gregarious, females and young in groups which may combine in winter; adult male solitary. Mainly diurnal, grazing and browsing. Vocal: adults whistle, young bleat. **Habitat** mountain pastures, coniferous and deciduous woodland, generally close to tree line. **Distribution** mountain areas of A, AL, BG, CH, CS, D, DDR, E, F, GR, H, I, PL, R, RU, SU, YU and Crete.

Track small to medium: 6.5 × 4.5cm without dew claws; up to 8cm long with them. Cleaves long, narrow; sole deeply impressed, as is the point. Toe pads lightly impressed. Walls of cleaves generally straight, characterized by medial walls which diverge above toe pad and towards the point. Distinct tapering shape even in young tracks. Cleaves tend to splay; small dew claws show in soft ground or when animal moves at speed.

Trail walking trail shows near perfect registration; tracks parallel, close to median line; stride 40–70cm. Trotting trail shows partial over-registration, cleaves slightly splayed; adult stride about 60cm. Galloping trail on open land shows tracks in groups of 4 with cleaves splayed and pointing slightly outwards; dew claws often show; stride about 150cm.

trotting

165

White-tailed Deer *Odocoileus virginianus*

Medium-sized deer. Diagnostic feature is long tail with white underside (held aloft in running) and white rump patch. Antlers curve forward, never with more than 5 tynes. Coat reddish in summer, more grey in winter. **Behaviour** generally in small groups, although females and young congregate in winter. Diurnal, browsing. Otherwise similar to Red and Fallow Deer. **Habitat** woodland. **Distribution** introduced and established in southwest SF and spreading; escapes lead to short-lived groups elsewhere.

Track medium. Toe pads, outer and inner walls prominent. Medial wall concave for almost half of length. Cleaves round at back and on outer walls; very close together. Dew claws, slipping and splaying often present on soft ground.

Trail walking trail shows tracks close to median line; almost complete registration; stride about 90cm. On soft ground the dew claws show, cleaves splay, stride decreases and registration is total. Galloping trail shows tracks in groups of 4; 180cm or more between groups.

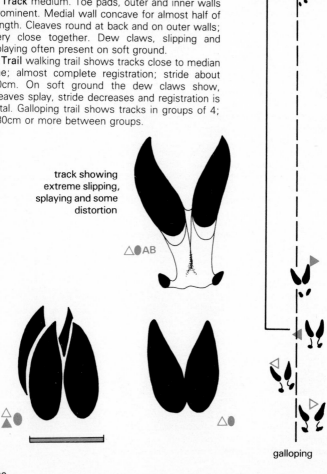

track showing extreme slipping, splaying and some distortion

galloping

Spotted Deer *Cervus axis*
Heavily spotted in all seasons. Male antlers simple with only three points, never flattened. Rump white, no black margin. **Behaviour** gregarious and diurnal; grazing and browsing, especially on tree fruits in autumn; highly vocal in rut. **Habitat** deciduous woodland, coniferous plantations. **Distribution** introduced and escapes: I and YU.

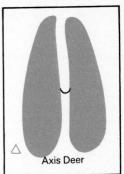

Axis Deer

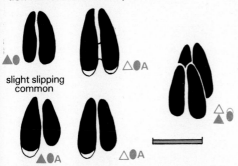

slight slipping common

Track small to medium. Cleaves tapering, rounded and frequently asymmetrical. Outer walls slightly convex, mesial walls generally parallel. Dew claws never show; splay limited. Membrane sometimes visible between cleaves.

Trail walking trail shows partially registered tracks; stride 60cm. Trotting trail shows heel-to-toe tracks in pairs; stride 90cm.

Domestic Sheep *Ovis aries*
The Sheep is very variable, but characteristic of domesticated breeds is the wool coat. **Behaviour** gregarious, active day and night. Always have distinct territories and pathways, even when enclosed. **Habitat** improved pasture, rough grazing, moorlands and open rocky hillside. **Distribution** widespread in many domesticated breeds and as more primitive, largely undomesticated types in remote upland areas.

Track small to medium: 6 × 4.5cm. Cleaves rounded at both ends; only a small gap; medial walls slightly concave. Dew claws do not show.

Trail tracks unregistered in trotting trail, pointing outwards and splaying in parallel rather than radially; slightly straddling median line; stride about 90cm. In walking trail registration is perfect; tracks lie close to median line; stride about 70cm. In the galloping trail tracks are in groups of 4, pointing outwards, splayed widely.

Roe Deer *Capreolus capreolus*

Smallest native deer (body to 120cm, shoulder up to 75cm). Male has small rough antlers with no more than 3 points. Coat reddish in summer, more grey in winter; fawns spotted. Plain white rump with virtually no tail is diagnostic. **Behaviour** solitary or in small family groups, especially in winter. Mainly nocturnal, but often active at dusk, on overcast days and constantly in areas where disturbance is limited. Browses on shrubs. Territories highly organized and marked. Both sexes vocal. **Habitat** deciduous and coniferous woodlands, especially where there are areas of open ground. **Distribution** widespread and common; absent only from IRL, IS, much of northern N, S, much of SU and coastal areas and islands in Mediterranean.

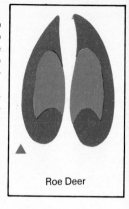

Roe Deer

Track small (5 × 4cm); slender and narrow towards front. Cleaves with convex outer walls, which are prominent, as are toe pads. Evenly imprinted tracks nearly heart-shaped. Medial walls diverge towards back, distinctly concave at front. Tips sharp, pointed. Splay and dew claws common on soft ground or at speed. Cleaves often appear uneven in deep or slipped tracks.

Trail walking trail shows near perfect registration; tracks close to median line; stride about 40cm. Trotting trail shows fore and hind tracks close together, unregistered; stride about 60cm. Galloping or bounding trails show tracks in groups of 4, cleaves splayed (especially fore) and dew claw showing; about 2m between groups.

distortion on one cleave due to deformity

Roe Deer tracks in soft ground showing some splaying, but no slipping.

Fallow Deer *Dama dama (Cervus dama)*

Medium-sized deer (body to 150cm, up to 110cm at the shoulder). Often spotted in the summer, generally unspotted and darker in winter. Flattened antler of mature male distinctive. Diagnostic features are white rump, edged with black; long tail with black mark on it. **Behaviour** gregarious and diurnal; extensive grazer and woodland browser; may form large herds, especially in park lands. Establishes territories which are marked (see page 235). **Habitat** prefers open deciduous woodland, but adapts to a range of conditions. **Distribution** A, B, BG, CH, CS, D, DDR, DK, E, F, GB, GR, H, I, IRL, L, NL, P, PL, R, S, SF and SU.

Track variable, generally medium (6.5 × 4cm). Medial walls near parallel or slightly concave; outer walls and toe pads very distinctly impressed. Sometimes raised areas are only part of track to show, especially tips which may be of unequal length. Tracks often distinguished by the straight, even concave, profile of outer wall. On steep banks and in soft ground 2 very small dew claws, close together and far behind main cleaves, may show. Splay limited, tending to be greater in fore tracks than in hind.

Trail walking trail shows near perfect registration, tracks close to median line; stride about 60 cm. Trotting trail shows heel-to-toe tracks; galloping trail shows tracks in groups of 4 with about 110cm between groups.

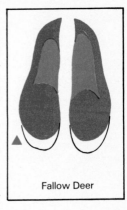

Fallow Deer

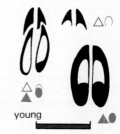

young

dew claws are unusual

Young Fallow Deer tracks. Imperfectly registered and broad in relation to length, indicating an immature animal.

169

Muntjac *Muntiacus reevesi*

Muntjac is a small deer. Colour dark, light-coloured rump area only visible when the tail is raised. Male antler very small and on permanent pedicles. **Behaviour** solitary, mainly nocturnal but diurnal if undisturbed; active all year. Establishes clearly defined territories. Browses on shrubs and eats tree fruits. Produces loud, frequent and distinctive barks. **Habitat** deciduous woodland with thick undergrowth. **Distribution** restricted to south and east GB.

Track small. Track of Muntjac is fully described on pages 38–39.

Trail walking gait shows parallel tracks close to median line; registration almost complete; stride 25–30cm. In trotting, tracks not registered, beginning to splay. Galloping tracks splayed; in groups of 4; dew claws show distinctly; stride often over 1m.

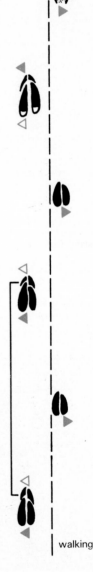

walking

Muntjac and Fallow Deer tracks on the same path. The Muntjac tracks are small, deeply impressed at the tips and asymmetrical.

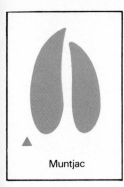

Muntjac

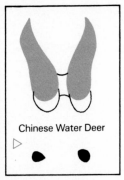

Chinese Water Deer

Chinese Water Deer *Hydropotes inermis*

Small, without antlers, but male has prominent tusks. Coat reddish-brown, rump patch not obvious, ears large. **Behaviour** mainly solitary and nocturnal. Grazes on grass and crop roots. Has well marked territories with regular pathways. Bucks whistle and bark at certain times of year, otherwise silent. **Habitat** open woodland, marshy areas and grassland. **Distribution** restricted to south and east GB.

Track minute; long, pointed and narrow. Cleaves nearly equal; medial walls flat or slightly convex, a diagnostic feature of this species; gap between cleaves is wide. Cleaves may show wide splay and small dew claws.

Trail in walking the tracks point straight ahead; slightly straddling the median line; registration nearly perfect; stride 30–40cm. Stride increases and registration disappears in trotting trail. Tracks in groups of 4, splayed and showing dew claws in galloping trail; often more than 1m between groups.

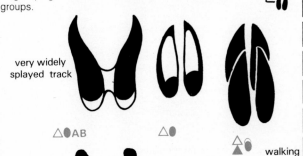

very widely splayed track

walking

171

Systematic list of the mammals of Europe

INSECTIVORA

Erinaceus europaeus	Hedgehog
Erinaceus concolor	Eastern Hedgehog
Erinaceus algirus	Algerian Hedgehog
Talpa europaea	Mole
Talpa caeca	Blind Mole
Talpa romana	Roman Mole
Galemys pyrenaicus	Pyrenean Desman
Sorex araneus	Common Shrew
Sorex minutus	Pygmy Shrew
Sorex coronatus	Millet's Shrew
Sorex granarius	Spanish Shrew
Sorex samniticus	Apennine Shrew
Sorex caecutiens	Laxmann's Shrew
Sorex minutissimus	Least Shrew
Sorex sinalis(isodon)	Dusky Shrew
Sorex alpinus	Alpine Shrew
Neomys fodiens	Water Shrew
Neomys anomalus	Miller's Water Shrew
Suncus etruscus	Pygmy White-toothed Shrew
Crocidura russula	Greater White-toothed Shrew
Crocidura suaveolens	Lesser White-toothed Shrew
Crocidura leucodon	Bicoloured White-toothed Shrew

CHIROPTERA

Rhinolophus ferrumequinum	Greater Horseshoe Bat
Rhinolophus hipposideros	Lesser Horseshoe Bat
Rhinolophus euryale	Mediterranean Horseshoe Bat
Rhinolophus blasii	Blasius's Horseshoe Bat
Rhinolophus mehelyi	Mehely's Horseshoe Bat
Myotis daubentoni	Daubenton's Bat
Myotis nathalinae	Nathalina Bat
Myotis capaccinii	Long-fingered Bat
Myotis dasycneme	Pond Bat
Myotis brandti	Brandt's Bat
Myotis mystacinus	Whiskered Bat
Myotis emarginatus	Geoffroy's Bat
Myotis nattereri	Natterer's Bat
Myotis bechsteini	Bechstein's Bat
Myotis myotis	Mouse-eared Bat
Myotis blythi	Lesser Mouse-eared Bat
Nyctalus noctula	Noctule
Nyctalus leisleri	Leisler's Bat
Nyctalus lasiopterus	Greater Noctule
Eptisicus serotinus	Serotine
Eptisicus nilssoni	Northern Bat
Vespertilio murinus	Parti-coloured Bat
Pipistrellus pipistrellus	Pipistrelle
Pipistrellus nathusii	Nathusius's Pipistrelle

Pipistrellus kuhli	Kuhl's Pipistrelle
Pipistrellus savii	Savi's Pipistrelle
Plecotus auritus	Common Long-eared Bat
Plecotus austriacus	Grey Long-eared Bat
Barbastella barbastellus	Barbastelle
Miniopterus schreibersi	Schreiber's Bat
Tadarida teniotis	European Free-tailed Bat
Lasiurus cinereus	Hoary Bat

MARSUPALIA
Macropus rufogriseus	Red-necked Wallaby

CARNIVORA
Thalarctos maritimus	Polar Bear
Ursus arctos	Brown Bear
Canis lupus	Wolf
Canis aureus	Jackal
Canis familiaris	Domestic Dog
Vulpes vulpes	Fox
Alopex lagopus	Arctic Fox
Nyctereutes procyonoides	Raccoon Dog
Mustela erminea	Stoat
Mustela nivalis	Weasel
Mustela lutreola	European Mink
Mustela vison	American Mink
Mustela putorius	Polecat
Mustela eversmanni	Steppe Polecat
Mustela furo	Domestic Ferret
Vormela peregusna	Marbled Polecat
Martes martes	Pine Marten
Martes foina	Beech Marten
Gulo gulo	Wolverine, Glutton
Lutra lutra	Otter
Meles meles	Badger
Procyon lotor	Raccoon
Genetta genetta	Genet
Herpestes ichneumon	Egyptian Mongoose
Herpestes edwardsi	Indian Grey Mongoose
Felis lynx	Lynx
Felis sylvestris	Wild Cat
Felis cattus	Domestic Cat

LAGOMORPHA
Oryctolagus cuniculus	Rabbit
Lepus capensis	Brown Hare
Lepus timidus	Mountain Hare

RODENTIA
Pteromys volans	Flying Squirrel
Sciurus carolinensis	Grey Squirrel
Sciurus vulgaris	Red Squirrel

Spermophilus (Citellus) citellus	European Souslik
Spermophilus (Citellus) suslicus	Spotted Souslik
Marmota marmota	Alpine Marmot
Tamias sibiricus	Siberian Chipmunk
Castor fiber	European Beaver
Castor canadensis	Canadian Beaver
Hystrix cristata	Porcupine
Hystrix hodgsoni	Himalayan Porcupine
Myocastor coypus	Coypu
Sicista betulina	Northern Birch Mouse
Sicista subtilis	Southern Birch Mouse
Eliomys quercinus	Garden Dormouse
Dryomys nitedula	Forest Dormouse
Glis glis	Edible Dormouse
Muscardinus avellanarius	Hazel Dormouse
Myomimus roachi (personatus)	Mouse-tailed Dormouse
Spalax microphthalmus	Greater Mole-rat
Spalax leucodon	Lesser Mole-rat
Micromys minutus	Harvest Mouse
Apodemus sylvaticus	Wood Mouse
Apodemus flavicollis	Yellow-necked Mouse
Apodemus microps	Pygmy Field Mouse
Apodemus agrarius	Striped Field Mouse
Apodemus mystacinus	Rock Mouse
Rattus rattus	Black Rat
Rattus norvegicus	Brown Rat
Mus musculus	House Mouse
Mus spretus	Algerian Mouse
Mus hortulanus	Steppe Mouse
Acomys minous (cahirinus)	Cretan Spiny Mouse
Meriones unguiculatus	Mongolian Gerbil
Cricetus cricetus	Common Hamster
Mesocricetus auratus	Golden Hamster
Mesocricetus newtoni	Rumanian Hamster
Cricetulus migratorius	Grey Hamster
Lemmus lemmus	Norway Lemming
Myopus schisticolor	Wood Lemming
Clethrionomys glareolus	Bank Vole
Clethrionomys rutilus	Northern Red-backed Vole
Clethrionomys rufocanus	Grey-sided Vole
Dinaromys bogdanovi	Balkan Snow Vole
Microtus agrestis	Field Vole
Microtus arvalis	Common Vole
Microtus epiroticus	Sibling Vole
Microtus oeconomus	Root Vole
Microtus nivalis	Snow Vole
Microtus guentheri	Gunther's Vole
Microtus cabrerae	Cabrera's Vole
Pitymys subterraneus	Common Pine Vole
Pitymys multiplex	Alpine Pine Vole
Pitymys bavaricus	Bavarian Pine Vole

Pitymys tatricus	Tatra Pine Vole
Pitymys liechtensteini	Liechtenstein's Pine Vole
Pitymys duodecimcostatus	Mediterranean Pine Vole
Pitymys lusitanicus	Lusitanian Pine Vole
Pitymys thomasi	Thomas's Pine Vole
Pitymys savii	Savi's Pine Vole
Arvicola terrestris	Water Vole
Arvicola sapidus	Southern Water Vole
Ondatra zibethica	Muskrat

PRIMATES
Macaca sylvanus	Barbary Ape

PERISSODACTYLA
Equus caballus	Horse
Equus asinus	Donkey

ARTIODACTYLA
Sus scrofa	Wild Boar/Domestic Pig
Cervus elaphus	Red Deer
Cervus nippon	Sika Deer
Cervus (Dama) dama	Fallow Deer
Cervus axis	Spotted Deer
Alces alces	Elk
Rangifer rangifer(tarandus)	Reindeer
Odocoileus virginianus	White-tailed Deer
Capreolus capreolus	Roe Deer
Muntiacus reevesi	Muntjac
Hydropotes inermis	Chinese Water Deer
Bison bonasus	Bison
Bos taurus	Domestic Cattle
Bubalus bubalus	Water Buffalo
Ovibos moschatus	Musk Ox
Ovis musimon	Mouflon
Ovis aries	Sheep
Capra ibex	Alpine Ibex
Capra pyrenaicus	Spanish Ibex
Capra aegagrus	Wild Goat
Capra hircus	Domestic Goat
Rupicarpa rupicarpa	Chamois

PINNIPEDIA
Phoca vitulina	Common Seal
Phoca hispida	Ringed Seal
Halichoerus grypus	Grey Seal
Monachus monachus	Monk Seal
Pagophilus groenlandicus	Harp Seal
Erignathus barbatus	Bearded Seal
Cystophora cristata	Hooded Seal
Odobenus rosmarus	Walrus

Bird tracks

Birds are more easily seen in the field than mammals. Because of this, field naturalists have tended to ignore bird tracks and signs and have concentrated on sightings. In addition, bird tracks are commonly found only in soft substrates, such as very wet mud, silt or snow. Many birds spend little (if any) time on the ground. They are often light and move only on their toes so that track impressions are very shallow. These factors mean that the location and interpretation of tracks, other than in waterside situations where waders and water fowl are well represented, is difficult. Despite these problems careful observation has shown that there is greater variation in morphology than many trackers accept, and tracks can be interpreted on a morphologically systematic basis. In a book of this length it is possible to cover only a limited amount of material, but this shows how much variety there is.

FOOT AND TRACK MORPHOLOGY

The typical bird foot has four toes, numbered I to IV. These radiate from the base of an enlarged fused metatarsal bone. Toe I, if present, points backwards and consists of three small bones. Toe II, nearest to the body, consists of three small bones. Toe III consists of four and is generally the longest toe. Toe IV consists of up to five small bones. Translated into track morphology this structure shows as an outline with a deepened central depression below the metatarsal (this depression is less well marked in perching and climbing birds). The small toe bones (phalanges) are covered by discrete pads which show in the tracks. Claws are normally present, and may be attached or discrete. This basic structure is modified according to the bird's way of life and the function of the feet.

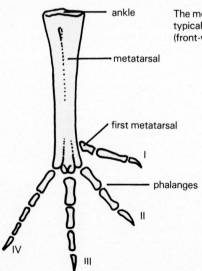

The morphology of a typical bird's right foot (front-view)

ankle
metatarsal
first metatarsal
I
phalanges
II
IV
III

Opposite: Heron tracks in soft estuarine mud. The vestigial web between toes III and IV may be seen in the upper left and lower right tracks.

Variations in bird track morphology
Number of toes in track The majority of tracks show four toes, but toe I may be reduced and/or lie high on the metatarsal so that only three toes ever show. Many four-toed tracks with a vestigial toe I show only three toes on harder ground.

Length of toes Toe I is the shortest toe on the track except in some perching and wading species, where it is very long. The rear lobe on toe I is called the hallux. Toe II is second shortest, III longest and IV second longest. This pattern is not invariable: in some game and wading birds toes II and IV may be of equal length; among zygodactyl tracks (see below) toes I and II may be markedly shorter than III and IV (woodpeckers and kingfishers), or of more equal length (owls).

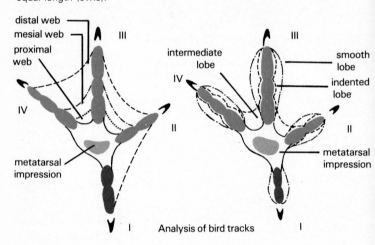

Analysis of bird tracks

Arrangement of toes In the majority of tracks three toes (II to IV) point forwards and one (I), even if only vestigial, points backwards. The toes radiate, with II and IV tending to lie more than 120° apart in the wading birds but no more than 90° apart in the perching birds. Sometimes toe I may lie to the side of the metatarsal impression rather than pointing straight back (e.g. grebes and pelicans). Some specialist tree-climbing and perching species are syndactyls – that is, toes II and III face forward and leave the central pad area in parallel. In these tracks toes I and IV always point backwards, although IV also points outwards to a variable degree. Birds with two toes pointing backwards and two forwards are known as zygodactyl (e.g. woodpeckers). In three-toed woodpeckers toe I is missing completely. Some owls are in an intermediate category in that toe IV may point sideways or backwards.

Symmetry In many tracks it is possible to draw a line down the centre of Toes I (if present) and III. Although the lengths of II and IV may be slightly different, in some tracks their angle with the line of symmetry is identical: this is particularly evident in perching species. In other tracks toe I is distinctly offset. The form of this asymmetry is useful in species identification of many waders and water fowl.

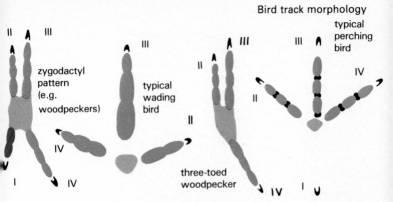

Bird track morphology

zygodactyl pattern (e.g. woodpeckers)

II   III

IV

I   IV

typical wading bird

III

II

II

three-toed woodpecker

IV   I

typical perching bird

III

II   IV

I

Webbing marks The tracks of most birds living on or near water show some degree of webbing between toes, although this has to be carefully looked for and is most apparent in deeply impressed tracks. Webbing may be simple or lobed. Simple webbing stretches between the toes and is classed as distal, mesial or proximal according to its distance from the central metatarsal area. Normally toes II to IV are joined by simple webbing, but sometimes I and II are also linked (e.g. in pelicans); such webbing is described as totipalmate. An important diagnostic feature of some wader tracks is the presence of a proximal web between toes III and IV only. Lobed webbing may consist of discrete, simple lobes on each toe, discrete indented lobes or simple or indented lobes connected by proximal webbing.

Claw marks Almost all bird tracks show claw marks, ranging from broad blunt attached marks in waders and ducks to sharp discrete points on bird of prey tracks.

Plumage marks Some game birds have stiff plumage around the lower metatarsal, particularly in winter, and the feathers show distinctly in soft substrates. The feather marks of other species may show in deep soft snow.

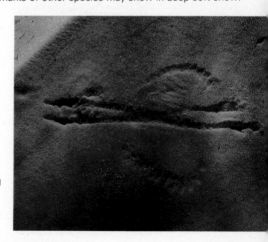

Impression of the wing tips, legs and body where a Blackbird has taken off in deep snow.

Bird tracks and trails

Broad webbed tracks of Black-headed Gull in sand dunes.

Heron tracks in the sand showing the asymmetrical structure of the toes.

Gallinule tracks in very soft silt. The tracks of these waders are enormous, being up to 20cm long and 18cm wide.

Track size and shape

There is considerable variation in the shape of bird tracks, particularly in length to width ratio. Many groups can be split on morphological features, but track size helps with species identification. In this book the same size categories are used as for mammal tracks, i.e. Enormous, Large, Medium, Small and Minute (see page 15). Larger, heavier ground-living species and those living close to the water tend to have very long toes, although the feet of the water birds are more delicately structured. Even the smallest perching birds have large feet relative to their body size because their balance is dependent upon only two feet; the supportive function of each foot, both flat on the ground and in perching, is obviously much greater than in four-footed animals. Birds of prey have large feet to enable them to fasten on to their prey.

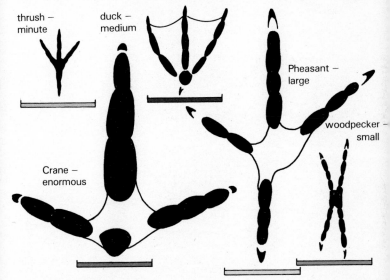

thrush — minute

duck — medium

Pheasant — large

woodpecker — small

Crane — enormous

BIRD TRAIL MORPHOLOGY

Bird trails are simpler than those of mammals since only two feet are involved, with occasional wingtip or tail feather marks.

Perching birds tend to leave trails in which the tracks lie parallel to or turn only slightly inwards towards the median line. Duck and goose tracks turn markedly inwards, while long-legged wader tracks lie parallel to the line or even point slightly outwards.

On the ground birds walk, run or hop. In the walking trail the tracks lie alternately on either side of the line. The individual tracks may lie in a straight line or may zig-zag; straddle is determined by the species. Unless the trail is in a soft substrate like snow, toe drag marks do not show. When the pace increases to a run the spacing between the tracks increases and toe drag marks are frequently present; straddle decreases. In the hopping trail the tracks are paired directly opposite each other and are normally close to the median line. Stride length is obviously determined by species, but the pattern

Bird tracks and trails

tends to be consistent. When the bird is forced to move quickly it will normally break into a run before taking off, although some will take off directly (e.g. crows). These patterns of behaviour are particularly apparent in snow, where a trail terminates in a series of paired wingtip marks which grow fainter as the bird becomes airborne.

Examples of variations in bird trail morphology.

**Walking trail
– Pheasant**

**Walking trail
– Pigeon**

**Hopping trail
– Crow**

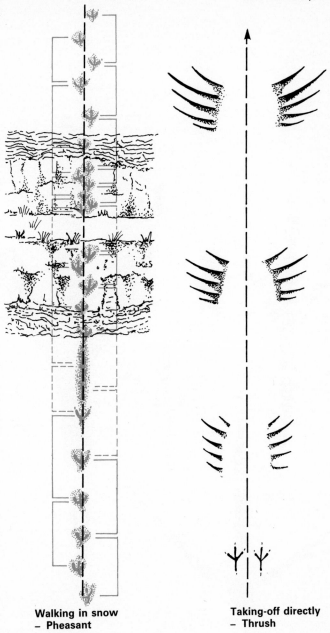

Bird trail morphology

Walking in snow – Pheasant

Taking-off directly – Thrush

BIRD TRACKS

Crow: 4-toed; phalangial and interphalangial pads present; toe I long; claw marks present; symmetrical

Pipit: 4-toed; pads not apparent; toe I long; claws long, I forming a spur

Pheasant: 4-toed; pads not apparent; large metatarsal area; toe I small; asymmetrical

Raven: 4-toed, large track; phalangial and interphalangial pads present; claws rounded and very long; symmetrical

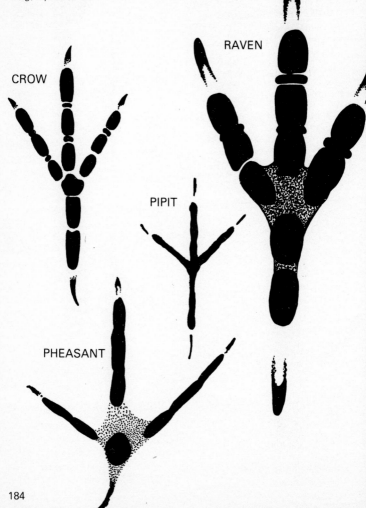

RAVEN

CROW

PIPIT

PHEASANT

Kestrel: 4-toed; phalangial pads well developed with small tubercles; toe I long; claws very sharp; symmetrical

Pigeon: 4-toed; metatarsal area indistinct; lobed; claws small and detached; slightly asymmetrical

Sparrow: 4-toed; small track; pads not apparent; toe I long; claws short; symmetrical

Magpie: 4-toed; phalangial pads long; hind toe slightly asymmetrical

Oystercatcher: 3-toed; medium metatarsal area; wide angle between very long toes; claws very small; symmetrical

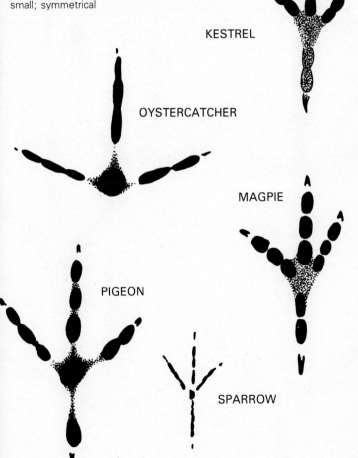

KESTREL

OYSTERCATCHER

MAGPIE

PIGEON

SPARROW

185

Bird tracks

Gallinule: 4-toed; small metatarsal area; toes very long and all similar in length

Turkey (male): 4-toed; toe III very long, all toes heavy including I; asymmetrical

Turkey (female): similar to male but slightly smaller; toes more slender, especially I

Night Heron: 4-toed; pads not apparent; no enlarged metatarsal area; small proximal web present between III and IV; claws long and slender; asymmetrical

Common Heron: 4-toed; continuous imprint, claws not apparent in example shown; proximal web present between III and IV; asymmetrical

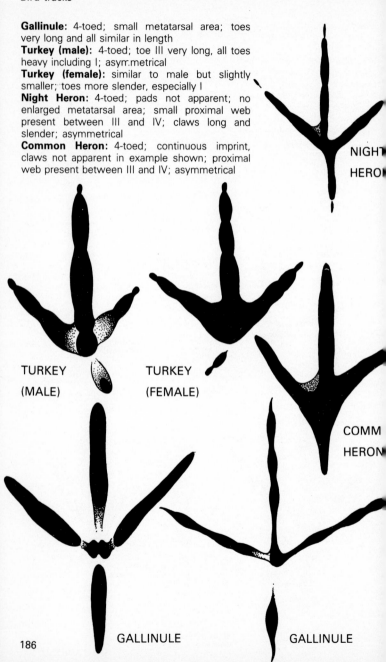

NIGHT HERON

TURKEY (MALE)

TURKEY (FEMALE)

COMM HERON

GALLINULE

GALLINULE

Goose: 4-toed; distal webbing present; toe imprints very heavy; toe I small and detached; asymmetrical

Black-headed Gull: 4-toed; distal webbing present; wide spacing between toes II–III and III–IV; toe I attached; asymmetrical

Duck: 4-toed; distal webbing present; toe imprints heavy; toe I slender and attached; asymmetrical

Crane: 3-toed; track large and widely spread; large metatarsal area; claws rounded and attached; nearly symmetrical

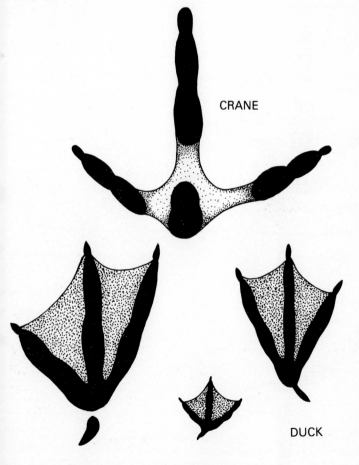

CRANE

DUCK

GOOSE   BLACK HEADED GULL

KEY TO BIRD TRACKS

There are too many species of bird for them all to be treated in the same detail as the mammals, and this key does not attempt to reach species level with every type of track. It has been developed around the morphological features already discussed individually: similarly structured tracks are grouped together and in some cases further differentiation, based on size, is given in the tables. In this way many common species or closely related genera can be identified.

Some species or groups are keyed out more than once since some birds' feet commonly make more than one distinct type of track – e.g. a four-toed foot may make a four-toed or three-toed track; and webbing, if present, may or may not show.

To use the key The key consists of 23 groups of multiple-choice statements. Start at group 1 (as numbered in the left-hand column) and choose between statement **a** and statement **b**. In some cases there may be up to four statements within a single group, but only one of them can apply to the track you have found. The relevant statement is followed by a further number, which identifies the group to which you should proceed next. Continue in this way until the key terminates in a group of birds (or a table) instead of another number.

Pheasant and Duck tracks, showing the widespread toes and small toe I of pheasant and the broad, distally webbed duck prints.

Bird track key

1 a Tracks with four toes 2
  b Tracks with three toes 17

2 a Three or four toes pointing forwards 3
  b Two toes pointing forwards 16

3 a Webbing present 4
  b Webbing absent 7

4 a Webbing totipalmate, distal: pelicans, cormorants, shags, gannets
  b Webbing not totipalmate 5

5 a Webbing present between toes II–III and III–IV 6
  b Proximal webbing between toes III–IV only: sandpipers, herons

6 a Webbing distal: swans, geese, ducks, gulls – see table I
  b Webbing mesial: terns

  c Webbing proximal: plovers, lapwings, pratincoles

7 a Fringes present on toes 8
  b Fringes absent 9

8 a Fringes fully lobed on each toe joint: coots

  b Fringes not lobed: grebes, Dabchick

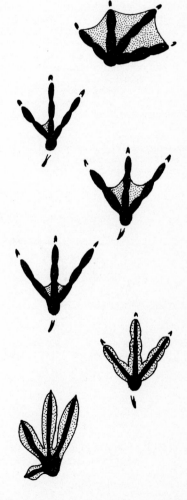

   c Fringe lobing intermediate:
      phalaropes

 9 a Track symmetrical about a line
      through toes I and III   10
   b Track not symmetrical as
      above   13

10 a Phalangial and interphalangial
      pads present; toe I approxi-
      mately equal in length to
      toes II, III and IV: crows,
      hawks

   b Phalangial pads only
      present   11

11 a Toe I approximately equal in
      length to toes II, III and
      IV   12
   b Toe I not equal in length to toes
      II, III and IV; claws short,
      attached: Pigeon

12 a Claws short, attached:
      sparrows

   b Claws long, discrete: eagles,
      shrikes, owls, pipits, larks,
      Blackbird, thrushes

13 a Phalangial and interphalangial
      pads present; toe I not
      equal in length to toes II, III
      and IV: turkeys, chickens

   b Phalangial pads only
      present   14

14 a Toe I approximately equal in
      length to toes II, III and IV:
      herons, bitterns, egrets,
      ibis, spoonbills, gallinules

b Toe I not equal in length to toes II, III and IV   15

15 a Toe I separate, showing as a distinct circular area on track: White Stork, cranes

b Toe I attached: game birds etc – see table II

16 a Toes I and IV approximately equal to toes II and III: cuckoos, kingfishers, owls, Osprey

b Toes I and IV not equal to toes II and III: four-toed woodpeckers

17 a Three toes pointing forwards   18
b Two toes pointing forwards; toes II and III parallel: three-toed woodpeckers, king-fishers

18 a Webbing present   19
b Webbing absent   20

19 a Webbing distal: gulls, skuas, petrels, fulmers, auks, shearwaters, Kittiwake, Golden Plover, swans, geese, ducks – see table I
b Webbing mesial, concave: terns, avocets, plovers, flamingoes

c Webbing proximal: Oystercatcher

Bird track key

    d Proximal webbing between toes III and IV only: Dotterel

20 a Fringes present on toes 21
      b Fringes absent 22

21 a Fringes fully lobed on each toe joint: coots

      b Fringes not lobed: grebes

      c Fringe lobing intermediate: phalaropes

22 a Toes approximately equal in length 23
      b Toes not equal in length: cranes

23 a Track symmetrical about a line through toe III: Oyster-catcher
      b Track not symmetrical as above: Red Grouse

Table I – tracks with distal webbing			
	Toes II and IV converge or become parallel towards front shown above		Toes II and IV diverge in a straight line
		Length of centre toe	
Four-toed tracks (three toes only show in some cases)	swans Mute Whooper Bewicks	16cm 14.5cm 11.5cm	gulls
	geese Greylag Brent	8.5cm 5.5cm	
	ducks Mallard	5cm	
Three-toed tracks			skuas petrels fulmers auks shearwaters Golden Plover

Table II – game birds			
Large metatarsal		Small metatarsal	
Capercaille Black Grouse Hazel Hen	Length of centre toe 10cm 7cm 5cm	(shown above) Pheasant Partridges Quail Willow Grouse Red Grouse Ptarmigan	Length of centre toe 7cm 4.5cm 2.5cm 2.5cm 4.5cm 3cm

Common Lizards, with the larger female at the top of the photograph. These are melanistic, but a wide range of colours occur. These lizards are most often seen basking in the sun.

Amphibians and reptiles

There are about 25 species of amphibian and about 20 species of reptile found in Europe. The amphibians comprise the salamanders, the toads, the frogs and the newts. Salamanders may reach 20cm in length, but amphibians are generally small in Europe.

The reptiles consist of the snakes, the tortoises and their closely related aquatic cousins the terrapins, and the lizards. The largest snake species, the Grass Snake, may reach 160cm; the tortoises may also be very large. There is considerable variety in the last group of reptiles, the lizards, ranging from the typical Sand Lizard through geckos to the legless Slow Worm.

The animals occur in many habitats. Viviparous lizards, slow worms and tree frogs are found in deciduous woodland areas. The venomous Adder is found on open land and woodland edges, although the majority of snakes and lizards are found in grassland and heath-type environments. The Grass Snake is semi-aquatic and will often hunt for frogs and tadpoles in ponds. Because of its size and habitat preferences the Grass Snake is the reptile most likely to leave a good track. Salamanders occur in damp situations, while the newts spend much of their time in water. The frogs and toads show varying degrees of dependence on water, ranging from the Tree Frog, which spends much time away from the water, to the Yellow-bellied Toad, which rarely leaves it. Frogs and toads have powerful webbed feet and leave distinctive hopping or walking tracks on land.

AMPHIBIAN TRACK MORPHOLOGY

The morphological variations illustrated below, although not distinct in every track, are worth inspecting carefully because details will impress in very soft ground and can be a useful guide to group if not species identification.

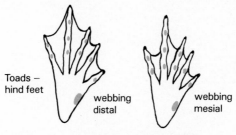

Toads – hind feet

webbing distal

webbing mesial

Examples of diagnostic features on amphibian feet
Fore feet
Midwife toads: proximal tubercles present, number varying according to species

Frogs: tubercles absent

Tree frogs: circular toe pads present, reflecting adaptation for an arboreal life

Hind feet
Spadefoots: the hind feet of these toads show simple structures with no tubercles on either the toes or the palm, with the exception of the very large 'spade' which is only present in some species

Toads: very variable in the arrangement of both palm and toe tubercles; a primary distinction may be made between paired and unpaired tubercles

Frogs: tubercles generally fewer; webbing may be distal or mesial

Midwife Toads – fore feet: proximal tubercles present

2 tubercles

3 tubercles

Spadefoots – hind feet

spades present

spades absent

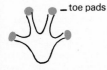

– toe pads

Frogs – fore foot

Tree frogs – fore feet: proximal tubercles absent

tubercles paired

Frogs – hind feet

tubercles single

Sand Lizard tracks in sand. The details of the tracks are obscured, but the body drag and feet impressions are clear.

TRACKS AND TRAILS OF AMPHIBIANS AND REPTILES

Tracks of amphibians and reptiles are not found often, but they do have distinctive features which enable them to be identified to type, if not to species. In previous works the tracks of amphibians and reptiles have been dismissed in a very general way but there are well marked differences as the following examples show.

Amphibians

Newts are extremely slight animals and trails are consequently rare. The individual tracks are very small and normally show only as toe prints, rarely as complete hand outlines. The hind tracks (0.5 × 0.6cm) have five toes, the fore tracks (0.4 × 0.5cm) have four toes. Often only three of four toes will show and there are no pad or claw marks.

The normal gait is a walk with a stride of about 3.5cm. The tracks are widely straddled, but point more or less straight forward; tracks never register. The trail is distinguished by very small tracks, wide straddle, lack of registration and marked oscillating tail and body drag, which is always present.

Toad and frog (the proportions are different but frog and toad tracks have much in common): the tracks are distinctive, although again rare with such light animals. The hind track is webbed and has five widely spaced toes. Sometimes only toe impressions are present, but there is at least one tubercle on the inner side of the track and this normally shows. The arrangement of tubercles varies between species. In a fully grown adult Common Toad the hind track may be 2.8 × 2.2cm. The fore feet show as a four-toed hand impression and are about 1.5 × 1.5cm in an adult. The trail shows the hind feet pointing straight forward with the fore feet at right angles to the median line; the straddle is about 1.5cm. In a slow walk the stride is about 4.5–5cm. In a faster walk or slow hop the stride increases to about 10cm, the tracks being grouped in fours. Registration never occurs. Long hops or jumps can cover 30 to 40cm.

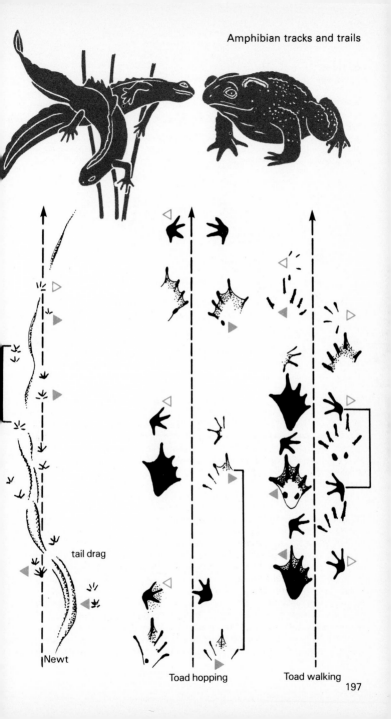

Amphibian tracks and trails

tail drag

Newt

Toad hopping

Toad walking

Reptiles

Tortoise: tracks and trails vary in size according to the age of the individual, but they remain morphologically similar. The example shown here is from a well grown 40-year-old male. The hind track is square-shaped with scales and tubercles on the rear and four distinct forward-pointing claws; most of the track normally shows. In this example the track is relatively large at 3 × 2.5cm. The fore track normally shows as a crescentic impression with four toes in a line; sometimes tubercles and scales are present. In this example the average size is 3 × 1cm.

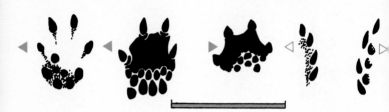

The trail is unmistakable. The straddle is very great (10cm for the hind feet in this case). At any pace the hind feet point straight forward; in the slow walking gait the fore feet lie inside almost on the median line; a stride of about 5cm is taken and toe drag shows between the fore and hind tracks. At a faster walk the stride increases to about 10cm and the fore tracks lie immediately inside the succeeding hind. At a fast walk the fore feet lie in the same line as the hind, although the stride only increases marginally (14cm in this example).

Lizard: tracks and trails are rare from these very light animals. There is variation with species and size, but the animals are mostly extremely small and the track and trail are minute. In the example shown opposite the tracks are 5-toed and measure 1.2 × 0.6cm. In some cases only toes show. Tracks generally lie parallel with the median line; tail drag is present but almost straight; tracks slightly straddled. The normal gait is a run; tracks do not register and in the example shown the stride is 6.5cm.

Salamander: tracks are extremely rare; when found they are similar to but slightly larger than those of newts.

Snake: the snakes have no limbs and move by a series of muscular contractions. Generally the body is propelled forward on a curving course which leaves a faint sinuous furrow. Although snake trails are uncommon, and vary in size according to species, they are unmistakable in the field.

Gecko: the tracks are unique and are distinguished by small circular discs on the end of each toe. Five toes on fore and hind tracks; toes always show; hand outline present on soft ground. No pad or palm detail apparent. Hind track 1.4 × 1.6cm; fore 1 × 1.1cm.

Trail is very distinctive: fore tracks point slightly outwards from median line; hind tracks are at right angles or even pointing slightly backwards. Tracks widely straddled; not registered but hind track close behind fore. Walking stride 7–7.5cm. Tail drag complex as tail is partially lifted with each stride. Acute angle of tracks to median line results from the foot arrangement of these arboreal species.

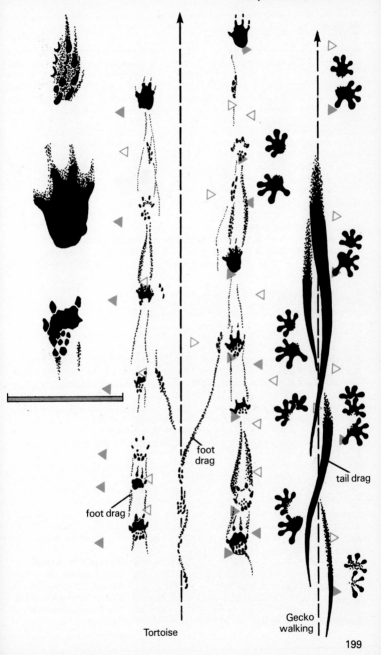

foot drag

foot drag

Tortoise

tail drag

Gecko walking

Pathways and runs

Most mammals and some ground-living birds follow regular routines in their daily activities. Set paths, tunnels and other permanent signs of movement become well established with time. These routes and temporary runs (such as in winter snow) occur in distinctive forms which give information both about the presence of species and their patterns of daily and seasonal activity.

It is not possible to differentiate between the runs of many closely related species of small mammal such as the voles. The pathways of larger mammals living in similar habitats may also be nearly identical. However, the intelligent use of distribution, habitat and habit data, coupled with careful observation of tracks and other signs, makes it possible for the tracker to learn a great deal about patterns of animal activity from paths and runs.

The overall dimensions of a pathway are determined by its largest user, but it should be remembered that several species may use the same route. This is particularly true in dense woodland, or at an easy crossing point over a stream (as illustrated opposite, where the tracks and signs show clearly that deer, badger and fox are all using the same path). It is important therefore not to dismiss paths and runs with too simple an explanation.

Entrance to Badger sett showing compressed, long-established paths radiating across the woodland floor.

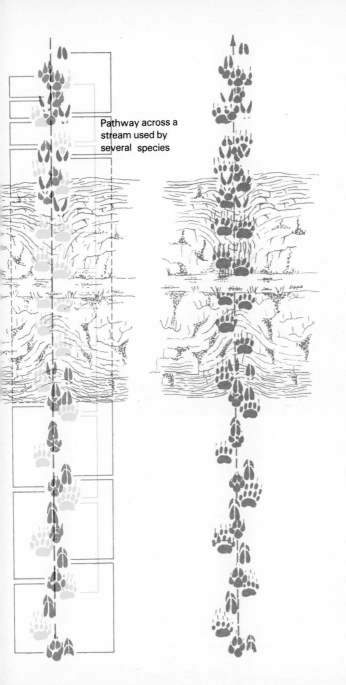

Pathway across a stream used by several species

Tunnels and runs below ground

Only the **moles** live a truly subterranean existence. Small piles of earth in a straight line mark the progress of a deep tunnel, while larger mounds may cover a nest. Shallow runs and furrows almost at the surface are created at certain times of the year; later these may collapse completely. They are thought to be used for either breeding or feeding purposes.

The **Water Vole** creates extensive surface runs which lead to tunnel entrances in the river bank. In winter, in the northern part of its range, the Water Vole sometimes seeks roots in cultivated land. It then creates a series of earth mounds which look very like molehills, but are not generally in a straight line.

The **Northern Root Vole** normally tunnels in vegetation, but when population densities are high it goes below ground and small earth mounds resembling miniature molehills are thrown up.

Both **Wood Mouse** and **Yellow-necked Mouse** make extensive underground systems in woodland floors.

Mole hills in permanent pasture. The large number of hills suggests much activity.

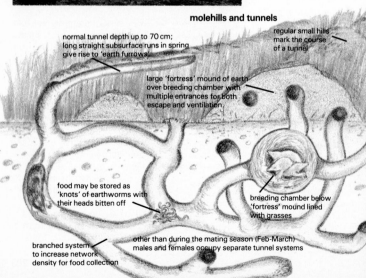

molehills and tunnels

normal tunnel depth up to 70 cm; long straight subsurface runs in spring give rise to 'earth furrows'

regular small hills mark the course of a tunnel

large 'fortress' mound of earth over breeding chamber with multiple entrances for both escape and ventilation

food may be stored as 'knots' of earthworms with their heads bitten off

breeding chamber below 'fortress' mound lined with grasses

branched system to increase network density for food collection

other than during the mating season (Feb-March) males and females occupy separate tunnel systems

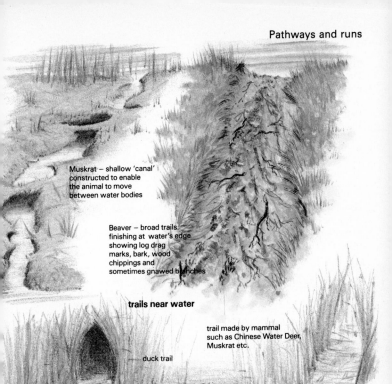

Muskrat – shallow 'canal' constructed to enable the animal to move between water bodies

Beaver – broad trails finishing at water's edge showing log drag marks, bark, wood chippings and sometimes gnawed branches

trails near water

trail made by mammal such as Chinese Water Deer, Muskrat etc.

duck trail

Riverside tunnels and runs

The **Coypu** makes large but shallow burrows, and these frequently collapse and undermine the river bank. It also tramples enormous areas of aquatic vegetation and there are regular bare runs up to 40cm wide radiating from 'climb outs' on river and canal banks.

The **Muskrat** also produces extensive tunnel systems and linking systems between water bodies. It creates wide paths in reed beds, but not on the same scale as the Coypu, with which it does not overlap geographically.

The **Beaver** has distinct waterside trails (see page 59), and these often show drag marks where logs have been pulled along; also there are wood chippings where felling and cutting has taken place.

The **Raccoon Dog** follows well marked waterside paths, which follow the edge rather than going to the water. By contrast the **Otter** has regular bankside paths which lead to 'swimways' in the water. On steep banks, slides may be created. There may be many other signs of Otter activity on the river bank too, but rolling places, where vegetation is flattened, are small compared with those made by Coypu and Muskrat.

Chinese Water Deer create pathways in reeds which are open from the ground upwards. **Duck** and other water bird paths in reeds take the form of tunnels, the upper parts of the vegetation remaining undisturbed.

Woodland paths

Paths in woodland are often long established and well worn into the ground. Paths used by deer have a variable vertical extent: **Muntjac** opens the vegetation up to about 60cm high and 15–20cm wide, whereas **Roe** opens it to about 100cm high and 30cm wide. The **Elk** opens it to about 250cm high and 100cm wide. If the path is only being used by smaller animals, such as **Badger** and **Fox**, then the actual width on the ground is about 25–30cm, but the height of disturbance is no more than 40cm in the case of badgers and 50cm in foxes.

Wild Boar creates very wide paths, marked by snaffles, scratching places and wallows.

Brown Bear paths are very wide and well worn, although obviously rare in Europe.

Some of the smaller woodland mammals, such as **squirrels**, leave paths radiating from trees which are regularly used as marking or climbing points.

Woodland paths used by deer and Badger

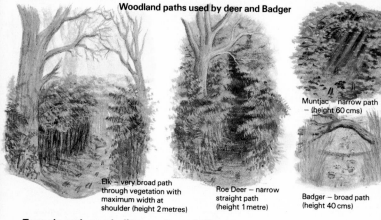

Muntjac – narrow path – (height 60 cms)

Elk – very broad path through vegetation with maximum width at shoulder (height 2 metres)

Roe Deer – narrow straight path (height 1 metre)

Badger – broad path (height 40 cms)

Tunnels and runs in litter and vegetation

All of the smaller voles make oval tunnels in vegetation, and on top of it when under snow. It is difficult to distinguish species, but examples show the range which can be found. The **Grey-sided Vole** makes runways in thickets, moss, lichens and grasses, while the **Bank Vole** makes extensive runs in dense cover and litter, and burrows into the ground. The **Common Vole** makes runways in grasslands only, mainly the long grass marginal to cultivated land. Such runs may reach 6m long.

Brown Rats create extensive tunnel systems in hayricks and have continuous pathways 5–10cm wide, keeping close to cover across farmland. The **shrews**, especially **Common Shrew**, create small, extensive, vertically flattened tunnels in the litter layers.

Runs across open land

Paths used exclusively by **deer** lead across open land from dense cover, such as woodland, and make for openings rather than cutting through hedges. They are very narrow and distinct.

Rabbit holes forming tunnels

Bank Vole hole in soil bank

large opening and well-trodden path created by Fox and Badger

Paths through hedges

Badger paths also follow distinct directions, but are broader and will pass through hedges. They normally lead from a sett to latrines, feeding places, sunning places or water.

Rabbit runs lead from hedges and banks and are distinct in the long vegetation, becoming less distinct as they lead out to grazing areas in the fields. They are marked by urine patches.

The **Mountain Hare** creates conspicuous trails up and down heather hillsides and mountains, the paths being maintained by the biting off of shoot tips. **Brown Hare** paths are fairly distinctive in cultivated land and are characterized by bound marks, where continuous impacting of the large hind feet gives an irregular effect to the path surface.

Fox paths, which also run through hedges, are smaller than badger paths and larger than hare, but can often be identified by snared red-brown hair on bushes and wire.

Reindeer paths are large, wide and open since they are used by large numbers of migrating animals.

On open dry acid ground, especially in bracken-dominated areas, bare paths 20–30cm wide and with undisturbed dead plant stems lying only 1cm above the surface are found. Close inspection reveals that these are **ant highways** with large numbers of Wood Ants carrying food to and from the nest.

Holes in hedges
Rabbit runs lead to small separate holes 15–20cm in diameter. **Fox** and **Badger** holes are higher and wider (up to 50cm high) and run straight through the hedge rather than disappearing into it as with rabbits. In fox-hunting areas holes created by packs of hounds may be confused with those of wild animals.

Runs in buildings
Both **Black Rats** and **House Mice** follow regular pathways which are marked by dark greasy smears. Where these cross girders or bars 'loop smears' are produced as the animals swing round the obstacle. The rats and mice follow regular but often largely unmarked routes in buildings, although their gnawing activity, faeces, urine and obvious damage to stored food clearly indicate their presence.

Beech Martens sometimes make their homes in thatched roofs, establishing regular runs which can cause extensive damage.

Red Squirrel on a forest floor displaying the distinctive ear tufts. The fore limbs are well shown.

Left: Tree stump used as a feeding place by a Red Squirrel. The cone has been stripped of its scales to reach the seeds inside.

Feeding activity

All animals leave signs of their feeding activity and a series of such signs may tell much about the way of life and behaviour of the species which has left them. There are many types of remains – the partial remains of meals, plant or animal; associated signs of activity to obtain the food, such as digging and gnawing; stores of surplus food, and, finally, the waste products. All animals produce droppings and many birds, especially the carnivores and scavengers, produce pellets. The various types of sign are described systematically here. Discussion is restricted to birds and mammals, except for comparative purposes.

Some species leave many signs, others very few. Many species have a distinctive method of tackling a particular type of food, such as a cone or a nut. Feeding signs and remains are dealt with in categories to avoid unnecessary complication, but obviously several different kinds may be found at the same location at the same time and a flexible approach to identification is essential in the field.

Feeding remains

PLANT REMAINS

Tree roots Many animals dig around tree roots for associated food sources. Some, such as the **Coypu** and **Water Vole**, may cause undermining and even complete uprooting by their burrowing activity. The Water Vole may eat away much of the root system of young trees and these are then blown over by wind. **Wild Boar** also causes considerable damage to roots when digging for grubs and truffles.

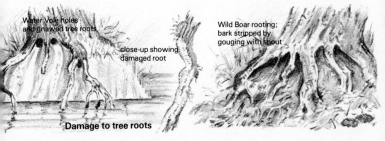

Water Vole holes and gnawed tree roots

close-up showing damaged root

Wild Boar rooting; bark stripped by gouging with snout

Damage to tree roots

Bark and tree trunks The lower cambium layer of bark in trees and bushes is an important part in the diet of a number of species, especially in winter. The bark on the trunk of the tree may be partly or totally stripped, even below snow. This can kill trees. Stripping and gnawing in terminal shoots of branches may severely deform a tree and stunt its growth.

Bank Vole, Red-backed Vole and Grey-sided Vole climb into the canopy of willow and birch bushes and young conifer trees. Bank Vole also strips elder bark in winter. With these species the outer bark layers are partially

Left: Rotten tree stump 'beaten up' by a Woodpecker to reach the invertebrates inside.

Opposite: Bank Vole gnawing on the terminal shoots of a tree. Note the partial removal of the bark and small teeth marks.

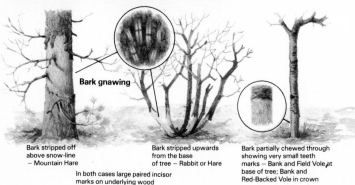

Bark gnawing

Bark stripped off above snow-line – Mountain Hare

Bark stripped upwards from the base of tree – Rabbit or Hare

In both cases large paired incisor marks on underlying wood

Bark partially chewed through showing very small teeth marks – Bank and Field Vole at base of tree; Bank and Red-Backed Vole in crown

stripped and the inner layers incompletely gnawed, leaving fine distinct teeth marks. In addition to winter activity, these voles feed on the new bark of growing shoots in the summer and may cause considerable damage in new plantations.

All voles are active at ground level; **Common Vole** and **Northern Root Vole** frequently gnaw through the bark of saplings and bushes beneath the snow. In the northern part of its range the **Field Vole** also strips bark in winter. These slightly larger voles have stronger teeth and so bark removal is more complete. **Water Vole** also strips the base of trees, especially willows, in winter.

Squirrels strip and loosen large areas of bark in the crown area of trees leaving big but indistinct teeth marks. The marks are vague because the bark is stripped off rather than gnawed as it is by lagomorphs. Frequently, long spiral twists of bark are removed by squirrels.

Damage to bark in the upper branches of trees in autumn and winter is usually caused by voles; in summer squirrels are more active.

Edible Dormouse may cause extensive damage by barking species of willow and plum, a sign which is often among the first indications of dormouse activity.

When **hares** and **rabbits** gnaw bark incompletely, the upper incisor marks

Deep, but small teeth
marks in root areas
of tree (small roots
may be bitten
through completely);
bark fully removed – Water Vole

Entire tree often felled
by gnawing; very large
incisor marks – Beaver

show clear longitudinal grooves from each tooth. In hard weather the lower part of the tree trunk will often be completely stripped and deeply gnawed: this is especially true of the **Mountain Hare** in the Arctic, where gnawing will start from the top of the snow line and extend more than a metre above this.

Beavers strip bark all year round, both for food (bark is important in their winter diet) and to reach the wood underneath. Aspens and birch felled and gnawed by beaver show large (up to 3cm) unmistakable incisor marks and have large chips of wood removed.

Larger herbivores gnaw bark, and the size of the bite marks and their height above the ground give some indication of the species involved. **Wild Boar** often bark trees at 60–80cm.

Deer bite into the bark, leaving deep distinct vertical marks. **Elk** strips bark up to more than 3 metres, while **Roe Deer** will not go much above 1 metre. **Red Deer** strip bark, especially conifer, up to 2 metres in winter and spring. **Mouflon** tends to bite on a slant, leaving oblique marks from the lower jaw incisors, while **horses** strip large areas from one side of any tree close enough to their fences by chewing with their incisors.

Badgers strip sycamore trees close to their setts to obtain sap.

Birds also strip bark. The **woodpeckers** will 'beat up' rotten trees, stripping bark and splintering wood to reach insects.

Horse Chestnut shoots killed as a result of earlier browsing and barking by Grey Squirrel.

Shoots of trees and bushes Many deer and voles feed on shoots at various times of the year. **Deer**, which have no upper incisors, tear off shoots at various heights according to species. They always leave a rough, uneven cut because of this tearing action. **Elk** concentrates on bark and shoots in winter, nipping twigs and buds up to 2.5m or more. Small branches are often completely torn off. The **White-tailed Deer** is a browsing species and takes shoots and leaves from trees and bushes, including conifers. **Red Deer** are fond of dwarf shrubs and shoots of trees and bushes in woodland, especially holly and yew, which they graze to 2.4m above ground level. **Roe Deer** take ash, hazel, oak and dwarf shrubs. **Muntjac** feed on brambles, ivy and tree saplings on the woodland floor. **Reindeer** also browse on tree and bush leaves in the summer, while the **Musk Ox** concentrates on the shoots of Arctic willow.

Brown Hares are fond of new shoots on bushes and tend to slice the ends cleanly and obliquely, a distinctive habit.

Squirrels feed on shoots (especially pine) and leaf buds in late winter and spring. The bud scales are turned back or stripped to expose the leaves.

Smaller mammals, such as the **Grey-sided Vole** and the **Bank Vole**, feed on the new top shoots of conifers, the former species also climbing dwarf birch for bark and twigs in winter. **Root Vole** will climb a short distance to browse leaves and shoot tips in the Arctic.

Browse Lines Browse lines occur in areas where there is a combination of relative food shortage and high population densities. In this situation all the available branches and foliage in a hedge or woodland habitat are stripped away up to as high as the browsing species concerned can reach. The result is a series of exposed trunks or stocks with a square clipped base to the foliage.

Rabbits produce a line normally not more than 50–60cm high and localized under hedgerows and in scrubland close to the warren.

Roe Deer normally create browse lines on the edges of both deciduous and coniferous woods to a height of 1.5m. In Finland high population densities

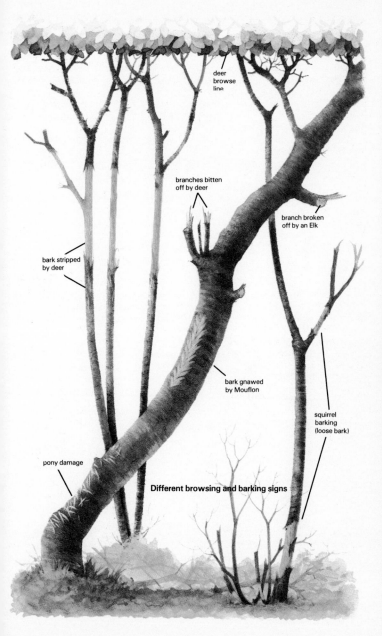

deer browse line

branches bitten off by deer

branch broken off by an Elk

bark stripped by deer

bark gnawed by Mouflon

pony damage

squirrel barking (loose bark)

Different browsing and barking signs

Feeding activity

of **White-tailed Deer** may cause whole forest areas to carry browse lines up to 2m high. Other browsing species can have the same effect, though less commonly. A combination of bark stripping and feeding to a browse line can kill large areas of trees and shrubs.

Cones Cones are a major food item for many birds and mammals and discarded parts are extremely useful for establishing species. The cones of pines and spruce are most frequently involved.

Spruce cones tackled by **Crossbills** have the scales split lengthways and are found beneath the parent tree. The same is true of pine cones, where the scales are split and pressed outwards.

Woodpeckers take cones to a favourite tree or rock crevice, where they can be jammed. These 'anvils' often have large accumulations of cones and nuts beneath them. Spruce cone scales are opened irregularly, while pine cones are pecked open lengthways. The twisting and tearing action always gives the cones a rough appearance.

Nutcrackers peck the scales off, often on top of a tree stump, but they do not leave such rough edges as woodpeckers.

Squirrels gnaw the scales off spruce cones, except at the apex where there are no seeds, but leave rough pieces. The scales are roughly gnawed from pine cones, which are reduced to an irregular central stem. Cones eaten by squirrels are often found in accumulations beneath trees or other feeding points, but also occur singly.

Mice, especially **Wood Mice**, strip spruce cones very cleanly. Scales on pine cones are also neatly nibbled off. Cones eaten by mice are sometimes found in sheltered places and sometimes on prominent feeding points.

Nuts and seeds Seeds and nuts such as hazelnuts, acorns and walnuts are

Bank Vole eating a nut. The characteristic position with the nut held in the forepaws away from the body is clear.

Pine cones

scales split
neatly – Crossbill

Cones and nuts

Hazel nuts; jammed
in bark and split
open – Nuthatch

a popular food source for many birds and mammals. The method of opening is again often distinctive.

Adult **squirrels** rasp the ends and then split the shells neatly in two; juveniles split them less evenly and leave large incisor scars by the break. The ground below bushes and favourite stumps or branches will often be littered with split shells and bracts.

Water Voles, **Bank Voles** and **Wood Mice** gnaw into shells. They all produce rough holes with corrugated edges. Shells opened by Woodmice show marks from the upper incisors on the outside of the hole, while those opened by voles and **Striped Field Mice** do not. Shells broken by woodmice are frequently found on tree stumps and stones on the woodland floor.

The **Hazel Dormouse** gnaws a hole, but the sides are neatly chiselled and smooth, a characteristic of this species. The nuts are normally eaten in the dense leafy canopy of bramble, wild rose and hazel bushes and have to be carefully searched for. **Edible Dormice** bite the nuts and leave large jagged holes; they do not split them.

Birds hammer the nuts open with their beaks. **Tits** punch small neat holes while holding the nuts between their feet.

Nuthatches and **woodpeckers** peck larger, more irregular holes; nuts opened in this way are sometimes found jammed in crevices in bark and below woodpeckers' 'workshops'.

Many seeds are nibbled or gnawed by small rodents, but on the basis of such remains alone it is not possible to establish species with certainty.

Birds peck open flower heads to reach seeds. **Goldfinches** peck thistle seed heads on one side and leave the remains littered below. Other finches peck open a range of flower heads, including dandelions.

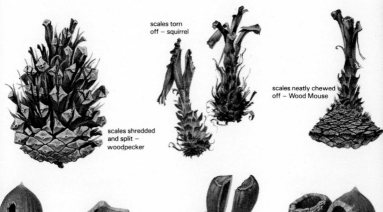

scales torn off – squirrel

scales neatly chewed off – Wood Mouse

scales shredded and split – woodpecker

neatly punched hole – Great Tit

neatly gnawed rim (with no incisor marks on surface) – vole

split open or broken open – squirrel

neat holes with faint lower incisor marks on surface – Wood Mouse

Feeding activity

Grazed vegetation Many herbivores graze grasses, herbaceous plants, mosses and lichens. Deer, voles and geese in particular are grazers. It is not possible to tell them all apart, but some species have distinct preferences and habits.

In northern Scandinavia **Reindeer** graze on mosses and lichens in winter. They create extensive, closely cropped areas which become very obvious in open Arctic woodland areas in the spring.

Rabbits and **Brown Hares** eat wild grasses and cereals; ground adjacent to rabbit holes is frequently closely cropped. (Where rabbits are still common they can be a major biotic factor: ling heath can be converted to grassland, and elsewhere vegetation removal can cause denudation and erosion, which may be a serious problem in sensitive areas such as sand dunes.)

The **Field Vole** and **Common Vole** make tunnels in matted vegetation, eating as they go.

Norway Lemmings, **Root Voles** and other voles create extensive tunnels and grazing areas beneath the snow in winter.

Field Voles feed on a variety of grasses and dicotolydons. The recent use of tunnels is signified by small mounds of short, nibbled grass stems or leaves. **Common Voles** leave similar signs, but favour heath rush (*Juncus squarrosus*) as a food source.

Water Voles graze riverbank vegetation closely for 10–15cm around their holes; another sign is tangled masses of the white inner pith of rushes, deposited along the bank in spring. Prominent feeding stones with chopped vegetation and Water Vole 'gardens' are also important signs.

The **Muskrat** grazes on the leaves and stems of aquatic plants in the summer, as does the **Coypu**. Both species create extensive tunnel and channel systems and trample large areas; banks may be seriously undermined.

The **Norway Lemming** carries food to favourite places leaving large accumulations of stems and shoots in the summer. The **Wood Lemming** leaves unique signs in that it grazes almost exclusively on forest floor mosses of the genera *Pleurozium* and *Hylocomium* and some liverworts: tunnels and large grazed areas in these mosses indicate this species alone.

Ducks and **Geese** are omnivorous, but graze on a wide range of vegetation. The **Brent Goose** relies heavily on sea-grasses (*Zostera*) in coastal regions, estuaries and tidal marshes in winter. Other species graze on foliage and root crops (e.g. **White-fronted Goose** on potatoes). Areas grazed by geese show large irregular patches of closely cropped vegetation.

Soft fruit and berries Fruits and berries are a major part of the late summer, autumn or even winter diet of many birds and mammals. Often the whole fruit is eaten, but smaller animals may leave distinctive marks on partially eaten fruit.

Squirrels leave broad double teeth marks on fruit which has been removed from the tree.

Fruit, especially apples, showing large incisor marks but still in situ on the tree is often the work of **Garden Dormice**.

All the voles and mice eat fruit and berries, but the teeth marks are not diagnostic. **Bank Voles** are fond of rosehips, eating the flesh but leaving the carpels (seeds), which may be found in piles in favourite feeding places above ground or in tunnels. **Wood Mice** eat the carpels from rosehips but leave the chewed flesh.

Plant remains

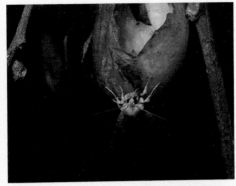

Plum opened by a bird and subsequently fed on by a moth and a wasp.

A store of hazelnuts left by a Wood Mouse underneath a tree.

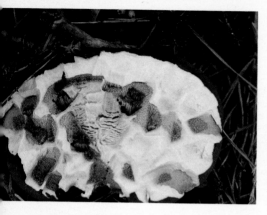

Left: Boletus fungus gnawed by a squirrel: paired incisor marks are 0.8cm across.

Opposite: Pigeon killed by a Sparrowhawk. The head has been torn off and the hawk has started to feed on the breast muscles.

Edible Dormice and even Beech Martens may leave remains of soft fruit under roofs when they are using these as nesting places.

Stored fruits eaten by House Mice and Rats are fouled with droppings and urine.

Seed-eating birds such as the Greenfinch peck out the flesh of fruits to reach the carpels. Rosehips eaten by seed-eaters are distinguished from those taken by Bank Vole by the smaller area of flesh pecked out.

Crossbills will peck away large areas of an apple to reach the carpels, while thrushes and blackbirds peck away and eat the whole fruit, leaving only the outer skin.

Slugs leave large gashes in the fruit and their activity is identified by the lack of teeth or peck marks, and often the presence of slime trails.

Various insects feed on fruit: wasps attack plums and other sweet fruit, leaving superficial but extensive cavities.

Fungi Fungi are another important element of the autumn diet of some animals.

Squirrels sometimes take the whole fruit of fungi into the branches of trees, where they may leave them partially eaten; they leave large incisor marks when they gnaw the caps.

Norway Lemmings, Bank Voles and mice leave small neat teeth marks. Rabbits also gnaw some fungi and leave very wide incisor marks.

Larger mammals such as Badger break or knock fungi over when they are foraging, although they rarely eat them.

Various birds peck at fungi, as their beak marks show. Slugs graze heavily on fungi, leaving slime trails and deep white holes with small pits from individual bites. There are many other invertebrates that feed on fungi, but their activities cannot easily be categorized.

ANIMAL REMAINS

Detailed identification of skeletal remains is discussed later (see pages 279–310); this section deals with the use of animal kills to identify the predator rather than the victim.

Carcases Animals killed by Fox or Wolf generally have bones crushed and broken. The Fox plucks fur or feathers from a kill and there is a strong musty

smell associated with the remains outside the earth. Hedgehog or rat skins which have been turned partially inside-out may be attributed to Fox; and frequently foxes partly bury or hide a carcase.

Larger animals (e.g. lambs or hares) killed by foxes often have teeth marks over the shoulder and crushed vertebrae; the prey is sometimes decapitated and the head buried.

The **Lynx** feeds on deer, hare and squirrels, and these are often decapitated. Separate carcases and heads, always unburied, are normally remains of Lynx feeding.

Wild Cats leave larger mammal and bird carcases neatly defleshed and without broken bones. Smaller prey may be partially buried; larger prey may have the head torn off and the brain eaten.

Both **Stoat** and **Weasel** kill with a bite on the back of the neck, which may be apparent on the carcases. Remains of small mammals and birds outside little holes and crevices point to Weasel activity.

Carcases of small mammals such as rats and squirrels which have been turned completely inside out may be the work of **buzzards**. Pigeons taken by **hawks** (e.g. **Peregrine**) show talon marks on the back and are sometimes decapitated. If found in the early stages such kills often have only the breast muscles torn out.

Remains of a Rabbit which has been turned inside out by a Badger.

Bones Many rodents gnaw on bones to sharpen their teeth: **squirrels, rats, mice** and **voles** all leave distinctive marks. All members of the dog family, including the **Jackal** and **Raccoon Dog**, leave bone remains outside their dens, while the broken bones of smaller prey and a strong musty odour indicate an inhabited **Fox** earth.

Skeletons of birds taken by birds of prey or Corvid scavengers often show 'V' beak marks on the sternum.

Fish Otters leave fish remains at favourite feeding places by riverbanks. **Mink** also leave remains of fish, often associated with a strong musty smell.

Muskrat and **Bank Vole** also eat fish, although probably only as carrion; **squirrels** have also been recorded eating fish as carrion.

Eggs Birds peck holes in eggs, often taking the tops off with ragged edges. Smaller carnivores bite into the shell and the distance between the incisors may help to identify the species. The **Fox** neatly bites off the end of an egg and may store unopened eggs for future consumption.

Molluscs and crustaceans Various mammals feed on these groups, especially on freshwater mussels and snails. Two factors give clues to the predatory species involved: the location of the shells and the way in which they are broken.

Perhaps the best known example of an indicator location is the **thrush anvil**. This is a large stone, or even a concrete doorstep, where snail shells with varying sizes of hole knocked in them are littered about. The thrush holds the lip of the shell and knocks it against the stone to expel the occupant. By contrast, snail shells opened by **Bank Voles** are nibbled down the spiral, and such remains are associated with vole paths.

Wood Mice open snail shells by biting through the shell away from the spiral, and these remains are often found on tree stumps or in other prominent places.

The **Garden Dormouse** is fond of snails and generally opens them by gnawing down the spiral, leaving larger holes than the vole.

Ducks such as the **Eider** feed on freshwater mussels, and remains of completely crushed shells may be found in reed beds. **Otters** eat mussels as well as many other molluscs and crustaceans, and the broken remains are left in prominent waterside feeding places. The **Coypu** crunches mussels, breaking the shells more or less in two. **Water Voles** nibble along the edge

Opposite: Salmon killed and partially eaten by an Otter. The fleshy areas have been removed first.

Right: Underground wasp nest dug out by a Badger for food.

of the shells, leaving small teeth marks. The larger **Muskrat** also opens mussels by chewing through the edges of the shells, but it removes larger, more jagged segments. Since the remains of mussels are always found on river banks or in reed beds it is important to examine them carefully to identify the predator.

Insect-hunting signs Signs of mammals and birds searching for insect or other invertebrate prey are common. Bee nests, both on and below ground and in trees, are broken open by **bears** and **badgers** to reach the honey. Both break nests open completely, but the Badger does not scatter the honeycomb over such a wide area as the Bear, and is obviously more common. Badgers also scrape out wasp nests.

Northern Birch Mice break open rotten trees and bark to find insects.

The **Greater Horseshoe Bat** will land on cow dung to feed on the Dor Beetles living in it: the distinctive track and slight disturbance of the surface of the dung may be a useful aid to identification in areas where Greater Horseshoe Bat roosts are thought to be present.

Species of **woodpecker** and birds such as the **Wryneck** feed on insects in rotten trees. The woodpeckers in general will attack the trees to reach insects, while the **Green Woodpecker**, which finds much of its food on the ground, will peck open Wood Ant nests.

The activity of **starlings** in pecking over moss-covered roofs for insects is familiar to most householders. A less familiar, but biologically very important,

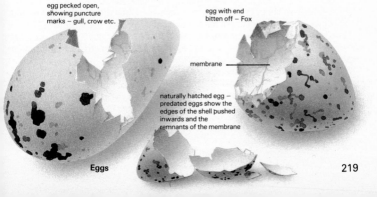

egg pecked open, showing puncture marks – gull, crow etc.

egg with end bitten off – Fox

membrane

naturally hatched egg – predated eggs show the edges of the shell pushed inwards and the remnants of the membrane

Eggs

219

process is the break-up of bare soil surfaces (such as peat or mineral over-burden) by flocks of starlings searching for Crane Fly larvae (Tipulids), which are often found in large numbers under such conditions.

Honey Buzzards feed largely on the ground and are particularly fond of bees and wasps, whose nests they break open in a similar way to badgers and bears. They do not take the honey, however, and this distinguishes their activity from that of the mammals.

Insect remains Recent research has shown that it is possible to identify **bats** to species from the size and type of bite mark on moth remains. This type of interpretation is highly specialized and not easy for the observer in the field. However, piles of moth wings and beetle elytra beneath porches or holes in trees, for example, indicate an occupied bat roost. Insect carapaces with small teeth marks are insectivore feeding remains, but species identification is not possible.

Feathers Individual feathers or a mass of feathers on the site of an obvious kill give an indication of the type of predator involved. **Birds of prey** pluck feathers out with their beaks, leaving a hole or broken area some way up the quill.

Small carnivorous mammals, such as **mustelids**, bite the feather off so that most of the quill is missing. Larger carnivores pull out mouthfuls of feathers.

The **Red Fox** often shears through primary wing feathers, leaving the quills broken and the plumes damaged. Individual feathers with quill and plume intact are normally moulted. In some cases piles of feathers and carcases show both plucked and bitten feathers, where an initial kill by a bird of prey has been subsequently scavenged by mammals.

COMBINED PLANT AND ANIMAL REMAINS

There are a number of feeding activities which involve both plant and animal foods.

Uprooting and digging Many mammals and birds dig to find food. The **Brown Bear** digs for roots, bulbs, insects and small mammals, the disturbed ground showing large claw marks at least 1cm apart. **Badgers** dig for invertebrates, especially earthworms, and also for the underground storage organs of woodland plants such as bluebells. The **dogs** will all scratch or dig after small vertebrate prey and leave shallow depressions with the soil kicked clear, but it is not possible to identify species from this activity alone.

The **hedgehogs** feed on a wide range of invertebrate food, small animals and carrion. Broken horse droppings and cow pats, superficially disturbed rubbish heaps and compost heaps are signs of their activity.

Moles obtain their food from the insects, myriapods, earthworms and molluscs which blunder into their semi-permanent tunnels.

Rabbits and, especially **Brown Hares** will scrape for roots and root crops (e.g. turnips) in winter, the species responsible being identified from the scattered droppings (see pages 225–226).

Voles feed in the root zone. Large areas of root crops may be killed in winter, the **Water Vole** causing particular damage to potatoes. The **Coypu** excavates basal meristems of waterside plants at certain times of year and causes extensive damage by digging and trampling. Root crops (e.g. turnips and sugar beet) gnawed by Coypu carry paired crescentic incisor marks up to 1.7cm wide. The **Muskrat** also digs for aquatic plant stems in winter.

The **Wild Boar** is a vegetarian omnivore which can damage enormous areas by trampling and uprooting with its snout and powerful teeth in search of larvae, truffles and roots. Bulbs, tubers, roots, acorns, beech mast, field crops (where large areas may be trampled and disturbed), grain, potatoes, sugar beet and vines are all part of its diet. **Domestic pigs** root in the same way, given the chance, and are sometimes used to clear rough, gorse-infested land.

Deer, rabbits and **hares** feed on the exposed sections of root crops. The size and shape of teeth marks indicate whether deer or lagomorphs are involved, unless the crops have been pulled out or grazed flat to the ground.

Birds dig for plants and invertebrate food. **Blackbirds**, for instance, create a series of small, shallow scrapes on the woodland floor.

Food stores Some mammals and birds store surplus food in an organized way. These examples help to demonstrate the range of species and food involved. **Arctic Fox** and **Red Fox** bury partially consumed carcases, often superficially; Red Foxes hide carcases and eggs as well as burying them. The **Brown Bear** is less inclined to cover partially eaten food than its American relatives. The **Wolverine** is a hoarder of food, especially in winter, and stores of up to 100 birds have been recorded. The **Wild Cat** partially buries its smaller prey in large quantities. **Hedgehogs** do not bury food, but they will dig up eggs buried by foxes. In **mole** tunnels food stores consisting of 'knots' of earthworms with the anterior segments mutilated are common.

Red Squirrels store small quantities of food (mainly nuts and fruit) in tree hollows and crevices in bark. The **Grey Squirrel** tends to bury food, either in single units or small groups, at 2 to 5cm depth. Sometimes seeds concealed in this way are not rediscovered and subsequently germinate. Both species occasionally store larger quantities of hazelnuts or acorns in tree hollows in so called 'acorn larders'.

Thrush's anvil in sand dunes with the remains of numerous snail shells broken open on the stone.

Feeding activity

Wood Mice store small nuts and seeds in some quantity in their tunnel systems, in old nests, under logs and in crevices in walls. Harvest Mice make stores next to winter nests, especially if these are in hayricks. The Bank Vole also stores nuts and chopped vegetation in its tunnel systems, as well as in old birds' nests and under flat stones. The Water Vole lines the floors of its tunnels with grass to provide food in winter.

Food storing among birds is less common, but the shrikes are a well known exception. The Red-backed Shrike impales insects, amphibians, reptiles, small birds and mammals on barbed wire or thorn bushes; the Great Grey Shrike stores small mammals, especially in winter in the northern part of its range, and may wedge these between branches rather than impaling them.

Feeding points

Specific feeding points have been discussed elsewhere according to the type of remains involved (e.g. thrushes' anvils will be found in the *molluscs and crustaceans* section). However, many mammals feed on a range of plant and animal materials, and some use particular places from which species may be identified. Among the more common species to use set feeding places are otters, which select a prominent boulder or overhanging branch. These are recognized by assorted remains of waterfowl bones, fish bones, crustaceans and molluscs. Pine Martens choose prominent points on open land, but these can often be more easily identified from droppings rather than unconsumed remains.

Water Voles have several small boulders or bare mud patches close to the water's edge, where chopped pieces of water plant and reed piled on them ready for eating may be found. Wood Mice use branches or tree stumps,

Root Vole killed by a Great Grey Shrike and then impaled on a branch for storage.

and these carry remains of shells and droppings. The **Edible Dormouse** often feeds on tree stumps or even window ledges. **Squirrels** sometimes select feeding branches, which consequently have the remains of nuts, hips and berries both on them and on the ground below.

Droppings

All animals produce solid or semi-solid faeces to void waste digestive products. In invertebrates these are small and have limited value for species identification purposes. In the amphibians, reptiles, birds and mammals, however, they can give a lot of information both about general food preferences and digestive processes; in herbivorous birds and carnivorous mammals they can be used to identify both the species which produced the faeces and the precise food species itself.

In the amphibians, reptiles and birds the faeces are voided from a clocoa (common opening) into which the alimentary canal, ureters and genital ducts open. White concentrated urine is associated with faecal matter from these groups. In mammals urine and faecal matter are excreted separately.

In the pages that follow, the mammals are discussed in considerable detail since their droppings are one of the most positive and easily locatable field signs the tracker is likely to encounter.

MAMMAL DROPPINGS

Mammals may be carnivorous, insectivorous, omnivorous or herbivorous. Species are morphologically adapted to feeding methods and have digestive processes which are modified according to primary feeding preferences. Droppings are often distinctive and, while there is variability within a species depending on contents and on age and condition of the animal, they frequently give a good indication of species, if not always positive identification.

Many mammals have regular routines which involve the use of latrines or regular defecating places. Some species deposit urine or scent from various glands at specific points in their territory, and these marking points may be associated with droppings. These signs make it possible to identify species and to learn something of their behaviour patterns.

The droppings of some animals weather in a particular way with age, and this can be a very useful indication of how recently an animal has been active in an area. The contents of droppings, particularly from carnivores, may give valuable information about prey species.

In this section droppings, latrines and associated signs of a range of European mammal species are described. Many are discussed as individual species, but some groups such as the bats, mice and voles are dealt with in a more general way since the signs are very similar and not diagnostic of species.

The carnivores

Despite the name, the droppings of most species in this order reflect a largely omnivorous diet. Faeces vary greatly in shape, content and colour but are generally well structured and contain the recognizable hard parts of prey, both animal and plant. Generally the droppings are dark when fresh, but tend to turn chalky with age. Sometimes droppings containing remains of small mammals and birds may be confused with bird pellets. However, the remains in faeces are twisted together and orientated parallel to the long axis, while remains in pellets lie at random, the fur often being compacted but not twisted.

Feeding activity

Domestic Dog droppings tend to be sausage-shaped, untwisted and generally without identifiable food remains. They vary in size and colour and are often deposited at random, although there may be preferred places associated with urinating points, especially with males. The musty odour associated with other members of the family is generally absent.

Wolf droppings are often found in large numbers outside their dens along with partially eaten food remains. They are twisted, contain hair, are generally grey in colour and are 5–20cm long.

Red Fox 'castings' normally contain large quantities of undigested hard parts of food. They are pointed, twisted and linked together by hairs in 'chains' 5–20cm long. Colour is variable, but generally dark, and they are moist when fresh with a strong musty odour. Often deposited on prominent places such as stones, molehills or branches, they frequently endure for weeks, becoming progressively bleached and less adhesive with age. If the indigestible content is low the castings are similar to Domestic Dog droppings and in this case they can only be distinguished by the strong musty odour (when fresh) and by positioning.

Arctic Fox droppings are, by contrast with those of other dogs, small (1–6cm), pointed and not twisted. They are generally dark when fresh, although they vary with contents, and are associated with a strong musty smell and urine patches when fresh. Large hard remains are not common. They are deposited at random, although accumulations may occur at entrances to earths.

Raccoon Dog: twisted and containing much hair as well as hard part fragments; 5–8cm long.

Polar Bear droppings are rarely found on land. When they are they form black amorphous masses, frequently with undigested pieces of meat in them reflecting the exclusively carnivorous diet of this species.

Brown Bears, by contrast, are omnivorous. The faeces are large, thick, blunt-ended and not tapered. They are 5–6cm in diameter, of variable length and generally brown in colour. Remains of both plant and animal food are obvious, although the digestive process is strong and macro-remains are not common.

Stoat 'scats' are dark, irregular and elongated. They are 4–8cm long and there are characteristic twists of fur at each end of the faeces, which are coiled and twisted within themselves. They have a strong musty smell when fresh, but weather to an odourless grey with time. Often piled in the den, but also deposited at random. They contain a wide variety of mammal, bird and reptile remains as bone fragments.

Weasel scats are generally similar in shape to those of stoat, but are relatively longer, more twisted and curled, 3–6cm long, dark with a strong musty smell when fresh. Often contain vole and mice fur as well as the weasel's own brown and white fur. Often found in large numbers in den.

American Mink droppings are twisted and coiled as with all mustelids, but can be identified by the fish bones they often contain. When fresh they are loosely constructed, dark coloured, extremely pungent and highly mucilaginous. They weather and disintegrate quickly. Frequently found on or near riverbanks, not always in latrines. Up to 8cm long.

Western Polecat: slightly coiled, often twisted and with tapering ends. Colour varies with diet but generally black, strongly musty when fresh. Up to 7cm long, about 0.5cm in diameter. Contain fur and bone fragments, but no fish remains, and often plant material. Frequently in regular latrines, which are sometimes in outbuildings.

Ferret droppings are generally similar to those of polecat, but are often less coiled.

Pine Marten scats are left in regular latrines, often in conspicuous places, e.g. on a boulder or log. They are 4–12cm long, dark, coiled, musty-smelling and bound by mucus when fresh. They often contain fur and feathers as well as bone fragments. The species is omnivorous and droppings may contain only plant seeds, but always have a proportion of vegetable remains, often leaves and grass.

Beech Marten: 8–10cm long, up to 1.2cm in diameter, cylindrical, twisted and pointed but not coiled. They are dark grey/black when fresh, contain fur, feathers and bones and are strong smelling. Often occur in large numbers on special latrine sites, such as tree stumps, old boxes and on the roofs of buildings.

Wolverine: faeces long, twisted and hairy; up to 15cm long. Does not use a regular latrine site like other mustelids.

Otter 'spraints' are black, mucilaginous and very musty when fresh. They are 3–10cm long and are deposited in groups of 1–4. Contain scales, fish bones and shells of molluscs and crustaceans. They are deposited in regular prominent places close to water, and weather quickly.

Badger droppings are generally elongated and neither twisted nor coiled. They have a musty smell when fresh, and range greatly in consistency with diet: they are loose and muddy if the diet is predominantly earthworms, but more firm if the diet is mixed. They often contain beetle elytra and other insect remains. There may be fur, feathers and bone fragments while at certain times of year grass husks may dominate and even sunflower seeds under some circumstances. Regular latrines are used; these are shallow pits close to the sett or on the perimeter of the home range. They are not covered after use.

Raccoon: these are sausage-shaped, variable in contents and colour as well as size. They are not strongly musty.

Lynx droppings are long, straight or only very slightly twisted and have pointed ends. They have a high fur and feather content and may contain very large bone fragments. May be up to 25cm long; colour varies according to content. The faeces are deposited in regular latrines, but are not buried. They are associated with scratching and urine deposits.

Wild Cat: compact, cylindrical and twisted with tapered pointed ends; 4–8cm long, about 1.5cm in diameter; contain few large bone fragments, but often insect remains. Deposited in regular latrines, although not buried, and at random, sometimes on prominent places such as rock ledges. Musty smelling when fresh.

Domestic Cat: similar to Wild Cat if living wild, but on a domestic diet faeces have little structure and no musty odour. Sausage-shaped with pointed ends. Sometimes partially or fully buried.

Seal droppings are infrequently found on dry land. Common Seal faeces are sometimes found on sand banks or stones: they resemble dog droppings, are irregularly shaped and round. They are 2–3cm in diameter, brown or rarely grey. Occasionally fish bones or shell fragments may be recognizable. Grey Seal droppings are also like those of dogs, but tend to be slightly larger (4–4.5cm in diameter) and are brown or putty-coloured. Often contain traces of shed hair, especially in spring.

The insectivores

Hedgehog droppings are long (1.5–5cm) and cylindrical (1cm in diameter). They are often hard, compressed and coloured dark with insect carapaces. Sometimes they contain the remains of small vertebrates, in which case they are grey or brown and may be confused with Arctic Fox droppings. They are sometimes slightly twisted, but always rounded at the ends (unlike Arctic Fox). Deposited at random and without strong odour.

Shrew droppings vary in size between species but this cannot be used diagnostically. They are very small (up to 0.8cm long and less than 0.2cm in diameter), elongated and contain the hard parts of insects which give them a dark colour, even when weathered. Deposited at random in tunnel systems and over territory. Detailed examination of contents distinguishes them from mouse droppings.

The bats

There is again great similarity between species, varied locations often being the only clue to the different species involved. Droppings consist almost entirely of insect remains; they are porous, crumble easily and are brown to black in colour. Often deposited in large heaps immediately below roosts in lofts, cellars or under perches. The outer, lower rim of tree holes inhabited by bats is frequently stained black by the accumulated droppings.

Marsupial

Red-necked Wallaby droppings consist of ovoid pellets which are 1.5–2cm long, have rounded ends and are composed of coarse fibrous material. They are deposited at random, loosely clumped, with only a few pellets in a string.

The lagomorphs

The droppings of the three species in this order are ovoid pellets composed of fibrous vegetation remains. All produce soft faeces in the day which are re-ingested.

Rabbit pellets are small (1cm in diameter) and circular, almost black to green when

Feeding activity

fresh; depending on composition. They weather to a light uniform brown after about three weeks. They are generally odourless, but territory-marking faeces are made pungent by glandular secretions. May be deposited in very large numbers on regular latrines such as molehills or in slight scrapes. Equally, they may be deposited at random, singly or in strings. Differentiated from lamb pellets by lack of faceting. Urine patches on grass or in snow are common.

Brown Hares produce circular pellets which are slightly flattened, paler and more fibrous than those of Rabbit, and slightly larger (1.25–1.5cm in diameter). Moist and adhesive when fresh, bleached and brittle with age. Deposited in numbers in shallow scrapes or at random over territory.

Mountain Hare droppings are small (1cm in diameter) and circular, fibrous, brown or grey-green in colour. Deposited in scrapes on open hillsides or at random.

The rodents

Red Squirrel faeces are small (0.6cm in diameter), dark and rounded, but not as spherical as those of rabbit. Found widely scattered on woodland floors containing recognizable plant remains and sometimes chitin. Strategic urinating points are widespread.

Grey Squirrel droppings are highly variable; may be cylindrical or round, up to 1cm long. Widely scattered on forest floors, again with strategic urine points in territory.

Flying Squirrel pellets are 1–1.5cm in diameter and are found at random on the forest floor.

Beaver droppings are small (2.5–3cm long, 2cm in diameter). They consist almost entirely of wood chips, coarse vegetation or bark remains which make them unmistakable. Defecation generally takes place in the water and so droppings are rarely found on land. Break up quickly in water and on land.

Coypu faeces are long, spindle-shaped and cylindrical. The sides are slightly curved and have longitudinal ridging. Size varies from about 0.7 × 0.2cm in the very young to 1.1 × 7cm in adults. Shape is always distinctive. Scattered on river banks or floating in water.

Voles, rats and **mice**

All vole and lemming droppings have rounded ends as opposed to the pointed ends of those from rats and mice.

Norway Lemming droppings occur in large numbers, frequently in the vegetation. They are cylindrical, light in colour, and 0.3–0.8cm in length.

Bank Vole faeces are round in section, 0.4cm in diameter and up to 0.8cm long. Brown to black when fresh, they may be in small or large groups in latrines off the main underground runs. They are smaller in diameter than Wood Mouse droppings, and they lack the green coloration of those of Field Vole.

Field Vole droppings are also found in concentrations in tunnels, running through vegetation. They are distinctly green in colour, because of the high grass content, and oval.

Water Voles make use of a series of regular latrine sites, often associated with piles of chopped grass on prominent rocks or on a raised river bank. When the species are more terrestrial latrines are found in tunnel systems. The droppings, which occur in large numbers, are perfectly cylindrical with rounded ends, 1–1.2cm long, of smooth composition and khaki to light green in colour.

Muskrat droppings may be confused with those of Water Vole, but tend to be slightly larger (up to 1.5cm), more elongated, and dark brown. They are found in small piles on logs, rocks and favourite resting places close to water.

Brown Rat faeces vary in colour with content, are about 1.7–2cm long, 0.6cm in diameter and taper to a point. They are deposited in groups in regular latrine spots, such as the rafter junctions in roofs.

Black Rat droppings are 1–1.2cm long and 0.2–0.3cm in diameter. They have rounded ends, are smaller than those of Brown Rat and are deposited singly and at random. In large samples the two rat species can be distinguished on diameter-to-length (D:L) ratios. If D:L is 0.31–0.37 – Black Rat; if D:L is 0.42–0.46 – Brown Rat.

Wood Mouse droppings are about 0.8cm long, rounded in section, short and thick. Initially pale, soft and moist, they darken, dry and harden quickly. Deposited on prominent places such as branches, which are also used as regular feeding points.

Harvest Mouse faeces are very small (about 0.2cm long), generally dark in colour and rarely found other than in the nest.

House Mouse: concentrations occur in favourite places. The faeces are rounded in section and smaller than those of Wood Mouse (about 0.6cm long and 0.2–2.5cm in diameter). Colour varies with diet. Associated with 'urinating pillars' which are accumulations of droppings, dirt, grease and urine in favourite places.

The artiodactyls

Wild Boar faeces are dark and resemble half-inflated rugby balls. They contain remains of plants, insects, bits of shell and small bones. They are scattered over the animal's territory.

Domestic Pig droppings vary with diet, but tend to be more cylindrical than those of Wild Boar.

Cattle 'pats' consist of large, semi-liquid irregular masses, which frequently show many signs of the activities of other groups of animals.

Musk Ox pellets are coarse and fibrous and contain remains of vegetation. They are 1–1.5cm in diameter and are scattered at random over the territory.

Domestic Sheep droppings are left in large, dark, faceted masses or 'crotties'. These may be 10–14cm in size, but break into individual pellets or small strings very easily. Lambs produce single pellets, similar to those of Rabbit except that they are faceted. These and the crotties are deposited at random over the range.

Mouflon pellets are faceted, dark and cylindrical. They are deposited in masses which break up easily. Even when these are cohesive they are much smaller than those of sheep (4.5 × 2.5cm).

Ibex and **Goat** droppings are similar. They are cylindrical, flattened at the ends, about 1cm long and non-adhesive. They are dropped in groups, but not in regular latrines.

Chamois pellets are black and bullet-shaped. They are deposited in small piles while the animal is on the move, and are not adhesive.

Red Deer 'currants' are black and sometimes adhesive, about 2cm long and 1.5cm in diameter. In the female they are rounded at one end; in the male they are acorn-shaped, pointed at one end and flattened at the other. Deposited in piles or strings at random. In summer miniature 'pats' 5–7.5cm in diameter are produced by males.

Sika Deer: smaller than Red Deer, but morphologically similar. Black and currant-like, often deposited in regular latrines.

Fallow Deer droppings are shiny, black, cylindrical pellets which in summer are deposited in partly fused piles; pointed at one end, indented at the other and measuring 1.1 × 1.5cm in the male; with rounded ends and measuring 0.8 × 1.5cm in the female. Deposited in lines or piles in summer but individually in winter.

Elk pellets are large, varying in length (2.5–5cm) and in number; hard in winter, but soft in summer resembling miniature cow pats due to variations in diet. Urine patches in the snow induce a bacterial response which gives yellow rings in vegetation in the spring.

Reindeer droppings are 1.5–2.5cm long. Winter droppings are dark greenish brown-black, bottle-shaped with one end flat or concave and the other pointed. Deposited in small groups, non-adhesive and not in regular latrines. In summer they are shapeless, semi-liquid and yellow-brown.

White-tailed Deer droppings are similar in shape to Red Deer; 1.5–2.5cm long.

Roe deer pellets are shiny, black and cylindrical. Short and oval in winter, they may also be light-coloured with a high fibre content. They are pointed at one end, indented at the other. Juicier food in summer gives larger, less well formed masses, often lumped together and deposited in regular latrines.

Muntjac 'currants' are black and shiny with rounded facets, striations and a single peak; small (1cm in diameter). Sometimes as an intact mass (crottie), more often widespread. Often deposited in shallow scrapes under trees or under dense scrub cover on a woodland floor. There may be very large accumulations of droppings in undisturbed areas, but these are spread around as individual pellets.

Chinese Water Deer droppings are small, cylindrical, non-adhesive and black; 0.5–1.5cm; dropped in small groups. Regular latrines may be used in reed beds.

The horses

Horse droppings are cylindrical and vary in size, but can be distinguished by their large size and the coarse remnants of unchanged stems of vegetation. They are yellow-green in colour, with imperfect cohesion.

Red Deer

♂ Fallow Deer

♀ Fallow Deer

Elk

Chinese Water Deer

Muntjac

Sheep

Mammal and bird droppings

Wild Boar

Fox

Rabbit

Hare

Bat

Field Mouse

Rat

Lemming

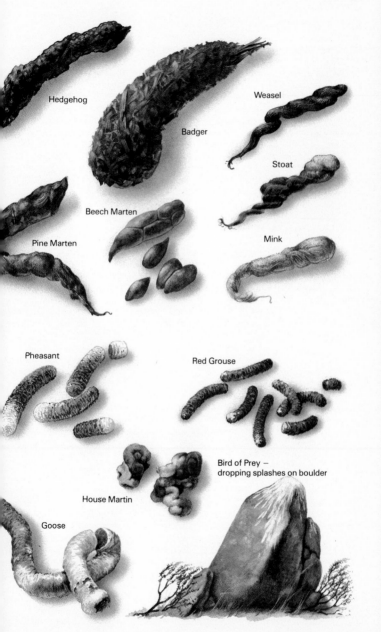

Mammal droppings

Hedgehog

Badger

Weasel

Stoat

Beech Marten

Pine Marten

Mink

Pheasant

Red Grouse

Bird of Prey —
dropping splashes on boulder

House Martin

Goose

229

BIRD DROPPINGS

In common with mammals, birds produce droppings which depend on both digestive adaptations and diet. The faeces may be completely liquid, semi-liquid or solid in consistency. There are a variety of shapes and structures, but droppings are generally (i) amorphous/liquid, (ii) round and twisted/semifirm or (iii) cylindrical and firm. Many droppings are accompanied by concentrated white urine, which is excreted from the clocoa (common opening) with faecal matter.

Unlike carnivorous mammals, which pass indigestible remains right through their alimentary tracts and excrete them in their droppings, carnivorous birds, including eagles, herons and gulls, produce (regurgitate) pellets containing hard parts (see pages 231–233) and excrete almost completely liquid faeces. The tail is lifted and faeces squirted as a near-horizontal jet. These liquid droppings below nests and roosting places stain vegetation and may kill it, thus identifying nesting sites. This is particularly conspicuous in heronries and under cormorant nests.

Insectivorous birds such as woodpeckers produce cylindrical hard droppings with the indigestible remains of chitin from insect bodies and a grey membranous covering.

Vegetarian birds produce more solid faeces. Game birds, feeding on coarse vegetation, produce fibrous cylindrical droppings which may be species specific: grouse, for instance, leave fibrous tubular brown faeces which are slightly curved, dry and firm, and are found singly or in groups on open moors. Under certain conditions they may turn semi-liquid and can be confused with the summer droppings of some species of deer. Capercaille droppings are large (1–2cm in diameter), larger in the male than in the female. In resting places, which are used for many hours, the faeces are initially solid but become more liquid as the contents of the upper intestines (caeca) are voided; this also applies to grouse. Capercaille faeces are yellow-green when fresh but turn brown-grey with age. Hazel Hen droppings contain the remains of alder, birch and hazel catkins and fruits. Black Grouse faeces are 1cm in diameter and often contain birch buds in spring. In winter they are pale yellow, turning brown-grey with age. Pheasant droppings have a well developed white cap of urine at one end, are about 2cm long and 0.4–0.5cm in diameter. They are brownish black-green and firm in winter, but semi-liquid in summer when lusher vegetation is available.

Swan, goose and duck droppings may be green when fresh and often contain undigested vegetable mater. Structurally they may be semi-liquid, especially when aquatic vegetation is being grazed. Often they are cylindrical and firm, and may, in the case of swans and geese, be very large. Goose faeces are 5–8cm long and 1–1.2cm in diameter and consist of highly compressed plant fragments. Swan droppings may be twice this size.

Perching seed-eating birds produce semi-cohesive droppings which are well formed and often contain undamaged plant seeds: this is important for the propagation of some plant species. Berries, such as elder, may colour the droppings of some species, such as thrushes, in autumn. The range of droppings around bird tables gives a lot of information about species and their feeding preferences.

REPTILE AND AMPHIBIAN DROPPINGS

As in other groups the form and content of reptile and amphibian droppings varies with diet. In carnivorous species such as Adder the droppings are dark and may be liquid or semi liquid with distinct urine cap. In vegetarian species the droppings consist of a brown or dark green, soft, moist, coiled, solid mass; associated with this is semi-liquid white urine. Small undigested plant remains are in evidence. In the insectivorous species chitinous remains are apparent.

INVERTEBRATE DROPPINGS

The number of invertebrates and the variation in their droppings is enormous. Often there is little to be gained from attempting to interpret them, even if they can be found; however, a number of the more commonly found examples is given to help illustrate the range.

Cockroach droppings are small and black, and being found in dark warm places in buildings may be confused with mouse droppings; however, the insect faeces have longitudinal ridges and truncated ends. Spider droppings are greyish-white and liquid when fresh; they may contain the hard remains of prey and are found under webs, where they may form grey stripes down walls or the woody parts of plants. Fly droppings consist of flat, highly adhesive black or dark coloured spots, normally grouped together and often seen on woodwork around windows.

Slugs and snails leave globular masses associated with slime trails. Earthworms pass soil and vegetable matter through their gut. Some species come to the surface, particularly when it is wet or at night, and leave worm-

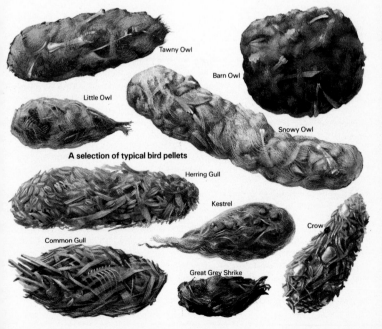

Tawny Owl

Barn Owl

Little Owl

Snowy Owl

A selection of typical bird pellets

Herring Gull

Kestrel

Crow

Common Gull

Great Grey Shrike

Feeding activity

Buzzard pellet containing fur and many small mammal bones.

casts. These are small, curled up piles of soil most often found on grass after a damp night. Castings are most apparent in autumn and early winter and may look like some bird droppings.

Whenever a stone or a log is turned over there are invariably masses of small globular droppings belonging to mites and woodlice, but it is not possible to attribute these to species in a field situation.

Bird pellets

Birds of prey, owls, gulls, crows and many smaller omnivorous birds regurgitate the indigestible remains of their food as pellets. The shape, contents, size and location of pellets can often be used to identify the bird which has produced them. They also give a great deal of information about the food available and the preferences of the bird. In the context of this guide, the main interest in pellets lies in the skeletal remains which many of them contain: these remains can be used as an indirect means of identifying the vertebrate fauna, particularly the mammals, of an area. Skeletal remains are more fully described later in the book, together with a full identification guide to the skulls and teeth of all mammal species treated in this book. Some species are too large to occur in pellets, or in the droppings of carnivores for that matter. However, single bones from larger domestic and wild mammals are frequently found and need to be identified.

The content of a pellet indicates the type of bird which has produced it. Generally a pellet will contain a variety of material, including fur, feathers, bones, chitin, indigestible plant matter and often small stones.

The small omnivorous perching birds, such as robin and chaffinch, produce little irregular pellets containing insect and plant remains.

Scavenging members of the crow family produce loose ill-formed pellets which include fur, feathers, bone fragments, mollusc shells, grasses and stones.

Gull pellets are irregular in shape, often large, and contain much fish, bird and shell matter.

232

Birds of prey have powerful digestive processes so that even those that eat their smaller prey whole, such as herons, produce tightly whorled masses of fur and feathers with small fragments of large bones and sometimes intact smaller bones.

Analyzing bird pellets – example: owls

There are thirteen species of owl in Europe, of which nine, including four vagrant species, occur in the British Isles. Owls swallow their prey whole, and as they have less abrasive primary digestive processes than the birds of prey, they produce pellets with many more complete bones, including whole skulls. Owl pellets vary greatly between species. Those of the Eagle Owl may be 15cm long and contain rabbit, lizard and bird (including other owl) skulls. The pellets of Snowy Owls are only a little smaller and contain a variety of species. By contrast, the pellets of the tiny Scops Owl are only 1cm long and consist almost entirely of insect remains. This variability helps to identify different owl species.

Accumulations of pellets may be found near the nests of many scavenging birds and birds of prey. Owls, however, tend to have a series of regular roosting sites, such as fence posts, farm buildings, ruins, telegraph poles and isolated trees. Pellets are deposited in large numbers under these roosts and can be used to make a study of the small mammal populations round about. It is important to be aware of the food preferences and hunting habits of owl species before attaching statistical significance to prey units in the pellets (see table). Pellets can be used to obtain information about both the predator and its prey, but perhaps their greatest value is as a non-destructive means of studying small mammal populations without elaborate live trapping programmes.

Food preferences of two owl species hunting the same moorland – grass upland				
	Short-eared Owl _Asio flammeus_		Long-eared Owl _Asio otus_	
Number of pellets analysed*	56		44	
Species of mammal in the pellets	Number of prey units	% of total	Number of prey units	% of total
Common Shrew _Sorex araneus_	32	38	8	8
Pygmy Shrew _Sorex minutus_	16	19	4	4
Wood Mouse _Apodemus sylvaticus_	0	0	12	12
Field Vole _Microtus agrestis_	36	43	80	76
Total	84	100	104	100

* Pellets accumulated under the roost of one individual of each species over a two-month period.

The Long-eared Owl appears to be hunting on the improved grassland, while the Short-eared Owl is obviously using the moor as well. Although producing fewer pellets, the Long-eared Owl produces significantly more prey units per pellet.

Roe Deer buck fraying the velvet from his antlers on a birch tree. The bark is scented and large gashes are torn in the trunk if the tree is used regularly.

Cast antler of Red Deer; note the three points.

Grooming and marking signs

All mammals and birds leave grooming signs, such as shed hair, feathers, and scratching and wallowing places. Reptiles and invertebrates shed their skins. It is impossible to illustrate all grooming signs here, but a selection of common examples can give an idea of the range encountered in Europe.

Marking points

Many mammals have marking points. These may be simply to identify territory, or they may have a dual grooming and territorial function.

In woodland situations both squirrels and deer have such marking points. Squirrels mark by gnawing and stripping sturdy trees near the roots or on the underside of the lowest branches. They also deposit urine, faeces and scent at such places, giving rise to a dark strong-smelling patch on the tree or the ground.

All male deer use saplings for fraying, mainly in late summer, at heights between 60 and 180cm according to species. The purpose of this is to remove the velvet from the buck's antlers. Red Deer fraying occurs between 60 and 120cm, whereas in Fallow it is rarely higher than 100cm. Sometimes these larger animals will choose a tree with a horizontal branch at about shoulder height, in order to rub both back and sides; in this case the underside of the branch shows signs of use as well as the trunk.

A post marked at a height of 40cm or less is likely to have been used by a badger.

Shed antlers

These are distinctive to the species from which they come. In many species the antlers tend to become progressively larger and more complicated with age, but the progression is not always a simple one and is related as much to nutrition and general health as to age. See also page 261.

Fallow Deer antler, showing wide palmate form.

Grooming and marking signs

Scenting mounds

A number of mammals build scenting mounds or spots by the edge of water. The Beaver creates piles of mud, often up to 90cm in diameter, which are scraped together and contain grass and sticks. These are then regularly scented.

The Muskrat creates scenting posts as territorial markers; these are made from reed stems mixed with mud.

The Otter has marking spots, normally associated with sprainting and feeding places which are marked by both scent and urine.

The Atlantic Seal produces an oil which may adhere to the places where it has been resting for a long time; the oil has a pungent and easily recognizable odour.

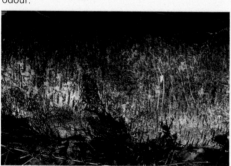

Badger claw marks on a birch tree. These marks may have a territorial function as well as being the result of claw sharpening and cleaning activity.

Rubbing and scratching posts

All mammals scratch to deal with irritations caused by parasites, dirt or moulting fur. Hoofed animals have to use objects such as wire, posts or trees since they are unable to reach all parts of their bodies with their feet.

Some of the more agile mammals such as cats and badgers also like to scratch against objects. Badgers often get the long claws of their front feet clogged with mud, and scrape them clean on a convenient post or tree near to the sett. Elder trees can stand more root disturbance than many other species and will grow close to setts, so they are often chosen for this purpose. The Badger's five long claws score deep scratches into the bark, and the use to which the mud-stained tree is put is often obvious from some distance away.

This scratching is often referred to as 'sharpening the claws' but this is probably not its main function. Fragments of the outer sheath of the claw may, however, be pulled off and lie in the earth at the base of the scratching tree.

Larger mammal species rubbing against trees may remove bark and impregnate the trunk with mud and grease. Rubbing places and associated hair deposits (see below) can be helpful in identifying deer, Wild Boar and sheep scratching activity.

Shed hair

Shed hair is common. It is sometimes found in large quantities as the result of a moult, or as a few strands on a bush, a length of wire or the entrance to a home.

Fox earths show scratch marks with strands of red hair in the debris at the entrance.

Black and silver Badger hair is found in debris outside setts, on the lower bars of gates or on barbed wire across pathways.

Rabbit fur is common on low bushes and fences and is mainly brown, grey and white. Early in the year the female Rabbit lines her nursery stop with grey underfur; also she often digs a scrape and pulls out tufts of fur to line it with.

Brown Hare fur has a higher content of black than that of the Rabbit. White Mountain Hare fur is often found in the form after the spring moult; white stoat fur is sometimes found by the remains of a kill in spring.

Dark brown hair is left on high branches and fences by deer: individual hairs are relatively short and thick since they contain large air spaces, and a tuft of deer hairs has a coarse spongy feel, unlike that of any other mammal. The Red Deer wallows in pools almost throughout the year, possibly to loosen dead hair, and a Red Deer wallow usually has a good deal of this around its margins.

Hair from cows and wool from sheep is common in all country areas.

The thick moulted hair of the Common Seal is often found on its hauling out places from July to September.

Similar to shed hair in many respects are the quills left by porcupines. Although the two species found in Europe are not widespread they both shed quills, which are really modified hair, and these may be found outside their burrows. The quills vary in length and shape according to which part of the body they have come from and the species involved.

Deep, water-logged depression in muddy ground created as a wallow by male Red Deer.

Tooth and claw sharpening

All rodents gnaw hard objects such as bones, stones and wood to sharpen their teeth. Squirrels and the Beaver produce very obvious gnawings. Squirrel claw marks on trees can be identified by the three parallel lines scored by the claws on the three longest digits. Red Squirrels have well established scratch points.

Superficial fraying of bark low down on trees or posts is often the sign of claw sharpening by Domestic Cats, Wild Cats or even Lynx.

Above: Cast skin from an Adder. It is rare to find a complete skin, but fragments from lizard and snake skins are not uncommon.

Left: Pheasant's dusting bowl. These depressions, which may be deep, are created by birds dust-bathing to remove parasites and freshen their feathers.

Opposite: Wild Boar wallowing.

Rutting scrapes

In the breeding season many male deer create rutting scrapes by continually scraping at the ground with their hoofs. This behaviour is associated with assertive activity. Roe and Fallow scrapes are particularly common. Rutting ring paths around trees are created by males walking round and round a tree chasing a female – again, particularly in Roe and Fallow Deer.

The Wild Boar creates large shallow depressions, and between April and October the Red Deer does the same. These may be wet or dry and probably serve the dual purpose of acting as a cooling/cleaning agent as well as dealing with some parasites.

Bare patches of ground known as 'leks' are created by male Capercaille in their display rituals.

Dust baths

Many birds take dust baths in saucer-shaped depressions in dry dusty earth. Sparrows, larks, game birds and chickens bathe in dust to keep their feathers in good condition. The size of the depressions and associated tracks and other signs may give an indication of the species involved.

Sloughed skins

While moulted fur and feathers may sometimes be used for positive species identification, sloughed skins from reptiles, although they give information about the size of their previous owners, cannot always be reliably used in the same way. Snake skins have no colour but they can sometimes be identified from the pattern of the scales.

Invertebrates also shed their skins, both in the process of maturing and, in some cases, to grow in size when adult body form is reached. The instar body cases of dragonflies which are sometimes found around ponds may be the only indication of the insect's presence in the area.

Homes and nurseries

Most animals do not have what human beings would call a home. Instead they usually have a territory within which they can find everything they need for their survival, and this may include a den or a number of sleeping areas; however, these are seldom permanent. The territory may belong to an individual, a pair or sometimes a social group, and other members of the same species will be excluded from it. Other species make different demands on the environment and will almost always be tolerated unless they venture too close to the breeding spot, which is in the home range from which all but the most inoffensive creatures are excluded.

The territories occupied by birds are bounded by lines between landmarks such as trees or buildings. The bird defends his boundaries by song and by posturing to warn others of his species away. Mammals, on the other hand, usually mark their territories visually or by scent; e.g. bears tear pieces of bark from trees, and deer fray trees with their antlers during the breeding season. This is not so much to mark boundaries as to announce their ownership of nearby females, and they will mark fresh trees should the females move to a new grazing place.

Scent is the more commonly used method of boundary marking among mammals, as it is effective both by day and by night. It is produced in a number of ways: some animals, e.g. wolves, dogs and deer, use urine, while many others, e.g. rodents, insectivores and badgers, use droppings. Carnivores may use their powerful musk glands for this purpose. Badgers mark not only the tracks they take when foraging, but also the other badgers that make up their colony, using a scent from a pair of glands under the tail.

The territorial boundaries of most animals are difficult for the casual observer to identify, and this is partly because the area required by many creatures is very large. However, they have been mapped very accurately by animal behaviourists who have watched groups of animals or individuals over long periods of time.

Many animals change their dens with the season, making a nursery in which to rear young in the summer and retreating to warmer quarters during the colder months. The most extreme example of this is furnished by the migratory birds, which may regularly travel over distances of thousands of miles. The nests they make in Europe usually disintegrate during the winter, although certain hole-nesting species, such as Sand Martins, can leave structures permanent enough to house parasites through the year.

Besides the birds, many rodents make summer nests in trees. Squirrel dreys are probably the most familiar, but dormice and Black Rats can also live in the canopy during the summer. When their nests are abandoned at the approach of winter they may be taken over by other species. Owls may roost in a squirrel's drey and Wrens may cram together to sleep in a drey or in the domed nest of a Magpie.

Beaver dam across a small stream. Large scale dams are found on some lakes in Europe but generally beavers have adapted to smaller water courses and structures on this scale are more typical.

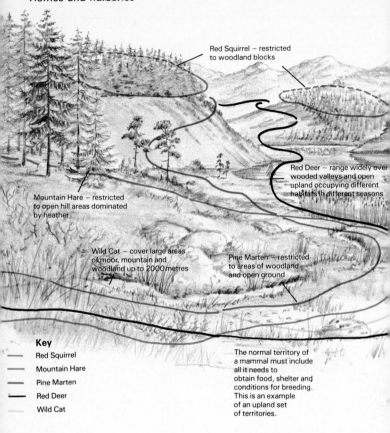

Red Squirrel – restricted to woodland blocks

Red Deer – range widely over wooded valleys and open upland occupying different habitats in different seasons

Mountain Hare – restricted to open hill areas dominated by heather

Wild Cat – cover large areas of moor, mountain and woodland up to 2000 metres

Pine Marten – restricted to areas of woodland and open ground

Key

—— Red Squirrel

—— Mountain Hare

—— Pine Marten

—— Red Deer

—— Wild Cat

The normal territory of a mammal must include all it needs to obtain food, shelter and conditions for breeding. This is an example of an upland set of territories.

It is not always easy to tell whether or not a particular den is in use. Birds' nests are occupied during the breeding season, but in the case of single-brooded species this may be quite short. Double or triple-brooded species such as Swallows may continue to use their nests until late summer. The summer nests of squirrels or Garden Dormice will be used until the onset of cold weather. Some species, e.g. Wild Cats, have several dens scattered through their territory and they use these in rotation, moving on whenever prey begins to become depleted in one part of their range. Wild Cats often have several dens at about the same level on the side of a mountain, and only the observation of other signs will reveal which one of these is in use at any given time.

Signs of fresh digging often denote that an underground den is occupied. Newly removed soil is often relatively damp, and is sometimes a different

Magpie — large untidy layered structure with loose dome of twigs, located in forks of outer branches

Squirrel — drey consists of 'ball' (over 30cms) of twigs and leaves together with moss, grass etc, usually located in a fork close to trunk

Domed nests in upper sections of trees

colour from that which has weathered for a few months. Field Mice often dig new breeding dens in the spring, and the tip heaps round the entrance to these are an indication of activity within.

Bedding freshly removed from a Badger sett shows clearly that it is occupied; and in the winter a column of condensed water vapour from the breath of the badgers proves their presence beyond doubt. Also, on a cold day ice crystals round the lip of a mouse hole can betray the presence of an occupant. Droppings near a rodent's nest are a clear sign, for all rodents are clean animals and do not soil their living places.

The summer dens of many animals are easier to see than their winter homes, but the latter are often more permanent. A suitable hole in a tree may be used by generations of animals, and as it becomes enlarged with the passage of time, a succession of different types of animal may use it.

Homes and nurseries

Underground homes

Badgers' setts have a rare degree of permanence, sometimes being occupied for centuries on end, and they have often been refurbished and enlarged over the years. Badgers prefer to make their homes where digging is fairly easy and the drainage is good; thus many badger earths are dug on the side of a hill where the slope prevents water from lying. A big old sett may extend for 100 metres or more along a hillside and have many entrances and tunnels. These do not penetrate far into the hill, but the sleeping chambers which lie at the ends of the passages are up to 90cm wide and 60cm high. The growth of the sett probably occurs chiefly when young badgers dig tunnels for themselves on first leaving their parents. These are later incorporated into the general structure of the sett. Sometimes a badger will leave the sett in which it has been living and dig a new hole elsewhere. This may be temporary, the badger moving back to its former living place quite soon, or it may become the nucleus of a new colony.

The entrance hole to a sett may be as little as 20cm in diameter, although it is often much greater. The spoil heap is often very large, and usually contains discarded straw and bracken bedding as well as shed hairs. The disturbance of the soil in and around the sett reduces plant growth: small trees are often killed by root disturbance, and nothing grows in the tip on the downhill side of the entrance holes. Any entrance which is stuffed with dry leaves or has a spider's web spun across it is not in current use.

Many other creatures may take refuge in a badgers' sett. The commonest of these is the Fox; there are occasional records of badgers eating foxes and, if they can, foxes will take very young badgers. Another animal that may take over part of a badgers' earth is the Raccoon Dog, which digs latrines not unlike those of the badgers; however, the droppings are distinctive (pages 224–225).

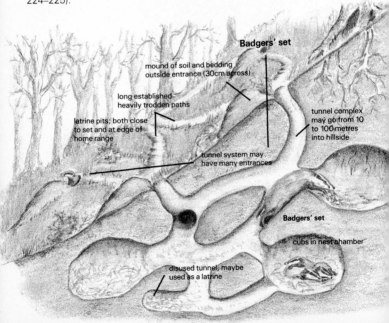

Badgers' set

mound of soil and bedding outside entrance (30cm across)

long established heavily trodden paths

latrine pits; both close to set and at edge of home range

tunnel system may have many entrances

tunnel complex may go from 10 to 100 metres into hillside

Badgers' set

cubs in nest chamber

disused tunnel, maybe used as a latrine

Rabbit warrens are a familiar sight over much of western Europe. Like many burrowing species, rabbits prefer to live in places where the soil is well drained and will remain dry even in wet weather; they often obtain additional shelter by making their holes under a hedge or in the edge of a wood. The burrow entrance is rarely more than 10cm in diameter and does not usually

Extensive Rabbit warren under old tree stumps in a bank which marks a former boundary.

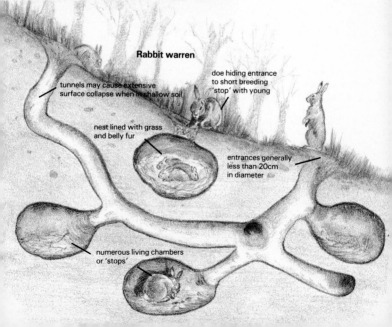

Rabbit warren

tunnels may cause extensive surface collapse when in shallow soil

doe hiding entrance to short breeding 'stop' with young

nest lined with grass and belly fur

entrances generally less than 20cm in diameter

numerous living chambers or 'stops'

go more than a metre or so into a bank, although if the warren is built on flat ground a large area may be honeycombed with shallow runs, tunnels and chambers. Ground disturbance may be easily seen from a long way away, long before individual holes can be seen, for rabbits can alter their habitat almost more than any other European species except the Beaver. All edible vegetation is removed in the immediate area of the warren, and in seriously disturbed areas only some thistles and viper's bugloss may survive. Tree growth is inhibited by the close nibbling, although a fine sward may also result from this, as on the Downs of southern England. A warren is occupied by a colony of individuals in which there is a fairly strongly developed hierarchy, with the dominant animals living in the centre parts of the warren and subordinates on the fringes. Central territories are marked with droppings and urine and with scent from glands under the chin, but those on the edge are less well demarcated. Does produce their young in short blind-ended tunnels or 'stops' on the edge of the colony. These are rarely deeper than 45cm, but if the colony is thriving they may be enlarged and deepened to become part of the overall system.

Sousliks inhabit the dry grassland of eastern Europe. Like rabbits they occupy big systems of underground runs with many openings to the surface, although these are little more than half the diameter of rabbit holes. The European Souslik may occupy headlands between fields, while the Spotted Souslik can occupy arable land, for its burrows are deeper and it is not disturbed by normal ploughing. Both species hibernate, and both make large stores of food to which they retreat at the end of summer, feeding underground until hibernation starts.

The **European Hamster** is a stout-bodied creature occurring in grasslands and the moister steppes of central and eastern Europe. The diameter of its burrow is about the same as that of a rabbit, and it descends to a depth of about 2m. There may be large numbers of burrows in close proximity, but each one belongs to a single individual, and is marked with scent from glands high on the flanks and on the underside. Each burrow includes sleeping quarters, a latrine area and a larder. Up to 14kg of grain has been recorded from a single larder; hamsters are agricultural pests.

The **Alpine Marmot** has been reintroduced into many areas in Europe and is beginning to increase in numbers. It is a social animal, several individuals sharing a complex of burrows, which are usually dug into stabilized scree where soil is plentiful between big blocks of stone. The tunnels may go as deep as 3 metres, although about 1 metre is more usual. The main resting chamber is an enlargement of the tunnel, warmly lined with dry grass which is taken down at the end of the summer, and which will be replaced after hibernation. Before hibernation marmots use earth from side tunnels to block off the entrance to the tunnel system. This has the dual advantage of making the entrance less conspicuous and increasing the insulation of the sleeping chambers.

Alpine Marmots are reputed to love the sun, and their burrows are almost always made on south or west-facing slopes, where the sun will be very strong.

Three species of **mole** live in Europe. All construct tunnels and runs which radiate from a central nest area into their feeding grounds. Moles have front feet very much widened for the purpose of digging. When burrowing, the mole braces itself with its hind feet and one fore foot against the side walls of the tunnel, and loosens the earth ahead of it with its other fore foot, probably changing hands every few minutes. Some of the earth is consolidated against the walls of the tunnel, but the remaining loose material is forced up to the surface, making a molehill. The number of molehills made depends to some extent on the depth of the tunnels and the stiffness of the soil: in light loamy areas fewer molehills will be formed than in heavy ground. Some runs, known as rutting runs or *traces d'amour*, are so close to the surface that they leave a raised area across a field, or even an open furrow. Other runs are deeper, down to a maximum of about 70cm. The central nest area may be merely an extension of the tunnels, or, especially in wet areas, it may be located in a structure that looks like a large molehill, called a 'fortress'. This contains a nest lined with grass or leaves, and a larder which generally contains worms, bitten behind the head to immobilize but not kill them. Moles have been seen collecting nest material, pushing their head and shoulders out of the ground and feeling about for a piece of grass or a leaf, which is quickly taken back into the tunnel. This action is repeated until the animal has enough material to line its nest cavity.

Mole-rats live mainly in the grassland areas of eastern Europe, where they make extensive burrows much like those of true moles. However, their feet are quite small and they dig by loosening the earth with their teeth, consolidating it mainly with their head and shoulders, although they push any surplus to the surface to make molehill-like mounds.

In parts of central Europe the **Water Vole** lives away from streams, usually colonizing pastures instead, and making extensive burrows just below the surface of the ground. As it does so it throws up hillocks similar to molehills, but they can be distinguished by the exit holes, for the Water Vole is able to forage on the surface.

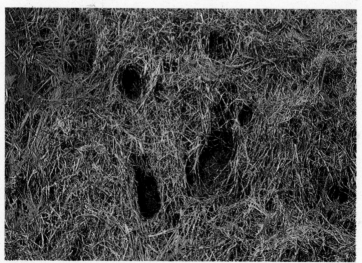

Field Vole holes in a grassy bank. The tunnel complexes in deep grass litter may be very extensive.

Homes and nurseries

Tunnels in stream banks

Many waterside animals make their resting places in the banks of streams. The size and length of the burrow cannot usually be guessed from the outside, because there is no telltale heap of soil as there is with land animals – the water normally washes away all traces of activity except for the hole itself.

Water Voles make holes about 8cm wide at different levels on the bank; as these animals live in places which are liable to flooding, they almost always have underwater entrances as well as those above water level. There is usually a resting place just inside the main dry entrance, and another deeper inside the network of tunnels. Both are lined with shredded grass and the pith from rushes. During the summer, Water Voles may extend their burrows to include holes reaching to the river bank a metre or so from the edge. Attention may be drawn to these by the mown grass look of the surrounding vegetation. Feeding lawns are rarely more than about a metre across, because the voles are timid and return quickly to their homes at the least disturbance.

In parts of Spain, the Pyrenees and western Russia, **Desmans** make short tunnels into the banks of rivers or canals. Such tunnels lead upwards to a den which lies only a short distance below the surface of the ground. Desmans do not make bolt holes or breathing holes, as they obtain enough air through cracks made by tree roots, or between the rocks among which they have burrowed. Their only way of escaping enemies, most of which are land-based, is to slip as quickly as possible into the water.

There are two introduced rodents which burrow into stream banks. The **Muskrat** has established itself widely in western and central Europe. It tunnels deeply into stream banks, making a hole about 15–20cm wide (and sometimes said to be as much as 6 metres deep) before it widens to make a resting or breeding chamber. It may also make a nest above water, building up a great pile of reeds and other vegetation as much as a metre high and with a diameter of 1.5 metres. The nest is in the middle of this, and is approached from below the water. If the river freezes the Muskrat is still safe, for there is usually air trapped beneath the ice and plenty caught in the nest material also.

Beavers have been exterminated over most of their former European haunts, although a few survive in Scandinavia, the valleys of the Rhône and the Elbe, and in Russia. Heavy persecution has probably altered their behaviour and today most European Beavers do not make dams or build obvious lodges, but tend to burrow into the banks of streams, although they do make a lodge of sticks, mud and stones which extends from their home in the bank. This gives them an underwater entrance to a feeding area, where they can eat by the edge of still water (as they prefer), and a nest chamber at a higher level where they can sleep and breed. In places where the Beaver is totally free from molestation it may build a dam like those familiar in North America. In this case the lodge will be within the structure of the dam, which may be 3 metres high and over 2 metres wide and contain several thousand cubic metres of wood, stone and mud.

Small burrows in banks

A number of birds tunnel into natural or artificial banks to make secure nests. The **Kingfisher** typically does so well above the water level of a stream with high banks: it loosens soil and stones with its beak and scrapes the spoil back with its feet, making a straight tunnel up to a metre in length. The end of this

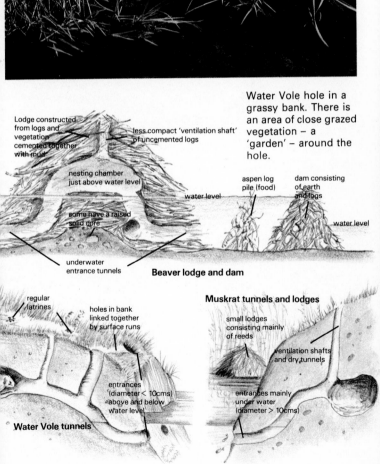

Water Vole hole in a grassy bank. There is an area of close grazed vegetation – a 'garden' – around the hole.

Lodge constructed from logs and vegetation cemented together with mud

less compact 'ventilation shaft' of uncemented logs

nesting chamber just above water level

water level

aspen log pile (food)

dam consisting of earth and logs

some have a raised solid core

water level

underwater entrance tunnels

Beaver lodge and dam

regular latrines

holes in bank linked together by surface runs

entrances (diameter < 10cms) above and below water level

Water Vole tunnels

Muskrat tunnels and lodges

small lodges consisting mainly of reeds

ventilation shafts and dry tunnels

entrances mainly under water (diameter > 10cms)

249

Homes and nurseries

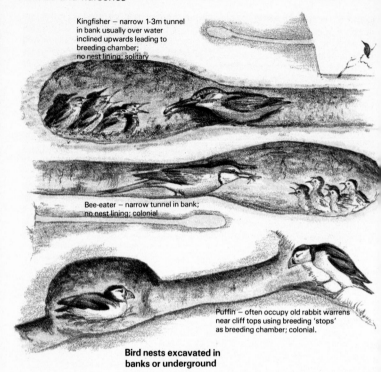

Kingfisher — narrow 1-3m tunnel in bank usually over water inclined upwards leading to breeding chamber; no nest lining; solitary

Bee-eater — narrow tunnel in bank; no nest lining; colonial

Puffin — often occupy old rabbit warrens near cliff tops using breeding 'stops' as breeding chamber; colonial.

**Bird nests excavated in
banks or underground**

is slightly enlarged to make a nest chamber. No nest material is taken in for the eggs, but the chicks are eventually surrounded by a mass of regurgitated fish bones cemented together by droppings.

Other birds may burrow into banks away from water, such as the sides of sand quarries. The **Bee-eaters** and **Sand Martins** are examples; neither gives its young any protection other than the hole it has excavated. Unlike the solitary Kingfisher, insectivorous Bee-eaters and Sand Martins are colonial and several hundred birds may nest together.

Puffins nest in burrows on the grassy slopes rising above many sea-cliffs. They may excavate these with their beaks and feet, but more often they take them over from rabbits.

On more level ground away from the sea, **Manx Shearwaters** also nest underground, often in burrows which may be no more than the depth of the turf, and which may also be taken over from rabbits.

Shallow burrows and surface nests and dens

Many small rodents and insectivores simply adopt whatever shelter their surroundings offer, burrowing in many cases, but merely tunnelling through the base of grasses or other vegetation when the ground is hard or water-logged. **House Mice** and **Wood Mice** both make burrows in the soil, which differ from those of shrews in being round, rather than oval, in cross-section.

Some of these runs last for more than one generation, as shallow roots can act as a support for the roof: the strong, spreading surface roots of nettles are often used in this way, and the walls of the tunnels below are polished smooth by the passage of many small rodents. House Mice retreat to buildings during the colder months and gnaw through obstructions such as wainscoting or roof timbers. Wood Mice rarely take such shelter, but the Yellow-necked Mouse tends to do so in Britain, although it usually climbs into the roof space rather than remaining on the ground floor.

In southern Europe **Black Rats** may live in trees all year round, but elsewhere they live in buildings, often in the upper storeys, where they climb readily on joists and rafters. Indoors both Brown and Black Rats make nests of any material to hand, including paper, string, sacking, and pieces of bone. The **Brown Rat** can also survive out of doors in most of Europe, making runs up to 400 metres long and tunnels up to 50cm deep. The nest is an untidy pile of leaves, grass etc., and will have a number of bolt holes and passages which nearly reach the surface of the ground. These can be broken through in emergencies.

Other small mammals which live on the ground or just under the surface include **voles**. The Common Vole and Root Vole live in pasture with very little cover, and hence burrow more than other voles. The nest of the Grass Vole is usually made of grass leaves and stems chopped into lengths of about 2cm, and is usually just underground; but the Root Vole often lives in damp areas and is more likely to make its home in the base of a clump of rushes. The Red-backed Vole often makes its nest above ground in the protection of a log or projecting tree root. It normally incorporates longer grass stems and leaves and moss.

Shrews' nests are usually just on the ground and are made of grass stems and leaves. The animal builds by pulling in nesting material from outside; this method ensures a tight tangled construction, but one through which the animal can exit at any point.

The **Balkan Snow Vole** often builds its nest under a stone or in a rock crevice, and many larger animals share this habit. Carnivores such as the **Pine Marten** and the **Wild Cat** often make their lairs in similar places. Normally, however, they do not use any bedding material, being well protected by their heavy coats; the only clue to the occupation of such a den is the pathway leading to it, and perhaps some footprints. Most carnivores are very wary, and the den often offers a good view over the surrounding countryside. The breeding den of the **Wolf** must also have water fairly close by, because the bitch does not leave her cubs alone for more than a few minutes in their first weeks of life.

Many carnivores, e.g. **otters**, **mink** and **bears**, may den up at the base of a hollow tree: they too use little nesting material except for dead leaves which may have blown into the cavity, although a she-bear, which gives birth to her cubs in the winter den, may partially close the entrance by dragging sticks and stones into it.

Bears and other animals sometimes make their lairs in a cave, if a suitable one is found. Caves and man-made shelters such as tunnels, mine shafts and roof spaces may also house **bats**, whose presence can usually be detected by droppings (see page 225) and sometimes also by discarded inedible insect remains. The preferred position of individual species within a cave may change at different times of year. Horseshoe bats, for instance, usually start their hibernation near the entrance of a cave, then move to a deeper part of the system as winter progresses. Smooth-faced bats always hang against a wall; some, such as Natterer's Bat and Whiskered Bat, prefer a vertical surface, while Daubenton's Bat likes to squeeze into a narrow crevice, often lying in a horizontal position.

Large resting places on the ground

Large European animals such as **deer** or the **Bison** do not make dens as such, but lie up in sheltered places within their feeding range. The depressions made among leaves or grass by deer, which often rest or chew the cud in close-packed groups, are easy to see. The long-term effect of animals resting in a sheltered spot, especially in rather barren country, is that they enrich the ground with droppings, forming a small fertile area. This is often marked by a growth of nettles, which require a highly nitrogenous soil.

Forest-dwelling creatures such as **Bison** often rest and give birth to their young at the base of a large tree, but such places must usually be identified from tracks and other signs. Depending on environment, **Wild Boar** may simply rest in the shelter of a tree or may dig a shallow trench, and this may or may not have dead leaves dragged into it.

Medium and small homes on the ground

Shrews often excavate small tunnels and their nurseries are frequently half underground.

In summer the **Fox** normally rests in thick cover above ground, but when the weather becomes harsh will turn to any cover, such as a corner of a badger's earth or an old drain, before making a den; this is often no more than an enlarged rabbit hole.

Some animals such as **martens**, **Wild Cat** or **Genet** may shelter in a rock crevice, or above ground in hollow trees or in old birds' nests.

The **Mongoose** normally lies up on the ground and in Europe frequently finds a secluded place in a reed bed for its home.

The **Brown Hare** lies up in the slightest of shelters, known as a form, in open fields. The more northerly **Mountain Hare** may make a short burrow into a slope of snow or peat, but more often than not this is more like a trench, mostly open at the top; the animal sits largely in the unroofed part.

Hedgehogs usually make a nest of some sort. In spring the female makes a football-sized nest in a quiet spot, often in woodland or a hedge, but sometimes near human habitations such as under the floor of a shed or outbuilding. The nest is built chiefly of grass and lined with leaves and moss. In late autumn hedgehogs build a hibernating nest or 'hibernaculum' which incorporates large quantities of leaves, dry bracken and grass neatly packed down to make the structure weatherproof. This will be in a sheltered position such as at the base of a tree, inside a hollow trunk or even in the mouth of an old rabbit hole.

Birds' nests on the ground

Many birds are either too heavy to nest safely in trees, or simply live in treeless places. All European seabirds nest on or under the ground, although in some cases the ground consists of nothing but a precipitous ledge. All European game birds also nest on the ground, often making a substantial but well camouflaged nest of grass or twigs.

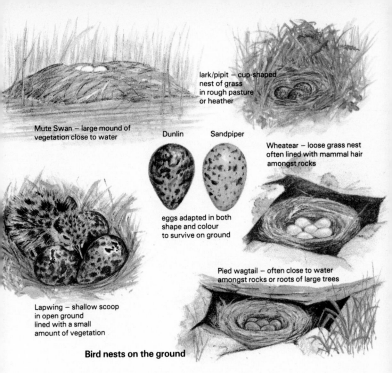

lark/pipit – cup-shaped nest of grass in rough pasture or heather

Mute Swan – large mound of vegetation close to water

Dunlin

Sandpiper

eggs adapted in both shape and colour to survive on ground

Wheatear – loose grass nest often lined with mammal hair amongst rocks

Pied wagtail – often close to water amongst rocks or roots of large trees

Lapwing – shallow scoop in open ground lined with a small amount of vegetation

Bird nests on the ground

Swans and geese nest on the ground, the swan making a large pile of twigs and reeds. Some **ducks** nest in trees, but no European species does so invariably. Usually the nest is in a slight depression, lined with plant material to which down is added. All waders lay their eggs in a slight scrape, which is usually unlined; their eggs are well camouflaged and are extremely difficult to find.

Snowy Owls and some other owls nest on the ground, but usually make no attempt to protect their eggs except by brooding. **Larks**, **wheatears**, **pipits** and **wagtails** are among the small birds which usually nest on the ground; **dippers**, **wall-creepers** and some others use natural crevices. Birds' nests can almost always be distinguished from mammals' nests because they are characteristically cup-shaped rather than closed at the top.

Mammal nests above ground

Climbing mammals often build nests in trees or shrubs. Low above the ground dormice may make a den among the cut stumps of coppiced trees, always using the papery bark of honeysuckle as a building material if this is available: honeysuckle twigs stripped of their outer cover are a good sign of dormice.

Other species of dormouse may also make winter nests close to the ground, but are as likely to hibernate in holes high up in trees. The **Harvest Mouse** also nests within a few centimetres of the ground. During the winter this animal lives in scrub or hedgerows, but its nursery nest, made in early summer, is unique. Traditionally it was built in the stalks of growing grain crops, but today is more common in the rank grasses of damp waste land.

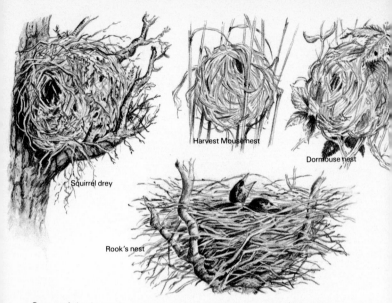

Harvest Mouse nest

Dormouse nest

Squirrel drey

Rook's nest

Some of the lower leaves from several stalks are split lengthwise into ribbons and woven together, without being detached. The nest is well camouflaged since the leaves are still living and retain their colour; by the time the grass dies the nest has long since been deserted. The height of the nest above the ground increases as the grasses grow, but the Harvest Mouse is an agile climber.

In the far north of the continent **Birch Mice** often excavate holes in rotten logs and build nests of pine needles and moss in them.

Other mammals may make nests much higher above the ground. The most familiar are squirrels' dreys, which can be seen in trees throughout Europe. The **Red Squirrel** usually builds its drey against the trunk of a tree at the junction with a large branch, 6–15 metres from the ground. Other sites include the crotch of big old deciduous trees and the crown of conifers. The Red Squirrel drey is usually a compact sphere of twigs, woven together and lined with shredded bark, mosses, grass and leaves. There is no special entrance hole – the outer framework is loose and springy enough to allow the squirrel to pass at any point. The **Grey Squirrel** nest is bigger and less tidy. It usually has an entrance on the side nearest the trunk. Height is much more variable than in Red Squirrel, being from just over 2 metres to 16 metres or more. It may be in use for long periods and may be refurbished or have more lining added; a drey in a particularly favourable position may be used by several generations of squirrels. The Grey Squirrel may also make a temporary summer nest in the outer branches of a tree, usually over 10 metres above the ground. These are often blown down in winter gales. The winter or breeding dreys are used by many other animals including Pine Martens, owls and some birds of prey.

Other animals which make nests high in the tree canopy include the **Fat Dormouse** and the **Forest Dormouse**, which build compact little nests during the summer months, but retreat to a lower level for hibernation.

254

Rookery: the flat-topped nests occupy the higher branches of a single tree or several trees close together, and may contain many pairs of birds.

Birds' nests in trees

Birds are more efficient builders than mammals and have developed many kinds of nests. It is impossible to give detailed descriptions here, but the following notes should enable some nests to be identified.

The larger members of the **Crow** family make obvious stick nests high up in trees. The cup is usually quite deep and a sitting bird is not easily seen. A solitary nest probably belongs to a Hoodie or Carrion Crow; if nests are grouped in the upper branches of a large tree they are likely to be rooks' nests. **Magpies** also make stick nests high in trees, but these are usually domed.

Large stick nests with a very broad base are built by some of the larger **birds of prey**. Eagles and other birds of prey often return to the same nest for many years, bringing new sticks and lining to it, so that it may eventually measure several metres in diameter.

Herons and **storks** also make large stick nests: Grey Herons, and occasion-

255

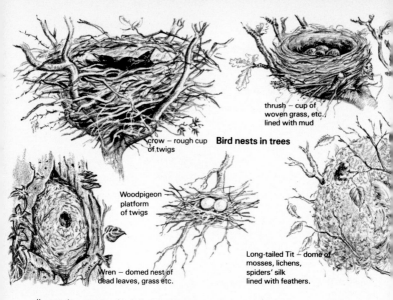

Bird nests in trees

thrush – cup of woven grass, etc., lined with mud

crow – rough cup of twigs

Woodpigeon platform of twigs

Wren – domed nest of dead leaves, grass etc.

Long-tailed Tit – dome of mosses, lichens, spiders' silk lined with feathers.

ally storks, nest colonially in tall trees. All other members of the family either nest on the ground in swamps or reed beds, or sometimes in bushes and small trees close to the water's edge.

Members of the **Thrush** family build a deep-cupped mud-lined nest, or sometimes on buildings or on the ground. It is built of fine twigs and branches, usually on a base of mud. **Blackbirds** are often numerous in built-up areas and sometimes build their nests in the vicinity of buildings. In such areas birds often obtain unusual nest-building materials such as polythene bags.

The majority of town pigeons are feral pigeons nesting on the ledges of buildings. Some, however, are tree-nesting **Wood Pigeons**, and these nest in fragile platforms among the branches of planes or other city trees. After the leaves have fallen these nests can still be seen. Nests of a similar kind are made in the countryside by **Turtle Doves** and **Collared Doves**, but they are situated in low and shrubby growths.

Most other European perching birds build their cup-shaped nests in dense vegetation. The size, location and materials used depend on species. In general, **buntings** build near to or sometimes even on the ground; **finches** build at fairly low to moderate height in trees; **warblers** make small nests from tree stump level to the upper branches of small trees; **Wrens** and **Long-tailed Tits** both make domed nests, the former usually against a tree trunk, the latter decorated with lichens and hung in dense, often spiny bushes. The **Golden Oriole** slings its nest between a horizontal fork in high branches, often close to water, while the tiny hammock nests of **goldcrests** and **firecrests** are hung from the tips of whippy conifer or other branches.

Mammal nests in hollow trees

A cavity in a tree can make a secure dry den for many mammals, and a tree which is hollow to the ground may be used for shelter by **bears**, **Raccoon Dogs** and a number of other species. Hollow trees are especially important to **bats**, and some, such as the Noctule and the Serotine, are known as tree bats because of this. The hole need not be very large – even old woodpecker holes may be taken over by Noctules. The lower side of a bats' roost is often stained by droppings, which make a dark streak down the tree trunk; the roost also has a characteristic musky smell. A large hole may contain many bats; in winter they will be huddled together for warmth.

The **Grey Squirrel** prefers a small cavity and may gnaw one in the trunk of a tree where a dead branch has fallen off: recent tooth marks may be visible. In the far north **Flying Squirrels** den up in trees, but leave few signs or none at all.

Among dormice the **Garden Dormouse** and the **Edible Dormouse** are most likely to use a tree hole for nesting and hibernation.

Many carnivores will nest in the base of a hollow tree, but only the **martens** are agile enough to use a hole high up in the trunk.

Genets sometimes find a suitable cavity in a small tree and **raccoons** often find a suitable hole high up in a big tree. Identifying such dens depends largely on the discovery of other signs such as footprints or feeding remains.

Remains of Dor Beetles eaten by Greater Horseshoe Bat. The large, ridged droppings of the bats are distinctive.

Holes in trees which are regularly used by bats can be detected by staining caused by grease, urine and faeces from the bats.

Left: Nuthatch taking food to its young. Mud has been plastered into the hole to make it the right size for the bird.

Opposite: Young Little Owl emerging from the nest at the base of an oak tree at dusk.

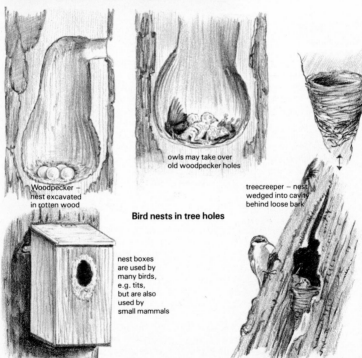

Woodpecker – nest excavated in rotten wood

owls may take over old woodpecker holes

Bird nests in tree holes

treecreeper – nest wedged into cavity behind loose bark

nest boxes are used by many birds, e.g. tits, but are also used by small mammals

Birds' nests in hollow trees

Most **woodpeckers** make their nest holes in wood already weakened by fungus growth, although the Great Black Woodpecker and some others can chisel their nurseries from apparently undamaged wood. They carry the telltale chippings away and drop them some distance from the nest, but often a few fragments remain to give a clue to their activity. The nest hole of the Great Black Woodpecker is nearly 50cm deep; other woodpeckers make smaller holes, but all species make a new hole each year.

Other animals use the abandoned holes: mammal activity has been described above, but woodpeckers open up the environment for other birds as well. **Owls** often adopt such holes, but leave no signs to indicate this. A succession of other birds may use the old woodpecker's hole: **Stock Doves** take the larger holes, while **starlings** and **bats** may fight for possession of smaller ones. Small holes are also used by **titmice, flycatchers** and **tree creepers**, all of which bring grass, moss and feathers to them. **Nuthatches** sometimes take over larger holes and plaster up the entrances with mud to exclude bigger birds. They are the only European birds to do this; the sign is quite distinctive.

With use a circular hole becomes oval in shape as its lower edge gets worn away. The amount of wear depends partly on the condition of the wood, but an old hole can easily be distinguished from a recent one.

In managed woods there are few hollow trees, and in recent years concerned parties have begun to install nest boxes to replace them. Boxes of many sizes are used, but not always by the species for which they are intended – a squirrel, for example, may gnaw at a small entrance hole to enlarge it, and to prevent this some boxes have metal tacked round the entrance hole. Even Pine Martens have been known to nest in large boxes.

In some woodlands roosting boxes have been set up for bats, although these mammals appear to be highly conservative and will not use the boxes for some years after installation.

Miscellaneous

There are many things to be seen in the countryside which do not fit conveniently into categories. Some are genuinely rare; others puzzle the finder because they are incomplete or damaged in some way.

Objects discarded in the process of growth
Deer antlers are shed each year, generally at the end of the winter. A naturally cast antler shows clearly the point from which it grew and is not broken or cut at the base. In some countries deer live in an environment where the minerals required for antler growth are hard to obtain, so shed antlers are eaten. They are therefore scarce, even in areas where deer are common. When an antler is found it bears the marks of the incisor teeth of the deer: the long, shallow grooves are distinctive.

After giving birth, the **placenta** is expelled by female land mammals. In most instances it is eaten almost immediately by the mother; occasionally, however, it is left. A placenta is most likely to be found in the uplands, where sheep are abundant; but it will not last long, as other scavengers, e.g. foxes, kites and ravens, will soon eat it. A sheep's placenta is a red, glandular mass, 45cm across, showing the point of attachment of the foetus.

A normal **hatched egg** is broken into two approximately equal pieces. The parents often remove the shells from the vicinity of the nest, so that the whereabouts of the young is not betrayed to predators.

The papery shells of lizards' and snakes' eggs may sometimes be found. Those of some species may contain a substantial amount of yolk which was not used by the reptile in its embryonic development.

Cast insect skins are mostly inconspicuous, but large insects of southern Europe leave noticeable skins. Stick insect skins and the final moult of dragonflies may be seen attached to leaves or twigs. Cicadas, which can be numerous, all emerge from the soil to moult on the same night, so that large numbers of cast skins may briefly be found.

Opposite: Bark Beetle galleries on the trunk of a fallen tree from which the bark has been stripped.

Cicada moulting. The old skin has split along the back of the thorax.

Miscellaneous animal signs

Silk

Silk is produced by a number of insects and also by spiders and some of their relatives. Many **caterpillars** depend on it for their safety: in late spring the larvae of Oak Tortrix Moths roll leaves round themselves, holding them tight with silk. They will fall, if disturbed, hanging on a silk thread.

Butterfly caterpillars do not usually produce silk, but a few strands, dotted with hairs on nettle leaves, indicate the presence of Peacock or small Tortoise-shell caterpillars. The webs spun by Brown-tail Moth caterpillars are more obvious. These animals may entirely defoliate a stretch of hedge, and then the strong silver webs are visible from a distance. *Note* It is very unwise to handle these webs, since their barbed hairs penetrate the skin and cause intense irritation.

Over much of Europe, Processionary Moth caterpillars are major defoliators of various tree species, including oaks and pines. They make rugby-football-shaped nests on the ends of the branches. The silver-coloured silk can be seen from a considerable distance, and when these larvae are very numerous the nests seem to dominate the trees.

Almost all **butterflies and moths** use silk to some extent in the construction of cocoons, or pupal cases. These are usually well camouflaged, but empty pupal cases still suspended by their silk are found.

Most moths pupate underground, but some pupate above ground and may use silk for protection. The Large Thorn spins a cover using leaves; the Puss-moth incorporates wood chips into the surface of the cocoon, and cuts its way out leaving the lid raised, revealing the silk interior. Six-spot Burnet Moths make papery cocoons attached to grass stems or twigs. Brown-tail Moth cocoons are made of loose silk and may enclose several pupae. The Emperor Moth also makes a cocoon entirely of silk, but uses two different types to

The caterpillars of a number of species devour plants as a group, anchored and sheltered by a web like structure. These Peacock Butterfly caterpillars on a Stinging Nettle are a good example.

Pupa of an Emperor Moth on the stems of heather (*Calluna vulgaris*), its preferred habitat.

Plants defoliated by the Brown Tail Moth: the web complexes contain the larvae.

make a soft outside and a harder internal layer. This can be seen on heaths or moorland, placed high in heather shoots where it is well protected against most small predators.

Some wasp-like insects also produce silken cocoons. Many of them are parasitic on caterpillars, which die at about the time that they would otherwise have pupated, and the full grown parasite larvae emerge and pupate round the dead skin of their host. The tiny brown silk pupae of *Apanteles* can sometimes be seen surrounding the remains of a Cabbage White Butterfly caterpillar, often on a fence post where the caterpillar has crawled to pupate. A similar parasite affects some adult ladybirds but the host does not necessarily die as the parasite emerges. A ladybird may occasionally be found with the pupa of the parasite attached to it.

Spiders' webs
There are many species of spider in Europe. These are often very difficult to identify, but their webs, which in sheltered places may last for long periods, are characteristic of the families to which they belong. The webs most frequently seen are the work of female spiders: the males are almost always smaller than their mates and in some cases do not build webs at all.

Orb webs made by Garden Cross Spiders and their relatives may be seen through most of Europe. They are generally placed across corridors between plants or in other similar spaces. A Y-shaped framework is the basis of the whole trap which, when complete, hangs from the first line. The spider may sit head down at the centre or at the end of a signal thread which is vibrated by any trapped insect.

Miscellaneous animal signs

Several sorts of silk are used in the construction of the web, not all of them sticky. This shows clearly in the webs of spiders belonging to the genus *Argiope*, which looks much like orb webs but in which there are two or more broad zig-zag bands of silk radiating from the centre. It is likely that these help to disguise the web and the spider in it, although the exact purpose is not certain.

Spiders of the genus *Zygiella* make webs which look like orb webs with two adjacent segments missing. From this area the signal thread runs to the spider's retreat.

Hyptiotes makes a snare which looks like about one-eighth of a complete orb web. It is usually hung among conifers and held under tension by the spider, which releases it with extra line when an insect blunders into the trap. The web springs back towards the fixed points at the far end, enmeshing the prey as it does so.

Whereas the orb web builders are all fairly large, the makers of another abundant web type are mostly tiny. These are the Money Spiders, which are responsible for the huge numbers of **hammock webs** which are mainly slung among grasses in the summer and in hedges later in the year. The common *Linyphia triangularis* lies in wait beneath her hammock and pulls through any insect which alights on the web.

Several species of spider enter houses, although it is only in sheds and uncared-for buildings that the webs are allowed to survive for long. The House Spider (*Tegenaria domestica*) needs humidity, so its web is not found in centrally heated rooms. It consists of a sheet of grey silk, generally in a corner; the spider usually lies hidden in a tube against the angle of the walls. The web is not sticky, but insects are caught with their legs trapped in the loose threads.

Pholcus, the Daddy-long-legs Spider, occurs in houses near the south coast of Britain and out of doors through much of western continental Europe. Its web is a fragile untidy tangle, insufficient to hold any substantial prey, but *Pholcus* uses it only to alert her: when it is shaken she throws silk over the prey from a safe distance. In this way large and strong insects such as wasps may be overcome and may be seen thoroughly trussed in silk hanging from the *Pholcus* web.

Many spiders live on outside walls or in crevices in bark. Several spiders of the genus *Ciniflo* make a web which looks like a fluffy mat of threads leading to a silk-lined hole. Spiders of the genus *Segestria* make a rather similar lair but with a series of fine radiating lines of silk spreading from it. The spider is alerted by the rapid vibrations of insects brushing against the web, but is not restricted to small prey, being a large spider which can cope with insects up to the size of a bee.

On slopes in dry or heathy land the web of *Amaurobius* spiders may be seen. This consists of a dense mat of threads surrounding a tunnel, up to 15cm long, among vegetation or even under stones and logs. Round the mouth of the tunnel the discarded husks of past meals may often be seen. In similar situations the curious traps of Purse-web Spiders (*Atypus* spp.) may be seen. These usually look like finger-sized roots either lying on or standing up from the ground; the silk is mixed with grains of soil which both strengthen and disguise it. What is visible is part of a closed tube up to 25cm long, most of which lines a hole excavated by the spider. *Atypus* bites through the silk and poisons any small creature which walks on to the tube, then cuts a slit

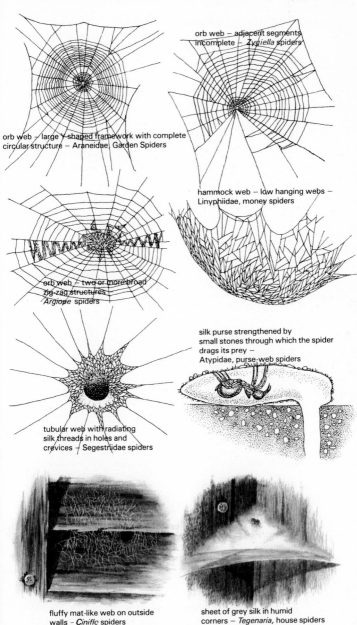

orb web – adjacent segments incomplete – *Zygiella* spiders

orb web – large Y-shaped framework with complete circular structure – Araneidae, Garden Spiders

hammock web – low hanging webs – Linyphiidae, money spiders

orb web – two or more broad zig-zag structures *Argiope* spiders

silk purse strengthened by small stones through which the spider drags its prey – Atypidae, purse-web spiders

tubular web with radiating silk threads in holes and crevices – Segestriidae spiders

fluffy mat-like web on outside walls – *Ciniflo* spiders

sheet of grey silk in humid corners – *Tegenaria*, house spiders in it through which the prey is drawn. The hole is mended at once, even before *Atypus* eats what it has caught. The southern European Trapdoor Spiders live in silk-lined crevices with hinged lids which, when closed, conceal the spiders perfectly.

Not all spiders make webs. Crab Spiders sit on flowers or foliage, which they usually match very closely in colour. They can often be detected from a distance because there is some damage to the petals or the edge of the leaf. A few thin strands of silk may lie across the flower, but the spider relies on surprise to snatch bees or flies before they can escape.

Jumping Spiders, which are often found on the walls of houses or fences, may lay down protective threads, which can be seen on the sides of buildings. They hunt by sight, leaping a distance of several centimetres on to their prey.

On the ground Wolf Spiders may often be seen, carrying a burden larger than their own abdomen: this silken bundle is an egg cocoon. Later they may be seen guarding a nursery nest containing over 100 young.

Many other spiders remain with their young, sometimes staying by them in densely woven shelters, or remaining nearby. In some the egg cocoons may be seen close to the normal web, as in the House Spider. In others, the eggs are encased in hard silk and attached to the underside of twigs or leaves, as with *Theridion*, whose cocoons at first sight look like tiny meringues, about 0.3cm in diameter, on the lower side of oak leaves.

Young spiders travel by releasing a long thread of silk, which on a fine warm day lifts them up in the ascending air currents. Sometimes the air seems full of the gossamer threads. This is an effective method of dispersal, and young spiders have been trapped thousands of feet above the ground in aerial plankton nets, while others have been recorded at very high levels in mountains. Most of them perish, but enough survive to continue the species.

Other insect homes

The longest-lived insects are large beetles which feed on dead wood as larvae, for growth using this un-nutritious substance requires a long period of feeding and lifespans in excess of 25 years have been recorded for some **Longhorn Beetle** grubs. These are not normally seen until they emerge from pupation in the wood, when exit holes ranging in size from about 0.1cm to over 1cm in width may be seen in European hardwoods and pines.

A number of species of beetle feed as larvae on the nutritious cambium layer underneath the bark of trees. Each beetle species has its own pattern of feeding and this may be seen when the tree dies and the bark falls off. After mating beneath the bark the female makes a burrow, aided by the male who helps to clean away the debris. This original tunnel is known as the mother tunnel and at intervals along it the female lays an egg. When these hatch the larvae begin to feed, making their tunnels at right angles to the original. In some cases they meander, although they never intersect another tunnel. In others they are straight, but the exit hole of the adult after pupation is at the furthest feeding point reached by the larva.

The female of many bee and wasp species provides for her young by stocking a nest with appropriate food. In the case of **wasps** this is always some kind of flesh, usually in the form of insects or spiders immobilized by a sting and placed in the nest, which is usually a burrow. These are found most commonly in sandy heathlands or dunes; however, it is impossible to identify the species from the burrow alone.

In heathland the small flask-shaped nests of **Potter Wasps** (*Eumenes*) may be seen. These are made of fine sand grains cemented by the insects' saliva and they contain a number of paralyzed caterpillars which are food for the grub. The **Heather Bee** (*Colletes*) digs a hole in heathland to make her nest and she provisions it with pollen for her grubs. Other digging bees include *Andrena* and *Halictis*, which are often called **mining bees**. They generally choose a light sandy soil for their nests, which are usually made in the spring, but some burrow into consolidated earth by the side of paths. The holes are about 0.5cm in diameter and are surrounded by the fine earth excavated by the bee; they may on occasion be very numerous. Each hole is the nest of a single individual.

The **Leaf-cutter Bee** cuts semicircles from stout leaves in the early summer and tries to find a suitable hollow for her nest. This consists of a column of cells made of the cut leaves, each containing one egg and some pollen. If a suitable hole is not available the bee will excavate one; the hole itself is insignificant, but there may be a considerable shower of sawdust below it.

Mason Bees burrow into soft mortar between bricks, mainly in old walls, and build wax combs in the cavities.

Truly social bees include the Bumble Bees and Honey Bee. **Bumble Bees**

Left: The gall-like mud nest of the Potter Wasp in a heather plant.

Below: Entrance to Dung Beetle hole in the ground. The entrance is distinct and surrounded by soil.

usually nest on the ground, taking over the nest of a Wood Mouse, the bedding of which the queen teases out as a basis for her wax comb. **Honey Bees** choose a large cavity for their nest. This may be any enclosed structure, such as a hollow tree, or the cavity wall of a house, for example. Honey Bee combs hang vertically and the cells open to one side. An old colony in a hollow tree may build combs down the side of the hole to a length of two or more metres. The entrance is likely to be quite inconspicuous, although during the summer time large numbers of bees may be seen entering and leaving the hole. If the colony is very long-lived and successful, surplus honey may seep out from the comb, staining the wall or tree and attracting many other insects.

Social **wasps** build their nests of paper, made of wood fragments chewed by the adults and mixed with saliva. Mated females are the only over-wintering survivors from a nest, however flourishing it may have been. These hibernate

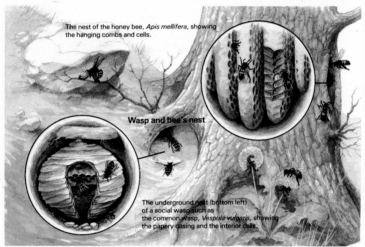

The nest of the honey bee, *Apis mellifera*, showing the hanging combs and cells.

Wasp and bee's nest

The underground nest (bottom left) of a social wasp such as the common wasp, *Vespula vulgaris*, showing the papery casing and the interior cells.

until mid-spring, when they look for suitable places for their nests. An early indication of a wasps' nest is scrape marks on dry wood, such as fence posts. Often the grooves made by the queen's mandibles show quite clearly.

Wasps' nests are made so that the comb lies horizontally and each cell opens downwards. A fairly large cavity is needed by the insects for this type of nest. A few live in holes in the ground, others in trees or even in buildings. Again, the entrances are unobtrusive and although sometimes nests are built in the open this is not common in northern Europe. Nests may be raided by a number of creatures for the grubs and sometimes fragments of papery material with beautifully precise hexagonal cells may be found. Wasps are themselves hunters, mainly of other insects, for larval wasps are fed on flesh, not pollen. Few signs can be definitely ascribed to wasp hunting, but if it catches a strong insect, or one which is too big to carry, the wasp will strip the wings off its prey. Mostly these will escape notice because of their small size, but butterfly wings are sometimes encountered.

All **ants** are completely social and their nests have a great degree of permanence. They vary greatly in size and location, some existing entirely underground or inside rotting logs. The **Red Wood Ant** builds the most conspicuous nest. It may be a metre high and three metres or more long, usually found in woodlands. The capping of pine needles and small pieces of twig acts as a thatch to shed rain and drips from the trees; and their paths may sometimes be traced for 100m away from the nest.

Almost any area of light sandy soil may be peppered with little holes, up to 0.5cm in diameter. Some are made by solitary bees or wasps, but others are made by **beetles**, particularly dung feeders. There are many species of these, and they share the habit of furnishing a deep burrow (in the case of the **Dor Beetle** up to 60cm deep) with the dung of herbivores. The soil is not carried away from the nest, so a high collar of sand remains round the entrance. This distinguishes a beetle hole from one dug by bees or wasps, in which the tip is more spread out. Even so, it will not survive a heavy shower of rain.

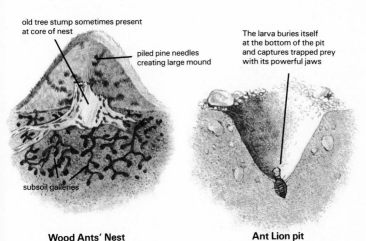

old tree stump sometimes present at core of nest

piled pine needles creating large mound

subsoil galleries

The larva buries itself at the bottom of the pit and captures trapped prey with its powerful jaws

Wood Ants' Nest

Ant Lion pit

Some holes are made by insect larvae, among them the **Tiger Beetle**. This insect makes a deep straight burrow in sandy soil, removing the grains so that there is no collar. The grub waits at the top of the hole to grab any passing insect; if alarmed it drops to the bottom of the tunnel, where it is safe. A few **moth** species also burrow for daytime concealment; small burrows in loose sand may belong to them.

The larvae of **Froghoppers** conceal themselves in a froth made of a sugary substance secreted from abdominal glands. In early summer small trees and herbaceous plants may be covered with the glistening white globs of froghopper froth.

Few insects make traps to catch their food, but the **Antlion,** which is quite common in southern Europe, does so. The larvae of these insects dig shallow pits in sandy places, burying themselves lightly at the bottom of the hole. The sides of the pit slope at an angle which is very near to the angle of rest of the sand grains, so when anything disturbs them, they roll to the bottom. When ants or other small insects step into the slope they roll to the bottom and are sucked dry by the Antlion.

Invertebrate feeding remains

Insect feeding remains vary greatly. In the case of defoliating larvae whole areas of woodland may be altered by their activity: frequently everything is blanketed in the droppings of the insects.

Most insects feed on a very narrow range of plant food, so identification of the plant can reveal the type of insect attacking it. Methods of feeding also vary: the larva of the **Chrysomelid Beetle** eat between the veins of the tough leaves of hogweed, while the **Figwort Weevil** larva merely sucks the soft tissue from between the upper and lower cuticles of the leaf, leaving withered brown patches over the plant.

Leaf miners, which are usually the tiny larvae of various moths, spend the whole of their early life within the thickness of a leaf; they excavate a meandering tunnel as they eat, and this widens with each moult.

Many larger caterpillars resemble their food plant in colour and pattern. One such is the caterpillar of the **Brimstone Butterfly**. This feeds on alder buckthorn or purging buckthorn, lying along the midrib of the leaf which it is eating. Starting at the tip of the leaf it moves backwards towards the twig, moving to a new leaf when its rear end touches the twig. Thus, when small it devours the whole leaf before its rear end touches the twig. As it grows this stimulus obviously comes earlier, so a buckthorn may show successive stages of leaf damage.

Although the feeding remains of carnivorous insects are rarely significant, there is an exception with **parasites of aphids**; the empty shell of the host remains attached to its food plant after the parasite has completed its growth and escaped.

Galls are formed when plant tissue is stimulated into abnormal growth by the presence of the eggs or larvae of various insects and mites. Galls vary in size: some are so tiny as to give a velvety feel to the back of beech leaves; oak apples may be several centimetres across. Oak trees are particularly affected by galls: in spring oak apples and redcurrant galls occur; later in the year there may be spangle galls on the leaves and a gall which causes a swelling of the acorn cup becomes apparent in the autumn.

The feeding signs of other invertebrates are sometimes easy to see, as with the destruction of soft foliage by **snails** or **slugs**. The slime trails left by these molluscs can be conspicuous, although very large populations may leave little trace on dense vegetation. Eggs of snails and slugs may be found buried in the ground, or sometimes in rotting wood. Slug eggs are generally soft while snail eggs have a parchment-like shell. The eggs of the Roman Snail are 0.2–0.3cm in diameter. The eggs of *Achatina*, a large African land snail sometimes imported into Europe as a pet or as exotic food, are over 1cm in length and have a hard, white shell.

Worm casts may be very abundant in pasture land. Some worms come to the surface at night and search for leaves which they pull into their holes. To this end the leaf is rolled about its midrib. Sometimes a leaf is too big to be pulled underground, or the worm is interrupted by the coming of daylight, so a rolled leaf, looking like a small cigar, is left standing out of a hole.

Luminescent signs

Luminous organisms are sometimes seen at night. Some fungi and bacteria are among these, and it is said that an owl may brush against a luminous fungus and give itself an eerie light; however, this is very unusual, and no

Marble gall neatly
pecked open by a woodpecker
to reach grub inside

land vertebrate is capable of producing light of its own. Several invertebrates may do so, however. The female **Glow Worm**, a wingless beetle, gives off a brilliant greenish light from the hind segments of her abdomen, and even the larva of this species has a faint light. The male has no luminous organ, but does have very large eyes and can see the light from a good distance away.

In southern Europe related species of **fireflies** are to be found. In these both male and female can fly, and the light is used in a kind of morse code signalling system between them. Sometimes large numbers of individuals synchronize their bright flashes.

Other luminous invertebrates include a worm in which the slime glows with a pale yellowish-green light. This is sometimes seen in rather damp places.

THE SEASHORE
The seashore is one of the richest and most varied of all environments, and the plants and animals which live there are all different from any found on land.

Tracks and trails on the shore
Footprints are often well preserved in sand (at least until the next high tide) and can indicate the presence of many animals which feed on the beach. These include **foxes**, particularly where there is a chance of stalking a duck or a seabird roosting above high water mark. The neat footprints sometimes reveal the search for stranded fishes or for refuse or carrion thrown up by the last high tide. **Otters** frequent the shore in some places, and although the animal itself is rarely seen, its tracks are distinctive. **Stoats** also forage on the beach and the **Lesser White-toothed Shrew** has taken to hunting for seaweed flies and sand-hoppers along the strand line in the Isles of Scilly.

If the shore has a band of dunes behind it the chances of finding interesting tracks are much enhanced, as dunes are usually ignored by holidaymakers and many rare animals flourish undisturbed. They include **lizards** and **snakes** and in some areas the **Natterjack Toad**, all of which leave distinctive tracks.

The dune fauna always includes **beetles**, and although their six-footed trail cannot be identified to species, they can give an idea of the size of the creature. In a beetle the legs are splayed widely on either side of the median line. As it runs it always maintains a three-point balance, so that while two feet (the first and the third) are in the air on one side of the body, on the other side two are on the ground and only one (the middle one) is moving

forwards. The track is a complex one, since the hinder of the two legs moving forwards reaches as far as the stationary leg, while on the other side the single leg in movement is set down just behind the front leg. This type of movement is typical of long-legged beetles such a carabids, or some of the hunting wasps which are found among the dunes. Other, narrower trails with the footprints more closely set are probably those of centipedes and millipedes; very light wider tracks are made by spiders and harvestmen.

Gulls and ducks often leave their web-footed prints in the lower sand. These are easily distinguished from the long-toed tracks of waders, in which the hind toe is absent, or the long four-toed track of a heron. The sprawling tracks of seals may sometimes be found coming up from the sea.

In rock pools the movements of various invertebrates may be traced. The tracks of crabs have a lacy look; although they walk sideways they travel in the direction of their long axis, and this must make their progress easier than if they were to travel broadside on.

The trails of periwinkles and top shells may be seen in the same places as the crabs. They consist of a groove in the sand or silt with small ridges of displaced material on either side.

Holes in shells and rock

On a rocky shore the presence of many animals such as limpets and barnacles is obvious. Other animals, however, may be hidden. Seashores from the Mediterranean to the Baltic which have outcrops of soft rock, such as chalk or limestone, may have these areas pitted with tiny holes, each about 0.2cm in diameter. These are the work of the Boring Sponge (*Clione celata*), which creates a network of tunnels filled with the sponge body, and this may project from some of them.

Holes about 1.2cm in diameter burrowed into soft rock, wood such as pier pilings, or peat on the shore is likely to be the work of the Common Piddock, although several related species of bivalve mollusc exist in European water. The Shipworm (*Teredo navalis*) and its close relatives bore only into wood; the deep holes which they make are lined with a hard calcareous secretion. The Shipworm may be seen in pier timbers, but is much more likely to occur in a baulk of wood which has been cast up on the shore. In some places circular grooves cut in rock indicate places where limpets once lived. These

Opposite: Tracks of a crab across rippled sand.

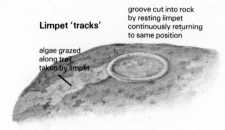

Limpet 'tracks'

algae grazed along trail taken by limpet

groove cut into rock by resting limpet continuously returning to same position

animals always return to exactly the same spot after feeding and on a soft rock their shells mark this position.

Many creatures burrow in sand, including the **Lugworm** (*Arenicola*), which makes a U-shaped tunnel. A slight depression marks the head end, where water is sucked into the tube to give food and oxygen to the worm; the other end is marked by a worm cast. Many bivalves lie hidden in the sand, but it is usually difficult to tell their exact location although a slight depression may show where some, such as the razor shells, lie. Soft-bodied worms may hide themselves under stones or in calcareous tubes, while others cement sand grains together to form a protective tube. These animals are very wary and so are rarely seen, but some, such as the **Peacock Worm** and *Lanice*, the **Sand Mason**, leave their armour standing above the surface of the seabed while they retreat to safer levels.

Growth signs on the beach

Shore arthropods, like their terrestrial counterparts, shed their skeleton-armour periodically. In many cases this is more substantial than that of their land-living relatives and may even be strengthened with calcium salts. **Cast crab shells** may often be found in vast numbers on the beach, while in rock pools the moulted skins of **shrimps** and **prawns** hang ghost-like in the water. Since all of the invertebrate animals of the beach are cold-blooded they are active and growing almost entirely in the summer time. This is reflected in various ways – many shells, for example, show signs of alternate rapid and slow growth as growth rings on the shell.

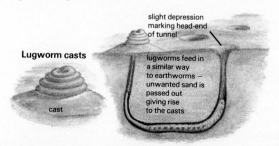

Lugworm casts

cast

slight depression marking head-end of tunnel

lugworms feed in a similar way to earthworms – unwanted sand is passed out giving rise to the casts

Miscellaneous animal signs

Feeding signs on the beach

Visitors such as **foxes** do great damage to nesting seabirds, killing more than they can possibly bury or use. There are also clear signs of the diet of many seashore animals. **Limpets** graze small algae from the rocks, clearing the area immediately round their home. The side to side swing of the limpet as it moves forward can be clearly seen in its curved, zig-zagging feeding pattern. Where the rock is soft the marks of the animal's horny teeth can be seen where they cut into the substrate.

On the open beach, holes made by the probing beaks of **waders** make vertical shafts from which small worms or molluscs have been taken. **Oyster-catchers** take cockles, hammering them open in order to extract the soft body of the mollusc. **Gulls** probe rather more untidily in the sand, sometimes finding a buried small crab, which is quickly broken up. If they find bivalves such as cockles, which they cannot open, they carry them to nearby rocks or roads and drop them to smash the shells. Piles of shattered shells indicate that gulls have been feeding in this way.

Carnivorous shore-dwelling **snails** rasp at their living food with a strong file-like tongue. The **Necklace Shell** (*Natica*) feeds beneath the sand on the huge numbers of bivalve molluscs which live there. The shell of a victim has a neat circular hole, through which the flesh has been extracted.

On sandy beaches **flat fishes** may remain in the shallow pools formed in depressions on the shore. Camouflaged to match their background perfectly, they are virtually invisible, but the small pits from which they have sucked mouthfuls of sand in order to extract anything edible remain to show where they have been.

The strand line

The strand line is the highest point on a beach at which matter has been abandoned by the waves until it is swept away by a higher tide. Apart from jetsam resulting from human activities, the strand line may be marked by dead shells and the remains of sublittoral and oceanic animals. Skeletons of seabirds and mammals, beautifully white from prolonged submersion in seawater, are often present. The bones of birds can usually be distinguished from those of mammals by their extreme lightness.

Occasionally individual **whale bones** are washed up on the beach. Although many large species of cetaceans are recorded from European waters, bones of smaller species such as the **Pilot Whale** are more likely, as this animal is particularly prone to beaching itself.

The bones of most fishes are small and do not survive the pounding of the waves for long. An exception to this is the bone carrying the pharyngeal teeth

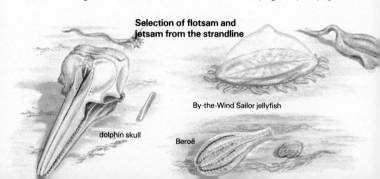

Selection of flotsam and jetsam from the strandline

By-the-Wind Sailor jellyfish

dolphin skull

Beroë

Large flock of Oystercatchers by the water edge.

of **wrasse**, and these small crushing teeth which lie at the entrance to the gullet are often picked up even though the rest of the skeleton has disappeared. **Sharks' vertebrae** are prized in some parts of the world, but they are rarely found round the coasts of Europe. However, the articular ends of the vertebrae of basking sharks occasionally become detached from the bone and are washed ashore.

Other curiosities include the remains of oceanic creatures swept in by the wind. The **By-the-wind Sailor**, a small relative of the notorious Portuguese Man o' War, is one. Like its cousin, which can give a painful sting (even when apparently dead) it has sting cells, but these cannot penetrate the human skin. Some inhabitants of the open ocean are so fragile that if cast up on the beach they collapse in the air, as the support of the water is withdrawn. Patches of clear jelly about 8cm across may be all that remain of the planktonic **comb jelly** *Beroë*; similar but larger patches are likely to be the remains of true jellyfish.

Many marine animals come into shallow water to breed, and their egg cases are often found on the beach. **Dogfish** and **skate** egg cases, each of which holds a single large-yolked egg, are often washed up after they have hatched. Due to their box-like shape they are known as **Mermaids' Purses**. The egg cases of **whelks** are common; the apple-pip-sized eggs of the **Dog Whelk** may be seen on the middle shore in spring.

Many **sea-slugs** lay their eggs in rock pools. Often these look like balls or whorls of jelly in which thousands of tiny dots can be seen, each one an egg. Occasionally a stiff collar-shaped object, rough with sand grains, is found. This is the egg case of the **Necklace Shell**.

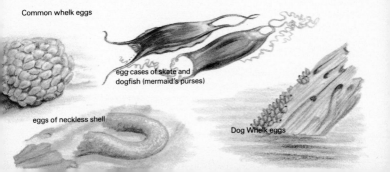

Common whelk eggs

egg cases of skate and dogfish (mermaid's purses)

eggs of neckless shell

Dog Whelk eggs

Field techniques

Each naturalist has to develop his or her own routines for field work. It is important to be systematic, however, and this chapter outlines a recording routine and looks at some established methods of studying tracks and signs.

Notebooks

There is no substitute for a well kept notebook, both as an immediate record for the naturalist and, over the years, as a systematic account of observations. When a track or other sign is to be recorded the surrounding area should be examined for further evidence of activity. If a trail is found it should be drawn to scale in the notebook before individual tracks are examined. A note should be taken of the exact location (using the appropriate national grid reference system), and of habitat, surface conditions, weather, date and time of day. Any other signs such as droppings, shed fur or feeding signs should be described and drawn or photographed before you disturb the site. Each track should be drawn to scale unless you are going to make a plaster cast.

Plaster casts

Although it is a time-consuming process, taking plaster casts provides the best permanent record of tracks. Some surfaces, such as snow or wet mud, may show good clear prints but they are not suitable for casting since the weight and heat given off by the material will severely distort the tracks. Before making a cast of a track it is always advisable to draw it.

Select a representative track and enclose it with a suitable liquid-tight container. Simple cardboard or wooden frames work well, provided they are liquid-tight. An alternative is to use a shallow plastic flower pot with the bottom removed. Place this over the track with the wide side down so that the plaster cast can be pushed out without pressure on the moulded surface. The casting mixture should be made from surgical or dental plaster. Add the powder to water in a suitable container and gently mix to a thin creamy consistency. Mix enough to cover the track and give a thickness of 1.5 to 2cm above. Once the plaster is poured, tap the edges of the frame to dislodge air bubbles. Leave the cast to set for at least 15 minutes, checking the hardening process by waiting for the plaster to warm up and then go cold (exothermic reaction).

Once completely cold, lift the cast, roughly clean it taking care not to damage details of the print, and wrap it in an absorbent material such as newspaper for transporting. It can then be properly cleaned under running water, labelled and picked out with paint if required.

Tracks of small mammals may also be collected on smoked glass placed in front of a known inhabited home, but definition is poor.

Measuring tracks and trails

The overall length and overall width of each track must be carefully measured. In tracks with pads the length should be measured with and without claws. Similarly the distance from the toe tip to the back of the interdigital pad must be measured if there are proximal pads.

In tracks with cleaves measure the splay (the distance between the tips of the cleaves) and the length of the toe pad and sole. Measure the overall length of tracks with only the two main cleaves, and measure separately the distance including dew claws if present.

In bird tracks the length of the centre toe print helps with identification between species having morphologically similar tracks, but which are of different sizes (e.g. swans).

Trails should be drawn and the following measurements taken. The *stride* is the distance between the front of one track to the front of the next track made by the same foot. The *straddle* is the distance between the tracks from left and right feet perpendicular to the median line. The *inclination* of the tracks (the angle made by a line through the centre of a track towards or away from the median line) is very useful in interpreting both species and gait.

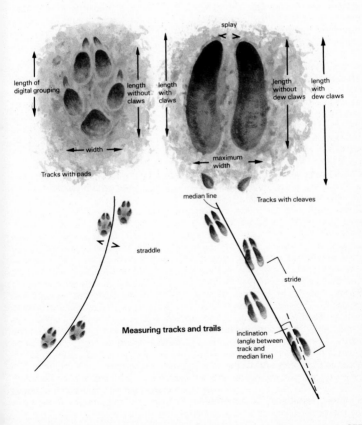

Measuring tracks and trails

277

Field techniques

Collecting and preserving material

Skeletal material Bones may be recovered from carcases in open country, the remains of kills outside carnivore dens, in carnivorous and scavenging bird pellets and in the droppings of carnivorous mammals. The best way of defleshing carcases is to bury them a few centimetres down in well drained soil, checking them every three weeks until they are clean. Methods of preparing bones in the laboratory are described in detail in a number of works listed in the bibliography (page 313). Bones which are already clean can be prepared quite easily by dilute bleaching. Skulls and jaws, even in a fragmentary form, can be used to identify many species of mammal. Label all bones before storing.

Plant remains Only hard parts of plants which show evidence of animal activity need be collected. These include bark and wood which has been gnawed or chewed and nuts and cones which have been opened in a particular way. Obviously only small items can be collected, but little preparation is required for this sort of material: simply dry it gently in a warm atmosphere. It can then be mounted on card and labelled.

Pellets and droppings Owl pellets and some carnivore droppings contain bones. In the latter case bones are fragmented and can only be used along with fur and feather remains to obtain an approximate idea of the prey. The digestive processes of owls are relatively gentle and entire skulls are common. In hawk pellets the remains are less complete.

The bones and hard parts can be removed from pellets by teasing. One method is to soak them in water in a shallow white dish and tease the bones out when the fur and feathers are softened. However, this can be unpleasant with older decomposing pellets, and you may prefer to tease the pellets out in alcohol: this has the advantage of cleaning the bones as well as reducing the odour. In addition to providing bones, pellets are useful in their own right for identifying the bird species which produced them. The only effective way of keeping a permanent record of whole pellets and droppings is by photographing them.

Grooming signs Fur, hair and feather can easily be kept by taping to card and labelling. Sloughed reptile skins and instar skins from invertebrates should be kept in airtight containers.

Photography Many modern cameras can be used to effect in relatively unskilled hands. It is often difficult to photograph tracks since the contrast is poor and the background is dark, so it is important to make sure there is enough light. If track shots are taken for reference purposes they must be truly vertical and a scale bar must be included. Photographs of signs, such as droppings, pellets and feeding remains, which cannot be stored, are valuable provided they are properly documented and always scaled in some way.

Sound recording Sophisticated sound recording apparatus enables the trained observer to collect a range of sound signs which are often not audible to the human ear or are too unfamiliar to recognize amongst general noise in the country. Such apparatus is expensive and this type of recording is the field of specialists. However, a small portable tape recorder taken to the same place at different times of day and in different seasons can be used to record an enormous range of sound. This is a useful exercise since it trains one to listen more carefully. It is quite surprising how loud and distinctive some sounds are. Once heard, sounds such as a badger scratching, hedgehog claws on a hard surface or fox calls in the night are never forgotten.

Skulls

It is not possible to include all of the diagnostic long and innominate bones of every mammal, let alone every vertebrate, in Europe. Attention is therefore focused on the skulls since partial skulls or even teeth (in mammals) can be used to identify species. The characteristics of the main groups of skulls are identified here and fuller descriptions of representative bird skulls follow; finally mammal skulls are described and illustrated in detail.

MAIN GROUPS OF VERTEBRATE SKULLS

MAMMAL
Teeth present,
different in shape.

FROG
Teeth present, similar
in shape; very small, in
upper jaw only.

LIZARD
Teeth present, similar
in shape; conical
(peg-like) in shape.

TOAD
Teeth absent; simple
unpointed tips on jaws.

TORTOISE/TERRAPIN
Teeth absent; point
on front of lower
and upper jaws.

SNAKE
Teeth present, similar
in shape; sharp and
pointing backwards.

BIRD
Teeth absent;
beak present.

Rarely, complete skulls are found, particularly in owl pellets. The following diagrams are sufficiently detailed to enable identification to be made from partial skulls, denteries or even teeth in some cases. Teeth cusp patterns can be used to identify many small carnivores, insectivores and rodents.

BIRD SKULLS

There is considerable variation in the morphology of bird skulls, particularly in the beak and beak sheath (outer chitin covering). The differences reflect adaptation to diet and habitat. With over 350 resident species in Europe alone it is possible to show only a selection of skulls which illustrate the range in structure and function.

The descriptions concentrate on obvious diagnostic characteristics rather than detailed anatomical keying. The examples shown were all collected from dead 'finds' in the field and are drawn in that condition rather than as text book specimens.

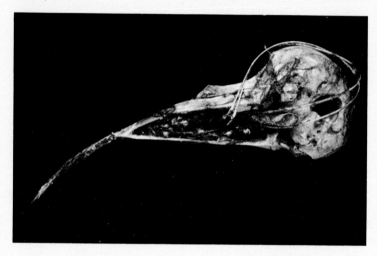

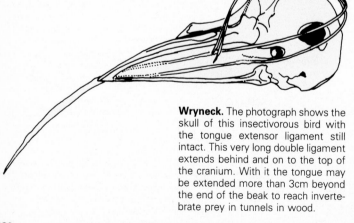

Wryneck. The photograph shows the skull of this insectivorous bird with the tongue extensor ligament still intact. This very long double ligament extends behind and on to the top of the cranium. With it the tongue may be extended more than 3cm beyond the end of the beak to reach inverte-brate prey in tunnels in wood.

Examples of bird skulls

House Sparrow
Small, 2.6cm. Thick, somewhat conical bill; slender cheek bone; feeds mainly on cereals, young plants, fruit, earthworms and insects.

Finch
Small, 3cm. Bill varies with species, but is generally strong, swollen at the base and conical in shape. Hawfinches have very heavy bills and strong muscular attachments as evidenced by the heavy cheek bones.

The finches' bills are adapted for crushing and extracting hard seeds.

Starling
Medium, 4.7cm. The bill is long and robust, but like the rest of the skull shows no special adaptations. Omnivorous species taking insects, but preferring cultivated fruits and seeds.

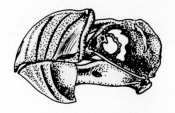

Puffin
Medium, 5.3cm. The bill, which is used as a weapon, digging tool and display feature, is very large and laterally compressed. With the brightly coloured sheath intact it is much deeper than the skull. Cranial area very small. Underwater feeder, taking small fish, molluscs and other marine organisms.

Curlew
Large, 11cm. The bill is distinctive, being extremely long and decurved

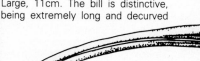

and often 80% of the skull length. The bill is adapted to search for deeper mud living invertebrates.

Barn Owl
Medium, 4.8 cm. The bill is triangular,

hooked and very robust as in all carnivorous species. The cranium is large and the orbits are extremely large and located on the front of the skull. The bill is designed for tearing the flesh of small mammals and birds on which the owl feeds.

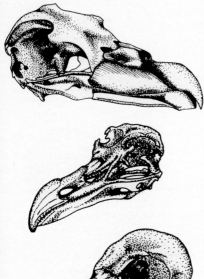

Fulmer Petrel
Medium, 6.7cm. The bill is hooked and broad with a system of filtering lamellae, forming tube nostrils. The skull is elongated. This is a scavenging species feeding on floating refuse and carcases as well as crustaceans and squid.

Greater Black-backed Gull
Large, 10.6cm. The bill is long, robust and hooked, especially with sheath intact. There are deep salt gland depressions above the orbital areas. The gulls are opportunist feeders, although they are adapted to removing shell fish from mud flats. This species feeds on a wide range including fish, reptiles, crutaceans and insects.

Carrion Crow
Medium, 5cm. The bill is robust, pointed, slightly hooked and often retains the fringe of feathers at the base long after the flesh has rotted off. As with all the crows this species is omnivorous, taking small mammals, young birds, eggs, frogs, molluscs, insects and vegetable matter.

Shag
Large, 12cm. The bill is cylindrical in section, long and has a pronounced hook at the tip. It is more slender than in cormorants. Skull elongated, orbits small and enclosed. Feeds mainly on fish taken below water.

Mallard
Large, 10.7cm. Bill robust, semi-circular in section, flattened on the underside and laterally extended. There are internal crenellations on the edges of the mandibles. Bill of ducks is generally designed to filter mud for food, but the diet is varied and the Mallard feeds on water and land plants, berries, grain, insects, molluscs and crustaceans.

TYPES OF MAMMAL SKULLS

The main types of mammal skulls are described and illustrated below. Page numbers refer to the sections dealing with the skulls of individual species.

INCISORS SEPARATED FROM CHEEK TEETH BY A GAP

Rodentia
One pair of incisors in upper jaw
(page 298)

Lagomorpha
Two pairs of incisors in upper jaw
(page 297)

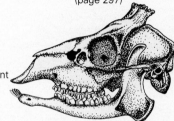

Artiodactyla
Pedicles in Male. Orbit prominent
and nearly circular (page 305)

INCISORS NOT SEPARATED FROM CHEEK TEETH BY A GAP

Carnivora
Large cranium; differentiated teeth
(page 290)

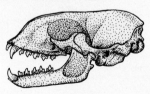

Pinnipedia
Large cranium; rostrum short,
bullae large (page 295)

Insectivora
Small cranium. Elongated facial
bones (page 284)

Chiroptera
Upper incisors or canines separated
by deep rounded concavity
(page 286)

Mammal skulls

ORDER INSECTIVORA

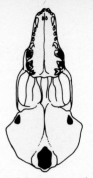

Family Soricidae (shrews)
Zygomatic arches absent; length of skull less than 2.8cm; tympanic bullae absent; mandible less than 1.5cm.

TEETH TIPPED WITH RED

Neomys species: 4 upper unicuspids; lower incisors without lobes on upper margins.

Sorex species: 5 upper unicuspids; lower incisors with 3 lobes on upper margins.

Sorex minutus Pygmy Shrew Similar to *S. minutissimus* but 1st upper unicuspid equal to 2nd.

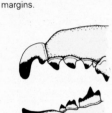

Neomys fodiens Northern Water Shrew
Lachrymal foramen over posterior part of 1st molar.

Sorex alpinus Alpine Shrew
Fifth upper unicuspid equal to 4th in profile, larger in crown view; 2nd lower tooth 2-cusped.

Sorex sinalis (*S. isodon*) Dusky Shrew
Fifth upper unicuspid smaller than 4th in profile, not larger than 4th in crown view; 2nd lower tooth 1-cusped; 3rd upper unicuspid smaller than 2nd; area of 1st upper unicuspid equal to 4 times the area of the 5th upper unicuspid.

Neomys anomalus Southern Water Shrew, Miller's Water Shrew
Lachrymal foramen over division between 1st and 2nd molars.

Sorex minutissimus Least Shrew
Fifth upper unicuspid smaller than 4th in profile; not larger in crown view; 2nd lower tooth single cusped; 3rd upper unicuspid as large as or larger than 2nd; 1st upper unicuspid larger than 2nd.

Sorex caecutiens Laxmann's Shrew
Similar to *S. isodon* but area of 1st upper unicuspid equal to 5 times the area of the 5th.

Sorex araneus Common Shrew
Similar to *S. isodon* but area of 1st upper unicuspid equal to 7 times the area of the 5th.

TEETH ENTIRELY WHITE

Suncus etruscus Lesser Pygmy Shrew
4 upper unicuspids; skull less than 1.4cm long; mandible less than 0.75cm.

Crocidura species: 3 upper unicuspids; skull more than 1.5cm long; mandible over 0.8cm.

Crocidura suaveolens Lesser White-toothed Shrew
Similar to *C. russula* but greatest length of skull usually less than 1.85cm; length of mandible usually less than 1cm.

Crocidura leucodon Bi-coloured White-toothed Shrew
Row of upper unicuspids short; distance between 1st incisor and large premolar at the root cavities equal to depth of rostrum; maximum length of skull 2.05cm.

Crocidura russula Greater White-toothed Shrew
Row of upper unicuspids long; distance between 1st incisor and premolar at root cavities at least 20% more than depth of rostrum in front of premolar; greatest length of skull over 1.85cm; length of mandible usually over 1cm.

Family Talpidae (moles)
Zygomatic arches present; tympanic bullae present; 11 upper and 11 lower teeth on each side; length of skull over 2.5cm; mandible between 1.3 and 2.5cm; skull widest across the auditory region.

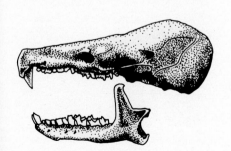

Galemys pyrenaicus
Pyrenean Desman
Upper incisor very large and canine-like; 1st and 2nd lower incisors large and followed by 6 smaller unicuspids.

Talpa species (moles): upper canines large and dominant; lower incisors and canines small; 4th lower tooth (i.e. 1st premolar) dominant and canine-like.

285

Mammal skulls

Talpa europaea Northern Mole
Length of skull over 3.25cm; mandible over 2.05cm and usually over 2.15cm; 1.1–1.3cm across cheek bones; upper incisors form a U and the largest (1st) is less than twice the size of the smallest (3rd).

Talpa caeca Blind Mole
Length of skull under 3.25cm; mandible under 2.15cm and usually less than 2.05cm; as for *T. europaea* but upper incisors form a V shape and the 1st is more than twice the size of the third.

Talpa romana Roman Mole
Skull 1.35–1.5cm wide across cheek bones.

Family Erinacidae (hedgehogs)
Tympanic bullae incomplete; 10 upper teeth and 8 lower teeth on each side; mandible over 3cm; skull widest across the zygomatic arches.

Erinaceus europaeus Western Hedgehog
Sagittal crest extending forwards only to the posterior end of the frontal bones; 3rd upper incisor with a single root.

Erinaceus algirus Algerian Hedgehog
Sagittal crest extending forwards to the centre of the frontal bones; 3rd upper incisor with 2 roots.

ORDER CHIROPTERA
The identification of bat skulls is based on dentition (the number and arrangement of the teeth), formulae for which are given in the following descriptions. The dentition of the bats is not dissimilar to that of the carnivores and the general skull shape is also similar. However, the bones in bat skulls are very thin and the largest bat skull in Europe is smaller than that of the smallest carnivore (the Weasel). In addition entire bat skulls may be easily recognized by a deep rounded concavity which separates the upper incisors. The rhinolophid (horseshoe) bats have bulbous projections behind the cavity. The zygomatic arch is long and slender and attaches to a conspicuous tympanic bulla. Size range in the skulls of European species is from less than 1.4cm to 2.3cm or more.

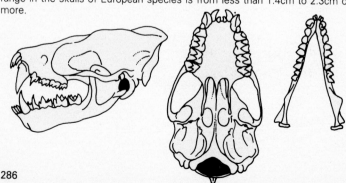

Family Rhinolophidae (horseshoe bats)

Rhinolophus species: two bulbous projections on top of skull behind nasal cavity. Dental formula: upper teeth – 1 incisor, 1 canine, 2 premolars, 3 molars; lower teeth – 2 incisors, 1 canine, 3 premolars, 3 molars; total number of teeth 32.

Rhinolophus ferrum-equinum

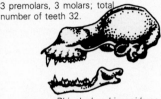

Rhinolophus hipposideros

Rhinolophus mehelyi

Family Molossidae (free-tailed bats)

Tadaria teniotis European Free-tailed Bat Bulbous projections absent. Dental formula: upper teeth – 1 incisor, 1 canine, 2 premolars, 3 molars; lower teeth – 3 incisors, 1 canine, 2 premolars, 3 molars; total 32.

Family Vespertilionidae

Vespertilio murinus Parti-coloured Bat
Total length of skull less than 1.7cm. Dental formula: upper teeth – 2 incisors, 1 canine, 1 premolar, 3 molars; lower teeth – 3 incisors, 1 canine, 2 premolars, 3 molars; total 32.

Eptisicus nilssoni Northern Bat
Total length of skull greater than 1.7cm. Dental formula as for *Vespertilio murinus*

Eptisicus serotinus Serotine Skull less than 1.7cm long; zygomatic arch expanded, cranial crest prominent at back; auditory bullae small; 1st upper incisor long, strongly bifid, twice as long as third upper incisor.

Mammal skulls

PROFILE OF SKULL
STRAIGHT AND ANGULAR

Nyctalus species: dental formula: upper teeth – 2 incisors, 1 canine, 2 premolars, 3 molars; lower teeth – 3 incisors, 1 canine, 2 premolars, 3 molars; total 34.

Nyctalus lasiopterus Greater Noctule
Total length of skull over 2cm.

Nyctalus noctula Noctule
Total length of skull between 1.8cm and 2cm.

Nyctalus leisleri Leisler's Bat
Total length of skull 1.7cm or less.

PROFILE OF SKULL
ROUNDED AT CRANIUM
AND CONVEX AT ROSTRUM

Pipistrellus species: 1st premolar easily visible in lateral view; incisors not equal in size. Dental formula as for *Nyctalus* species.

Barbastella barbastellus Barbastelle
Skull profile rounded at cranium and convex at rostrum; 1st premolar not visible in lateral view; incisors approximately equal in size. Dental formula as for *Nyctalus* species.

Pipistrellus savii Savi's Pipistrelle
Third incisor approximately two-thirds size of 2nd.

Pipistrellus kuhli Kuhl's Pipistrelle
Third incisor approximately half size of 2nd.

Pipistrellus pipistrellus Common Pipistrelle
First upper premolar small, partly concealed by the canine.

Pipistrellus nathusii Nathusius's Pipistrelle
First upper premolar not concealed by the canine.

Miniopterus schreibersi Schreiber's Bat
Profile of skull with prominent bulbous mound in mid-cranium. Dental formula: as for *Plecotus* species.

Plecotus species: profile of skull without prominent mound in mid-cranium. Dental formula: upper teeth – 2 incisors, 1 canine, 2 premolars, 3 molars; lower teeth – 3 incisors, 1 canine, 3 premolars, 3 molars; total 36.

Plecotus austriacus Grey Long-eared Bat
Total length of skull over 1.7cm.

Plecotus auritus Common Long-eared Bat
Total length of skull less than 1.7cm.

PROFILE OF ROSTRUM
DEEPLY CONCAVE

PROFILE OF ROSTRUM
WITH SHALLOW DEPRESSION

Myotis species: dental formula: upper teeth – 2 incisors, 1 canine, 3 premolars, 3 molars; lower teeth – 3 incisors, 1 canine, 3 premolars, 3 molars.

Myotis blythi Lesser Mouse-eared Bat
Total length of skull over 2.1cm.

Myotis mystacinus Whiskered Bat
Total length of skull less than 1.4cm.

Myotis emarginatus Geoffroy's Bat
Front of rostrum turning up.

Myotis nattereri Natterer's Bat
Total length of skull 1.5–1.6cm.

Myotis brandti Brandt's Bat
Similar to *M. mystacinus* but with an additional cusp on the 3rd upper premolar.

Myotis capaccinii Long-fingered Bat
Rostrum relatively short from zygomatic arch to front of premaxilla; front of rostrum turning up.

Myotis daubentoni Daubenton's Bat
Total length of skull 1.4–1.5cm.

Myotis bechsteini Bechstein's Bat
Skull larger than Natterer's, relatively narrow; cranial ridges prominent, bullae large; 1st premolar larger than second.

Myotis myotis Greater Mouse-eared Front of rostrum turning up; total length of skull over 2.3cm.

Mammal skulls

ORDER CARNIVORA
The skulls of this Order may be divided into two major groups according to whether a bony septum dividing the auditory bullae is present or absent (see table below). They can be further differentiated by the presence or absence of the alisphenoid canal.

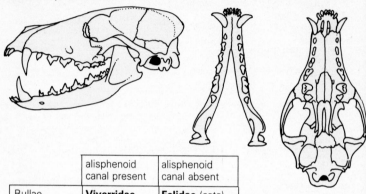

	alisphenoid canal present	alisphenoid canal absent
Bullae divided – Superfamily Feloidea	**Viverridae** (Mongoose and Genet)	**Felidae** (cats)
Bullae not divided – Superfamily Canoidea	**Canidae** (dogs and foxes) **Ursidae** (bears)	**Procyonidae** (Raccoon) **Mustelidae** (Mustelids)

Family Viverridae

Herpestes ichneumon Mongoose
Orbit completely or almost completely encircled with bone, forming post-orbital bar; bony palate reaching far beyond posterior molars and post-glenoid processes, projecting beyond level of glenoids; rostrum parallel-sided; *occurs in Spain only.*

Genetta genetta Genet
Orbit not encircled with bony ring but widely open; bony palate not reaching beyond posterior molar and post-pterygoid processes just extending to the level of the glenoid; rostrum long, slender and tapering.

Family Felidae

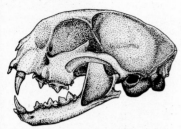 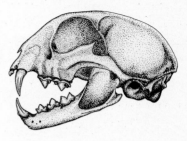

Felis sylvestris European Wild Cat
Condylobasal length less than 12cm; dental formula: upper teeth – 3 incisors, 1 canine, 3 premolars, 1 molar; lower teeth – 3 incisors, 1 canine, 2 premolars, 1 molar; total 30.

Felis lynx Lynx
Condylobasal length greater than 12cm; dental formula: upper teeth – 3 incisors, 1 canine, 2 premolars, 1 molar; lower teeth – 3 incisors, 1 canine, 2 premolars, 1 molar; total 28.

Family Ursidae (Bears)
First and 3rd upper premolars very small and single-rooted; 2nd premolar usually absent; carnassial (1st molar) flattened and tuberculate.

Ursus arctos Brown Bear
Second upper molar approximately twice as large as 1st, combined length equal to width of palate.

Thalarctos maritimus Polar Bear
Second upper molar approximately equal in size to 1st, combined length much less than width of palate.

Family Canidae (dogs and foxes)
Second and 3rd upper premolars double-rooted; carnassial adapted for cutting.

Canis species (dogs): region of post-orbital processes elevated; post-orbital processes strongly convex above.

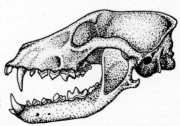

Canis aureus Jackal
Condylobasal length less than 18cm; cingulum on outer margin of 1st upper molar broad and conspicuous.

Mammal skulls

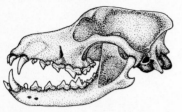

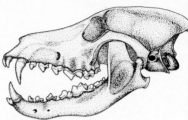

Canis familiaris Domestic Dog
Rostrum concave in front of orbit, not elongated as in Wolf; sagittal crest small, not extending to condyls; extremely variable due to variety of breeds.

Canis lupus Wolf
Condylobasal length greater than 18cm; cingulum on outer margin of 1st upper molar narrow and inconspicuous.

Nyctereutes procyonoides Raccoon Dog
Region of post-orbital processes not elevated; post-orbital processes not markedly convex above; upper tooth row less than half length of skull; 'false angle' in front of angular process.

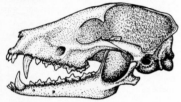

Foxes
Upper tooth row greater than half length of skull; no abrupt convexity anterior to angular process of dentary.

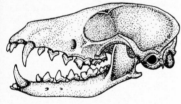

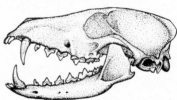

Alopex lagopus Arctic Fox
Frontal sinuses enlarged with consequent local expansion of skull; in apical view with jaws closed upper canine fails to reach lower end of jaw symphysis; 3rd upper incisor bearing on large lingual cingulum which often carries small tubercles.

Vulpes vulpes Red Fox
Skull not greatly expanded in region of frontal sinuses; in apical view with jaws closed the tip of the upper canine reaches or just fails to reach the lower end of the jaw symphysis; 3rd upper incisor with a weak or absent cingulum.

Family Procyonidae

Procyon lotor Raccoon
Upper cheek teeth 6, 2 upper molars; length of palate nearly two-thirds length of skull.

Family Mustelidae

Upper cheek teeth less than 6, 1 upper molar; length of palate half of or less than half of length of skull.

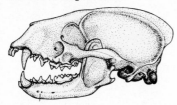

Meles meles Badger
Condylobasal length over 10cm; upper molar much larger than preceding premolar, not elongate; 1st lower molar low-crowned; 4 upper premolars.

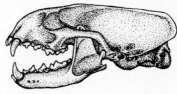

Lutra lutra Otter
Post-orbital constriction narrow, one-fifth or less of zygomatic width; sagittal crest not projecting beyond occiput.

Gulo gulo Wolverine
Upper molar equal to or smaller than preceding premolar, transversely elongate; 1st lower molar at least partially adapted for cutting; post-orbital constriction wide, one-third of zygomatic width; sagittal crest forming posterior projection above occiput; 4 upper and lower premolars.

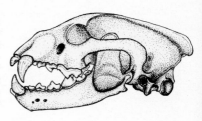

Martes species (martens): condylobasal length less than 9cm; 5 upper cheek teeth, 4 upper and lower premolars.

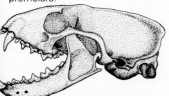

Martes martes Pine Marten
Distance between the bullae in the region of the carotid foramina is more than half the length of the bulla from its anterior end to the para-occipital process; length of bulla greater than the distance between the external edges of the jugular foramen.

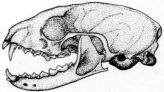

Martes foina Beech Marten
Length of the bulla is less than or (occasionally) equal to the distance between the external edges of the jugular foramen.

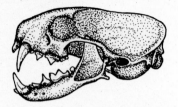

Vormela peregusna Marbled Polecat
Four upper cheek teeth, 3 upper and lower premolars; posterior process of pterygoid makes contact with the bulla; lower carnassial with accessory cusps on inner side of principal cusp.

Mustela species: posterior process of pterygoid does not make contact with bulla; lower carnassial lacking additional cusp.

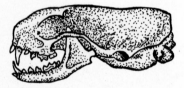

Mustela nivalis Weasel
Inner margins of auditory bullae running almost parallel, somewhat elliptical in shape; transverse diameter of infra-orbital foramen equal to longitudinal diameter of canine alveolus.

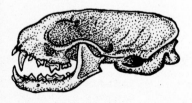

Mustela erminea Stoat
Similar to *M. nivalis* (above but transverse diameter of infra-orbital foramen is considerably larger than the longitudinal diameter of the canine alveolus.

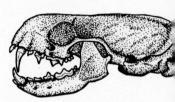

Mustela vison American Mink
Inner margins of auditory bullae not parallel, angular in shape; lower lip of auditory meatus expanded, in ventral view obscures roof of meatus; mastoid width half of condylobasal length.

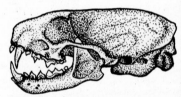

Mustela lutreola European Mink
Inner margins of auditory bullae not parallel, angular in shape; lower lip of auditory meatus not expanded and does not obscure roof of meatus; mastoid width less than half condylobasal length.

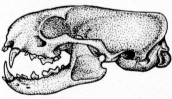

Mustela putorius European Polecat
Inner margins of auditory bullae not parallel, angular in shape; mastoid width over half condylobasal length; post-orbital region tapers gently to its junction with the braincase proper forming a constriction about one-quarter of the condylobasal length.

Mustela eversmanni Steppe Polecat
Inner margins of auditory bullae not parallel, angular in shape; mastoid width over half condylobasal length; post-orbital region tapers strongly towards the back at the same angle as the braincase tapers towards the front, forming a constriction about one-fifth of condylobasal length.

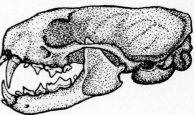

ORDER PINNIPEDIA

The skulls of the eight European representatives of this order are characterized by the very large cranium, constricted inter-orbital region, short snout and the absence of the lachrymal bone.

Family Odobenidae

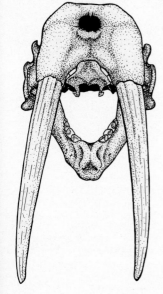

Family Phocidae (earless, true seals)
Nasal bones lengthened at rear between frontals; inflated, thin-walled tympanic bullae present; mastoid processes smaller than in Walrus; alisphenoid canal absent; canines in upper jaw remain small.

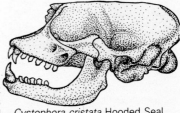

Odobenus rosmarus (Walrus)
The entire maxilla in front of each orbit houses the roots of the enormous canines, which develop into tusks; small tympanic bullae, alisphenoid canal and large mastoid processes present; bullae relatively thick-walled and flattened.

Cystophora cristata Hooded Seal
Two upper incisors and 1 lower in each side; premaxilla clearly does not reach nasals.

295

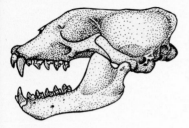

Monachus monachus Monk Seal
Two upper and 2 lower incisors on each side; premaxilla clearly reaches nasals.

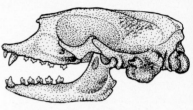

Pagophilus groenlandicus Harp Seal
Three upper incisors; jugal bone long and narrow, depth less than half of length; bony septum reaches or nearly reaches rear edge of bony palate; rear edge of palate forms a more or less straight line or shallow double arch.

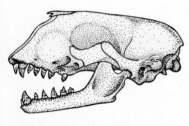

Halichoerus grypus Grey Seal
Three upper incisors; profile of nasals, frontals and parietals form a straight line.

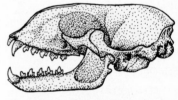

Phoca vitulina Common Seal
Three upper incisors; bony septum does not reach rear edge of bony palate; rear edge of palate forms a high arch, usually pointed at the top; nasal bones short and broad; teeth large; infra-orbital foramen small, its diameter one-third to two-thirds that of the root cavity of the upper canine.

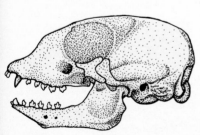

Erignathus barbatus Bearded Seal
Three upper incisors; profile of nasals, frontals and parietals convex; jugal bone short and deep, depth not less than half of length.

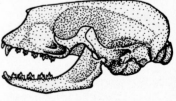

Phoca hispida Ringed Seal
Three upper incisors; bony septum and rear edge of palate as for *P. vitulina*; nasals longer and narrower; teeth small; infra-orbital foramen well developed, approximately equal in diameter to the root cavity of the upper canine.

ORDER LAGOMORPHA AND ORDER RODENTIA

Zygomatic arch large and complete; nasal cavities long; canines completely absent; palate narrow; diastema long. Post-orbital processes are absent and in some skulls there is an infra-orbital foramen. Incisors have open roots and wear to a chisel shape; molars are with cusps or ridges and may have open or closed roots; premolars reduced in number or completely absent.

ORDER LAGOMORPHA

Two pairs of upper incisors.

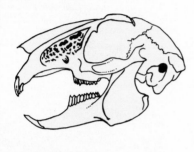

Family Leporidae (rabbits and hares)

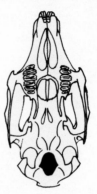

Oryctolagus cuniculus Wild Rabbit
Distinct suture between supra-occipital and inter-parietal bones; length less than 8.6cm; internal nares narrower than palatal bridge.

Lepus species (hares)
No distinct suture between supra-occipital and inter-parietal; internal nares wider than the narrowest part of the palatal bridge.

Lepus capensis Brown Hare
Pulp cavities of 1st upper incisors reach maxilla; fossa on zygomatic arch more forward than in *L. timidus*.

Lepus timidus Arctic Hare
Pulp cavities of 1st upper incisor do not reach maxilla; zygomatic fossa more backward than in *L. capensis*.

297

ORDER RODENTIA

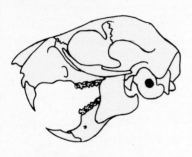

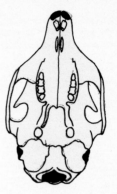

Family Hystricidae

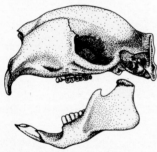

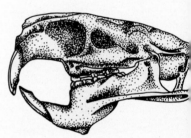

Hystrix cristata Crested Porcupine
Nasal bones over half the length of
the skull.

Myocastor coypus Coypu
Nasal bones less than half length of
skull; antorbital foramen very large,
almost as large as the orbit; skull
angular.

Family Spalacidae
Nasal bones less than half the length of the skull; occiput sloping forward so
that the crest is level with the posterior ends of the zygomatic arches.

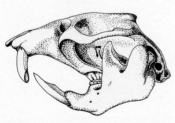

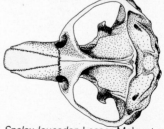

Spalax micropthalmus Greater Mole-
rat
Rostrum wide behind upper incisors;
perforations absent.

Spalax leucodon Lesser Mole-rat
Rostrum narrower behind upper incisors; small perforations present
beside the posterior opening.

Family Scuiridae

Occiput not sloping forward, very far behind zygomatic arches; 5 upper and 4 lower cheek teeth, 1st upper cheek tooth usually small.

Marmota species:
Length of skull over 6cm; length of mandible over 4cm.

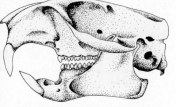

Marmota marmota Alpine Marmot
Narrowest part of post-orbital constriction visible in dorsal view.

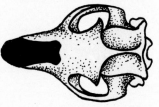

Marmota bobak Bobak's Marmot
Narrowest part of post-orbital constriction not visible in dorsal view, but obscured by the post-orbital process.

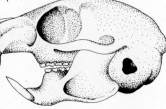

Pteromys volans Flying Squirrel
Length of skull less than 3.8cm, mandible less than 2.5cm; orbit very large; in lateral view zygomatic arch obscures part of tooth row.

Spermophilus species: orbit not very large; tooth row visible in lateral view; length of skull over 3.8cm; mandible over 2.5cm; 1st upper premolar at least half the width of the second; width of anterior and lateral faces of upper incisors approximately equal.

Spermophilus citellus European Souslik
Length of incisive foramina greater than width of upper incisors.

Spermophilus suslicus Spotted Souslik
Length of incisive foramina less than width of incisors.

Sciurus species: 1st upper premolar less than one-third the width of the 2nd; anterior faces of incisors about half the width of the lateral faces.

Sciurus carolinensis Grey Squirrel
Greatest length of nasal bones over 1.7cm; skull up to 5.6cm.

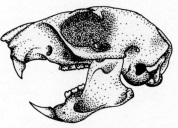

Sciurus vulgaris Red Squirrel
Greatest length of nasal bones less than 1.6cm; skull less than 5cm.

Tamias sibiricus Siberian Chipmunk

299

Mammal skulls

Family Muscardinae (Gliridae)
Cheek teeth 4 upper and 4 lower and with transverse ridges.

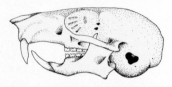

Eliomys quercinus Garden Dormouse
Length of skull over 2.8cm; occlusal surface of molars very concave; 2 central upper cheek teeth with prominent cusps.

Glis glis Edible Dormouse
Skull over 2.8cm; occlusal surfaces of molars not very concave; 2 upper cheek teeth with 5 or 6 low cusps on outer surface.

Muscardinus avellanarius Common Dormouse
Skull less than 2.35cm; 1st upper cheek tooth only half as wide as 2nd; upper tooth rows converge at front.

Family Castoroidea (beavers)

Castor canadensis Canadian Beaver
Antorbital foramen very small; nasals short with convex margins.

Castor fiber European Beaver
Similar to *C. canadensis* but nasals long with straight margins.

Family Zapodidae (birch mice)
Four upper and 3 lower cheek teeth. These two European species do not overlap geographically.

Sicista betulina Northern Birch Mouse.
Sicista subtilis Southern Birch Mouse.

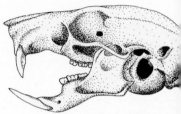

Dryomys nitedula Forest Dormouse
Skull less than 2.8cm; 1st upper cheek teeth more than half as wide as 2nd; upper tooth rows diverge at front; anterior palatal foramen short, ending far short of 1st cheek tooth.

Myomimus roachi Mouse-tailed Dormouse
Similar to *Dryomys nitedula* but anterior palatal foramen long, reaching level of anterior cheek teeth.

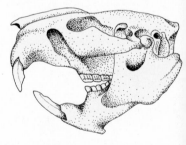

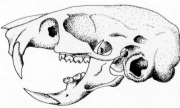

Family Microtinae (voles and lemmings)

Cheek teeth with patterns of alternating triangles.

Ondatra zibethica Muskrat
First and 2nd loops of 2nd and 3rd molars connected near the central line of the teeth; root of lower incisor crossing to outer side of the molars; length of skull over 4.5cm.

Lemmus lemmus Norway Lemming
First and 2nd loops of 2nd and 3rd molars connected at inner edges of the teeth; root of lower incisor entirely on inner side of the molars; length of skull more than 2.5cm; maxillary tooth over 0.8cm; mandible over 1.7cm.

Arvicola species
Teeth as for *Ondatra zibethica* but rear loop of 1st molar preceded by 3 closed triangles; length of skull over 3.1cm; cheek tooth row over 0.75cm.

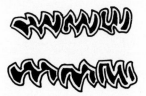

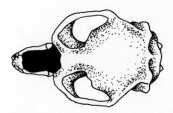

Myopus schisticolor Wood Lemming
Similar to *L. lemmus* but length of skull less than 2.5cm; mandible under 1.7cm.

Arvicola sapidus South-western Water Vole
Length of adult skull over 3.9cm; greatest width of nasal bones over 0.45cm.

Arvicola terrestris Water Vole
Length of adult skull less than 3.9cm; greatest width of nasal bones less than 0.45cm.

Mammal skulls

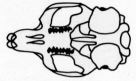

Clethrionomys species: posterior loop of 1st molar preceded by more than 3 closed triangles; palate terminating in a continuous or slightly interrupted transverse shelf (cheek teeth become rooted).

Clethrionomys rutilus Northern Red-backed Vole
Posterior margin of bony palate interrupted; 3rd molar with 4 outer ridges.

Clethrionomys rufocanus Grey-sided Vole
Posterior margin of palate continuous; 3rd molar with 3 labial ridges; upper tooth row over 0.62cm.

Clethrionomys glareolus Bank Vole
Posterior margin of palate continuous; 3rd molar variable; upper tooth row less than 0.62cm.

Pitimys species: palate terminating in a medium projection flanked by lateral pits; 4th and 5th triangles of 1st molar confluent excluding posterior loop (counting from back).

Pitimys subterraneus, P. incertus, (Alps), *P. tatricus* (Tatra Mountains), *P. bavaricus* (Bavaria) Root Voles
Third molar longer than 2nd; 3rd usually with 4 inner ridges.

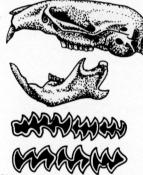

Pitimys duodecimcostatus Iberian Root Vole
Third molar not longer than 2nd, and usually with 3 inner ridges; length of diastema over 0.75cm; 2nd outer ridge of 3rd molar smaller than others.

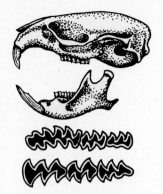

Pitimys savii Mediterranean Root Vole
Similar to *P. duodecimcostatus* but length of diastema less than 0.75cm; outer ridges of 3rd molar about equal.

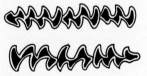

Dolomys bogdanovi Balkan Snow Vole
Fourth and fifth triangles of first molar separated; first outer groove of third molar shallower than second; upper tooth row usually over 0.7cm; molars root in adults.

Microtus species: first outer groove of third molar approximately equal in depth to second; upper tooth row rarely over 0.7cm; molars without roots.

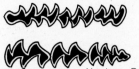

Microtus nivalis Snow Vole
First molar with three concavities on inner side, the anterior concavity deep, overhung by the anterior loop; third molar usually with three ridges on lingual side.

Microtus oeconomus Northern Root Vole
First molar with 3 concavities on inner side; anterior concavity of 3rd molar shallow, acute angle; 3rd molar with 4 inner ridges.

Microtus agrestis Field Vole
First molar with four concavities on its inner side; 2nd molar with 3 lingual ridges.

Microtus cabrerae Cabrera's Vole
Second molar with 2 inner ridges; 3rd molar with 2 outer ridges, 4th inner ridge very small; profile of cranium very convex.

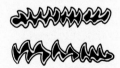

Microtus guentheri Mediterranean Vole
Second molar with 2 inner ridges, 3rd molar with 3 outer ridges, 4th inner ridge well formed; profile of cranium flat; bullae very large; in ventral view distance between bullae and 3rd molar less than length of 3rd molar.

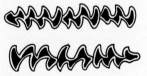

Microtus arvalis Common Vole
Similar to M. guentheri but with smaller bullae; distance between them and 3rd molar greater than length of 3rd molar.

Mammal skulls

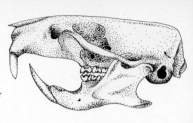

Family Cricetidae
Cheek teeth with cusps in 2 rows.

Cricetulus migratorius Grey Hamster
Cheek tooth row under 0.5cm.

Mesocricetus newtoni Rumanian Hamster
Cheek tooth row greater than 0.5cm but less than 0.7cm.

Family Muridae (rats and mice)
Cheek teeth with 3 rows of cusps.

Rattus species: cheek tooth row greater than 0.6cm.

Rattus rattus Black Rat
Temporal ridges widely curved on either side of brain case.

Rattus norvegicus Brown Rat
Temporal ridges approximately parallel on either side of brain case.

Acomys minous Cretan Spiny Mouse
Cheek tooth row less than 0.6cm; palate with posterior process; internal nares close to anterior margins of bullae.

Mus musculus House Mouse
Cheek tooth row less than 0.6cm; palate normal, terminating behind teeth; upper incisors with notch; first

Cricetus cricetus Common Hamster
Cheek tooth row greater than 0.7cm.

molar with three roots; third molar small, only half the length and width of second; nasal bones less than one quarter the length of the skull.

Micromys minutus Harvest Mouse
Upper incisor not notched; 1st molar with 4 or 5 roots; cheek tooth row less than 0.32cm; nasal bones one-fifth of skull length.

Apodemus species:
Maxillary tooth row greater than 0.32cm but less than 0.6cm; nasal bones approximately one-third of skull length.

Apodemus agrarius Striped Mouse
Second molar without antero-external cusp.

Apodemus mystacinus Rock Mouse
Second molar with antero-external cusp; 1st molar with 4 cusps on outer margin; width of 1st molar equal to half width of palate at that point.

Apodemus flavicollis Yellow-necked Mouse
First molar with 3 outer cusps; width of 1st molar less than half width of palate; length of skull over 2.5cm.

Apodemus microps Pygmy Field Mouse

Apodemus sylvaticus Wood Mouse
Similar to *A. flavicollis* but skull less than 2.5cm.

ORDER ARTIODACTYLA

The artiodactyls include pigs, deer, cattle, sheep and goats. Despite superficial similarities the skulls of this group are diverse; the Suidae (Pig) in particular is anomalous and is therefore treated in the miscellaneous section (page 310).

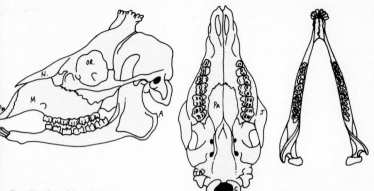

Family Cervidae (deer)

Deciduous bony antlers in males; post-orbital process complete; orbit prominent and nearly circular; palatines and pterygoids moderately large, squamosal small, para-occipital processes large. A summary of deer skull characteristics is given in the following table.

	Antlers present	Canines (tusks) present	Lachrymal pits present	Septum present dividing anterior nares	Pedicles present	Length of nasals (if present)	Lachrymal ridges present
White-tailed Deer *Odocoileus virginianus*	M			M F	M		
Reindeer *Rangifer tarandus*	M F			M F	M F		
Muntjac *Muntiacus reevesi*	M	M	M F		M	medium	M F
Roe Deer *Capreolus capreolus*	M				M	medium	
Sika Deer *Cervus nippon*	M	M F	M F		M	long	
Red Deer *Cervus elaphus*	M	M F	M F		M	long	
Axis or Spotted Deer *Cervus axis*	M	M F	M F		M	long	
Elk *Alces alces*	M		M F		M	short	
Fallow Deer *Dama dama*	M		M F		M	medium	
Chinese Water Deer *Hydropotes inermis*		M F	M F			long	

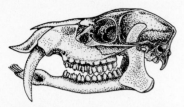

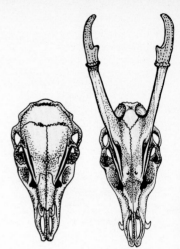

Hydropotes inermis Chinese Water Deer
Antlers absent in male and female; canines very large and tusk-like in male; lachrymal pits small, deep and slot-like.

long pedicles extending far beyond the skull; antlers, when present, less than half the length of the pedicles.

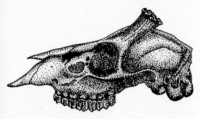

Odocoileus virginianus White-tailed Deer
Antlers present in male; canines absent; internal nares divided by bony septum; post-orbital bar approximately level with posterior molar.

Rangifer tarandus Reindeer
Antlers present in male and female; canines absent; internal nares divided by bony septum; post-orbital bar clearly backward of posterior molar.

Muntiacus reevesi Muntjac
Antlers present in male; canines in male small but tusk-like; viewed dorsally, prominent dorsal ridges over lachrymal pits and orbit in male and female: in male these continue into

Capreolus capreolus Roe Deer
Antlers present in male; canines absent; lachrymal ridges and pits absent; antlers, when present, are greater than half the length of the pedicles.

Cervus axis Axis or Spotted Deer
Similar to *C. nippon* but the two species do not appear to overlap geographically.

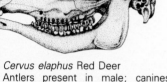

Alces alces Elk
Antlers present in male; canines absent; skull enormous; nasals very small, not or only just extending beyond a line level with the cheek teeth.

Cervus elaphus Red Deer
Antlers present in male; canines present in male and female; large lachrymal pits present: skull up to 40cm long or more.

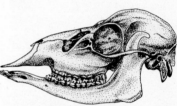

Dama dama Fallow Deer
Antlers present in male; canines absent; nasals clearly extend beyond the cheek teeth; long lachrymal pits present.

Cervus nippon Sika Deer
Antlers present in male; canines present in male and female.

Family Bovidae (sheep, goats, cattle)
Upper canines always absent; skulls in male always with horns, not always in female.

Ovibos moschatus Musk Ox
Horns down sides of skull; their tips, viewed laterally, never rise higher than the base: in older specimens they meet in the middle of the forehead.

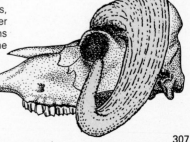

Mammal skulls

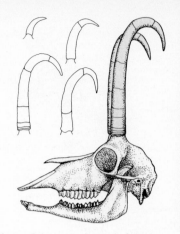

Rupicarpa rupicarpa Chamois
Horns rise straight and almost vertically, with a prominent backward-
facing hook at the tip.

Bubalus bubalus Water Buffalo
Horns flattened in cross-section,
sweeping in a crescent shape backwards beyond the back of the skull
(when viewed dorsally).

Cattle
Horns are at the back of the skull, well beyond the posterior end of the post-
orbital bar.

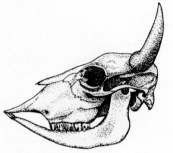

Bison bonasus Bison
Horns very short; skull with convex
profile; post-orbital bar almost in line
with posterior cheek teeth.

Bos taurus Domestic Cattle
Profile of skull flattened: post-orbital
bar not as in Bison.

Sheep and goats
Horns are directly over orbit; centre line passes through post-orbital bar.

Ovis musimon Mouflon
Rounded concavity (lachrymal pit) in
front of each orbit.

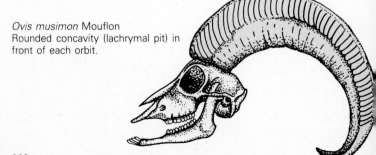

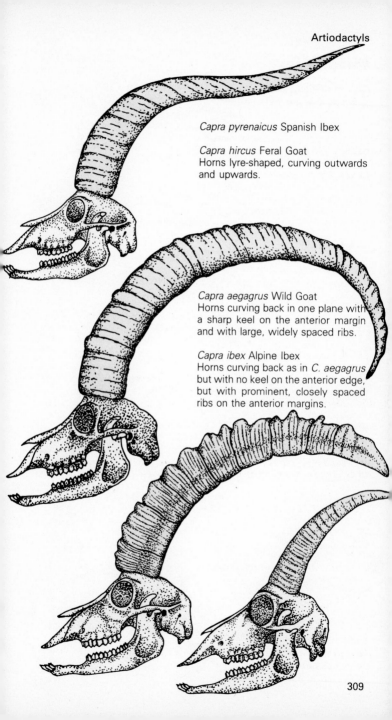

Capra pyrenaicus Spanish Ibex

Capra hircus Feral Goat
Horns lyre-shaped, curving outwards
and upwards.

Capra aegagrus Wild Goat
Horns curving back in one plane with
a sharp keel on the anterior margin
and with large, widely spaced ribs.

Capra ibex Alpine Ibex
Horns curving back as in *C. aegagrus*
but with no keel on the anterior edge,
but with prominent, closely spaced
ribs on the anterior margins.

MISCELLANEOUS

ORDER PERISSODACTYLA
Diastema present.

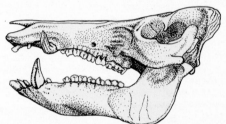

ORDER ARTIODACTYLA

Family Suidae (pigs)
Diastema absent; lower canines not incisiform, cheek teeth with rounded cusps (in these features pigs differ from the other artiodactyls described on the foregoing pages); dental formula: upper teeth – 3 incisors, 1 canine, 4 premolars, 3 molars; lower teeth – 3 incisors, 1 canine, 4 premolars, 3 molars.

ORDER MARSUPIALIA

There are several skull characters distinguishing the *marsupials* from the *placentals*, although here we are only concerned with the wallaby. Below are listed the *major* skull differences between the two groups.

Marsupial
(a) Four incisors in upper jaw
(b) Palatal vacuities in palate
(c) Angle of lower jaw inflected
(d) 2 ducts in lachrymal bone

Placental
(a) Three incisors in upper jaw
(b) Palatal vacuities *absent*; except in the Hedgehog *erinaceus*.
(c) Angle of lower jaw *not* inflected
(d) 1 duct present in lachrymal bone

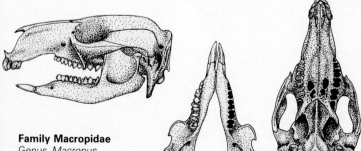

Family Macropidae
Genus *Macropus*
Macropus rufogriseus Wallaby

Glossary

Alveoli root cavities in jaw bones
Aquatic living mainly in water
Arboreal living in and around trees. eg. Red Squirrel
Bicuspid tooth having two cusps
Canine tooth between incisors and cheek teeth; prominent and conical in carnivores
Carnassials enlarged shearing cheek teeth found in most carnivores, one in each row
Casting (a) annual shedding of antlers by deer
      (b) **Cleaves** principal toes of a deer's foot
Couch (a) lying-up place of an otter
      (b) lying-up place of a deer
Crepuscular active at dawn and dusk
Crotties adhesive masses of ungulate droppings (sheep, goat, deer)
Currants hare droppings
Cusp projection on the biting surface of a tooth
Dew claws reduced second and fifth digits on an artiodactyl limb; sometimes never reach the ground
Diastema gap between the incisors or canines and molars or premolars
Digitigrade walking on the tips of the toes
Diurnal active mainly by day
Drey squirrel's nest
Feral escape from captivity and now adapted to living in the wild
Fewmets individual deer droppings
Fraying (a) removal of velvet from antlers
      (b) removal of bark from trees
Gait type of locomotion
Gallop fast gait in which all four limbs of a quadruped may be off the ground at once
Gregarious living in groups
Hibernation process of dormancy and sleep in some mammals during the winter. Body temperature is lowered; sleep is often preceded by feeding to increase body fat
Home range the area used by an animal in its normal pattern of activity
Hop slow gait in which the body is pushed off the ground from a standstill position using the hind feet
Incisor chisel-shaped teeth at the front of the jaws
Kennel surface resting-place of a fox
Latrine place, often a mound or pit, where droppings are deposited regularly
Maxilla large bone in the upper jaw of mammals carrying all upper teeth except incisors; sometimes used to refer to the whole jaw
Molars posterior grinding cheek teeth
Moult seasonal loss of hair or feathers
Nares (posterior and anterior) rear and forward areas of nasal region
Nasals bones protecting the nasal passages
Nocturnal active at night only

Glossary

Orbit bony cavity in skull containing the eye

Palatine bone forming the posterior part of the hard palate

Pelage coat of a mammal

Plantigrade walking on the flat of the feet

Premolars anterior cheek teeth

Prehensile tail tail which can effectively be used as a fifth limb, eg. in Harvest Mouse

Premaxilla bone at the front of the upper jaw which carries incisors, if they are present

Registration where fore and hind tracks on the same side of a trail partly or totally overlap

Run (a) regular, worn pathway used by mammals and ground-living birds
(b) fast gait in which the stride increases and the feet are lifted from the ground in diagonally opposite pairs

Rut autumn courtship and mating time of deer

Sella central part of the noseleaf in horseshoe bats

Slot deer track

Splay spread seen between component parts of a track, eg. between the cleaves of a deer slot

Spraint otter dropping

Straddle distance between the tracks left by the left and right limbs

Stop rabbit breeding burrow

Stride distance between two consecutive tracks made by the same limb

Subterranean living underground

Terrestrial living on dry land

Territory area that an animal defends against other members of the same species to ensure its own food supply and successful breeding

Tine prong on a deer's antler

Track single footprint in the ground

Tragus lobe growing upwards from the lower rim of the ear in bats

Trail pattern of tracks left by a moving animal

Tricuspid tooth with three cusps

Trot medium speed gait in which diagonally opposite feet are moved together

Tusk enlarged tooth, normally confined to males

Unguligrade walking on the tips of horny hoofs

Unicuspid simple conical teeth in the upper jaws of shrews

Velvet soft skin covering the growing antlers of deer

Walk slow gait at which the stride is short and normally at least two (in the case of quadrupeds) limbs are in contact with the ground at any one time

Wallow place where deer or boar roll

Selected bibliography

Bouchner, M. *Der Kosmos Spurenführer*. Kosmos Verlag, Stuttgart 1982

Brown, R. W. and Lawrence, M. J. *Mammals Tracks and Signs*. Macdonald, London 1983

Corbet, G. B. and Ovenden, D. *The Mammals of Britain and Europe*. Collins, London 1980

Corbet, G. B. and Southern, H. N. (eds.). *The Handbook of British Mammals*. Blackwells, Oxford 1977

Lawrence, M. J. and Brown, R. W. *Mammals of Britain, Their Tracks, Trails and Signs*. Blandford, Poole 1979

Leutsher, A. *Animals Tracks and Signs*. London 1979

Neal, E. *Badgers*. Blandford, Poole 1977

Rahm, Urs. *Die Saugetiere der Schweiz*. Basle 1976.

Saint Girons, M. C. *Les mammifères de France et du Benelux*. Doin, Paris 1973

Siivonen, Lauri. *Pohjolan nisakkaat*. Otava, Finland 1977

Thomassin, S. *Traces d'animaux*. Bordas, Paris 1982

Photographic Acknowledgements

AQUILA PHOTOGRAPHICS, STUDLEY: John Robinson 217 top, 238 top, C. J. Smale 137, M. C. Wilkes 212, 255; ARDEA, LONDON: Jean-Paul Ferrero 52, Richard Vaughan 275; BIOFOTOS, FARNHAM: Heather Angel 50, 156, 180 top, 249, 259; FRANK V. BLACKBURN 131 top, 267 top; ROY BROWN 59, 127, 180 bottom, 232; MICHAEL CLARK 19 top, 32, 79, 122, 131 bottom, 169, 170, 177, 179, 206 bottom, 217 bottom, 234 bottom, 235; BRUCE COLEMAN, UXBRIDGE: Jane Burton 81, 148, 150, 210, 234 top, Hans Reinhard 107, James Simon 94, Kim Taylor 117, 138, Rod Williams 87 bottom, Roger Wilmshurst 258 top; BOB GIBBONS PHOTOGRAPHY, RINGWOOD 196, 261: Robin Fletcher 5; HAMLYN GROUP: G. N. Dufeu 97, 215, 236, 245, 267 bottom; Peter Loughran 110, 168, 202, 208, 209, 219, 221, 237, 247, 262, 273; JACANA, PARIS: Nardin 240, 260, Varin 239; ASKO KAIKUSALO 87 top, 104, 113, 222; GEOFFREY KINNS 60, 66, 83, 89, 92, 96, 108, 109, 116, 129, 134, 140, 142, 151, 194, 206 top, 218; THOR LARSEN 55; MICHAEL LAWRENCE 280; NATURAL HISTORY PHOTOGRAPHIC AGENCY: L. Campbell 25, 200, Stephen J. Krasemann 180 centre, Walter J. C. Murray 188, Jany Sauvanet 71; NATURE PHOTOGRAPHERS LTD: Frank V. Blackburn 238 bottom, A. A. Butcher 263 top, Michael Leach 98 bottom, Owen Newman 121, Don Smith 119, Paul Sterry 98 top, Chris Wain 77; JOYCE POPE 215, 216, 257, 263 bottom, 272; LARS SVENSSON 19 bottom, 152.

Index

Numbers *italicised* indicate illustrations (other than in the main entry).

Index

Index

Index